THE COMPLETE IDIOT'S GUIDE® TO

Pleasing Your Woman

by Eve Salinger

ALPHA

A member of Penguin Group (USA) Inc.

To Gray, a true pleaser.

ALPHA BOOKS

Published by the Penguin Group

Penguin Group (USA) Inc., 375 Hudson Street, New York, New York 10014, U.S.A.

Penguin Group (Canada), 10 Alcorn Avenue, Toronto, Ontario, Canada M4V 3B2 (a division of Pearson Penguin Canada Inc.)

Penguin Books Ltd, 80 Strand, London WC2R 0RL, England

Penguin Ireland, 25 St Stephen's Green, Dublin 2, Ireland (a division of Penguin Books Ltd)

Penguin Group (Australia), 250 Camberwell Road, Camberwell, Victoria 3124, Australia (a division of Pearson Australia Group Pty Ltd)

Penguin Books India Pvt Ltd, 11 Community Centre, Panchsheel Park, New Delhi—110 017, India

Penguin Group (NZ), cnr Airborne and Rosedale Roads, Albany, Auckland 1310, New Zealand (a division of Pearson New Zealand Ltd)

Penguin Books (South Africa) (Pty) Ltd, 24 Sturdee Avenue, Rosebank, Johannesburg 2196, South Africa

Penguin Books Ltd, Registered Offices: 80 Strand, London WC2R 0RL, England

International Standard Book Number: 1-59257-464-5
Library of Congress Catalog Card Number: 2005934918

08   07   06   05   8   7   6   5   4   3   2   1

Interpretation of the printing code: The rightmost number of the first series of numbers is the year of the book's printing; the rightmost number of the second series of numbers is the number of the book's printing. For example, a printing code of 05-1 shows that the first printing occurred in 2005.

Printed in the United States of America

Note: This publication contains the opinions and ideas of its author. It is intended to provide helpful and informative material on the subject matter covered. It is sold with the understanding that the author and publisher are not engaged in rendering professional services in the book. If the reader requires personal assistance or advice, a competent professional should be consulted.

The author and publisher specifically disclaim any responsibility for any liability, loss, or risk, personal or otherwise, which is incurred as a consequence, directly or indirectly, of the use and application of any of the contents of this book.

Most Alpha books are available at special quantity discounts for bulk purchases for sales promotions, premiums, fundraising, or educational use. Special books, or book excerpts, can also be created to fit specific needs.

For details, write: Special Markets, Alpha Books, 375 Hudson Street, New York, NY 10014.

Publisher: *Marie Butler-Knight*
Editorial Director: *Mike Sanders*
Senior Managing Editor: *Jennifer Bowles*
Senior Acquisitions Editor: *Paul Dinas*
Development Editor: *Nancy D. Lewis*
Production Editor: *Janette Lynn*
Copy Editor: *Emily Bell*

Cartoonist: *Shannon Wheeler*
Cover Designer: *Bill Thomas*
Book Designer: *Trina Wurst*
Indexer: *Aamir Burki*
Layout: *Becky Harmon*
Proofreading: *Mary Hunt*

Contents at a Glance

Contents

Foreword

Most men will tell you that when it comes to relationships, they have a lot to learn. Few men today have a mentor to help them to perform the delicate balancing act that a fantastic long-term relationship requires. To be manly, yet not macho; sensitive, yet not weak, and to be sexually pleasing without being a bottomless pit is the universal dilemma of our times. As psychologists we are constantly helping men to understand what women really want, and how to please women without losing themselves in the process.

Every reader will have his own questions that he is afraid to ask even his best friends. *The Complete Idiot's Guide to Pleasing Your Woman* is loaded with the answers you are seeking.

We urge you to use *The Complete Idiot's Guide to Pleasing Your Woman* as your number one source for information on this all important topic. What really turns her on sexually? How to completely satisfy her. Learning how to convey the attitude she finds to be most irresistible and endearing. How to be there emotionally—both as a lover and a pal. Dozens of invaluable tips on day-to-day living that will enhance your lives together greatly. And, how this simple, loving attention will reap big benefits for you both—in and out of bed.

Eve Salinger offers you the kind of commonsense advice that you'll wonder how you never stumbled across before reading her book. If you have been through a divorce or a love relationship that broke up prematurely, you will undoubtedly gain some valuable insight as to why. But most important, you will understand exactly how not to make the same mistakes again.

She touches on areas such as etiquette, cooking for your partner, getting her gifts that make the right statement (and even where to get them), and romantic getaways (for any budget). Ms. Salinger even talks you through the challenge of finding your woman's "G" spot!

The Complete Idiot's Guide to Pleasing Your Woman truly gives you a look into the mind and heart of your woman as few books have ever done. Her easy to follow action steps will give you the direction you need. You need only choose the ones that apply to you to make wonderful things happen for you and your partner.

As you begin the adventure of learning new ways to please your woman, remember that you are setting in motion the best attitude and climate there is to make life optimally happy for many years to come.

Michael S. Broder, Ph.D., and Arlene Goldman, Ph.D.
Authors, *Secrets of Sexual Ecstasy*

Michael S. Broder, Ph.D., and Arlene Goldman, Ph.D. are psychologists, husband and wife, and co-authors of *Secrets of Sexual Ecstasy*. Dr. Broder's other books include *The Art of Living Single, The Art of Staying Together,* and *Can Your Relationship Be Saved?* They both have private practices in Philadelphia, Pennsylvania.

Introduction

Want to please your woman in bed? You go, guy! She'll show her gratitude in ways you'll never forget. But, wait, before you go rushing off to read one of those "how to give your woman an orgasm" books, remember this: if you want to do *anything* for your woman in bed, first you'll have to get her there. That's why you need *The Complete Idiot's Guide to Pleasing Your Woman.*

What kind of a guy reads an *Idiot's Guide* on how to please his woman? He's a catch, a peach, a real *mensch* (that's Yiddish for a caring, decent soul). Also he's the kind of guy who's about to get very, very lucky. He senses that women actually love sex as much as men do—*maybe more*—but he knows his woman will blossom under his touch only when he treats her like a flower, showering her with signs of attention, admiration, and devotion.

Wait! If that sounds like a lot of effort, have no fear. Your woman doesn't necessarily need bells and whistles. She just wants to know that her man values her. This book will show you how even the simplest romantic gestures and the right attitude can yield wonderfully gratifying consequences. *The Complete Idiot's Guide to Pleasing Your Woman* offers a man every tool he needs to get his woman in the mood for love.

How This Book Is Organized

This book is divided into six parts. Each will escort you through different aspects of pleasing your woman.

Part 1, "Please, Please Her," will offer an overview of what pleases and displeases women and what kind of guy they find most pleasing of all. It will help you to understand the subtleties of the romance dance, and inspire you to help your woman glow inside and out.

Part 2, "Intimate Companions," offers tips for constructive conversation as well as advice on laughing and playing together. It also includes advice for supporting your partner through life's rough patches.

Part 3, "Mr. Wonderful," helps you find ways to help out your lady around the house. It also offers a brush up course on etiquette and "bediquette," and contains grooming and fashion tips so you can look your most handsome for your honey.

Part 4, "Making the Mood," offers inspiration for taking your lady out on the town and also for creating a love nest at home. It suggests a number of ways to refresh and refuel your lady when she's running on empty.

Part 5, "Love to Love Her," provides techniques that will allow you to make the most of your partner's "mood for loving" and bring her to the height of satisfaction over and over again. No matter how good a lover you are, this part will make you an even better one.

Part 6, "Lovers for Life," offers tips for keeping your body in studly shape, your mind sharp and inventive, and your relationship strong for as long as you both shall live.

Pleasing Extras

Little notes have been placed throughout this book to make it even more user-friendly and to add some extra horsepower. Within them are all kinds of tips and information.

 Love Busters

Warning! These sidebars highlight male behaviors that are the cold showers of romance. Avoid them—or risk turning your loving woman to the "off" position.

 **He Says/She Says**

Women and men have lots to say on this subject. These contain advice and anecdotes from lovers who have pleased and have been pleased.

 Tongue Teasers

These offer an elaboration of terms related to woman pleasing that are mentioned in the text.

 Mood Makers

These contain tips for extra special pleasing that will get her in the mood and keep her turned on.

Acknowledgments

Thanks again to my editor, Paul Dinas, with whom working is always a pleasure. Also to Nancy Lewis, Janette Lynn, and Emily Bell for their expertise and tireless attention to detail.

Trademarks

All terms mentioned in this book that are known to be or are suspected of being trademarks or service marks have been appropriately capitalized. Alpha Books and Penguin Group (USA) Inc. cannot attest to the accuracy of this information. Use of a term in this book should not be regarded as affecting the validity of any trademark or service mark.

Part 1

Please, Please Her

Many men think women are a mystery, but we're easier to read than you might imagine. In this part of the book, I'll introduce you to the art of woman pleasing by exploring what women really want and debunking some myths. I'll discuss the connection between romantic and physical love, and help you to bring out the best, most confident side of your lady. You'll begin to be able to identify opportunities to please your woman by letting her know how important she is to you and how desirable you find her.

What Do Women Want?

In This Chapter

- ◆ Social versus emotional female needs
- ◆ Five things a woman needs to flourish
- ◆ Protecting and defending your lady
- ◆ The harmony of yin and yang

"What do women want?" is a question made famous by Sigmund Freud, the father of psychoanalysis. Some say it perplexed him so much that he was still asking it on his deathbed. That could be true, because he never did come up with a good answer during his lifetime.

With so many contrasting concepts and images of the female gender being floated nowadays, confusion about women's wants and needs has only gotten worse. Much of men's consternation is understandable—but a great deal of it can be straightened out once you learn to separate what *women* want as a *gender*, and what *your individual woman* wants from *you*. That's what this chapter is meant to sort out.

Public Women, Private Woman

Once upon a time, not so long ago, American women had astonishingly little political, economic, and social power. It was 1920 before the Nineteenth Amendment gave us the right to vote in every state. It was about half a century later when the contemporary Women's Movement began demanding increased rights for women in the workplace, such as equal pay for equal work and equal access to top-paying jobs.

Although there are still many issues for women to tackle, a great deal of progress has been made. But with all social progress comes a shifting of social norms and a period of adjustment.

The female gender, rightly insisting on respect from the male gender, has made it clear that condescending attitudes are out. We are not "little ladies" who "shouldn't worry our pretty little heads" about matters *above* our heads. We are as strong and as capable of doing any job—doctor, lawyer, firefighter, detective, CEO, scientist, secretary of state—as any member of the male gender.

Given these new dynamics and new realities, there's no need to, say, hold the door open for a woman you work with, or a woman you work *for* (though, of course, this is still your choice). For sure, you don't want to tell her how cute she looks in "that little outfit." First of all, her little outfit might be a thousand-dollar power suit; secondly, you could find yourself being called into the Human Resources department for a refresher course on avoiding sexual harassment.

By now, most men understand that the way to deal with any woman in a public setting is to treat her as he would a male. Women co-workers, managers, teachers, students, and so on are to be treated just as their male counterparts. They are not to be discriminated against, and neither are they to be afforded any special privileges as members of "the fairer sex."

Tongue Teasers

Political correctness refers to speaking and behaving in a way that gives no offense to any segment of the population. Being "PC" means showing that one is without prejudice or preconceived notions.

Fair enough, most men agree. But where does that leave men when it comes to knowing how to treat the one woman who means the most to them in their personal lives? Has *political correctness* killed off the possibility of true romance?

No, it has not—and thank goodness.

No matter what a woman's philosophy or politics, no matter if she considers herself "liberated" or "old fashioned," or just plain practical, she wants one man around who will treat her in private not just like everyone else but like the rare and special individual she is.

When it comes to her committed relationship, a woman wants to feel assured that she is the one at the center of her partner's universe, that it is she who is worshipped and adored. She wants to have the differences between maleness and femaleness celebrated. Oh, and does she want any special treatment? You betcha.

The Flower and the Gardener

There's a wonderful old saying: every relationship needs one flower and one gardener. If pleasing your woman is your goal, get your gardening tools ready and always remember—she needs attention and nurturing if she is to bloom in your presence.

Now, if that sounds a little one-sided, don't worry about it. Rest assured that as you nurture your woman, she will nurture you. Every relationship forms its own feedback loop, and what goes around comes around. When she is the center of your universe, you will surely be the center of hers.

Now, back to our gardening metaphor. What is it that a flower needs most of all so it can flourish? The answer, for all you budding botanists out there, is W-A-T-E-R, and as such:

- ◆ W is for Wooing

- ◆ A is for Adoration

- ◆ T is for Talking

- ◆ E is for Esteem

- ◆ R is for Restoration

W Is for Wooing

To woo a woman is to court her, to gain her acceptance and approval with the overall aim of making her yours—and you hers. It's a kind of nice, old-fashioned word, with traditional connotations. That's good, because most women do harbor a very traditional part of themselves when it comes to matters of the heart.

Most likely, you instinctively wooed your woman when you were first attracted to her—so attracted that it was beginning to dawn on you that she was "the one." Whenever you saw her, or spoke to her, or planned to see her, you went that extra mile, doing something to convey your ardor and your honorable intentions.

When you were with her, you concerned yourself with her comfort and well-being. You opened the car door for her; you walked closer to the curb so she would not be splattered by a passing car whooshing through a puddle. When you spoke with her, you hung raptly on her every word, perhaps searching for a hint that she returned your affections. When you made plans to get together, you thought carefully about what would make her most happy—and then you took charge of making it happen.

Then she made you the happiest man alive by becoming yours after all. And then what did you do? Well, although I don't know you personally, I'm willing to bet on one thing: you did a lot less than you did before when it came to wooing. It's human nature—or at least man's nature—to expend less effort once the hunt is over. Now it's time to enjoy the fruits of your efforts, right?

Mood Makers

Want to get back into a wooing mind frame? Imagine you're on your third date with your lady. Not the first date—you'd be too shy; not the second—too nervous. By the third date you knew you wanted her, and you also knew you had to work for it.

Well, yes and no. From a pure efficiency standpoint, there's no overt reason to continue chasing what one has already caught. But from an emotional standpoint, it's another story altogether. Increased familiarity, the passage of time, the bonds of commitment, the wearing off of novelty, do all take their toll on the rituals that accompany early courtship. But—and this is very important, so pay attention—no woman appreciates being thought of, or treated like, a sure thing.

No matter what stage of your relationship you're in—whether you've been together 1, 10, 20, or 50 years,—remember to dust off those courtship behaviors now and again. Yes, you have other responsibilities, and no practical woman wants you to ignore them. But despite other responsibilities, let her know she's your number one priority. Woo her, wow her—and then watch her blossom.

A Is for Adoration

Another thing your woman wants from you is your open adoration. While the trick of wooing lies in the things you do, the key to showing your woman your undying adoration lies in your attitude. Eying her with frank appreciation, peppering your conversation with subtle smiles, holding her hand, walking with your arm around her—these are all displays of your adoring attitude. But, underneath, the attitude itself must be heartfelt and genuine.

Adoration is strong affection *plus* complete faithfulness. Even if the woman in your life right now is not the only woman for whom you've ever had strong feelings, she wants to believe that in this case your feelings are strongest. She wants to be compared to no one. Certainly you're allowed to admire other women (after all, you're not dead, are you?). But the message you need to convey to your chosen love is that you admire no one—and never have admired anyone—the way you do her.

Adoration ties in to a certain kind of love. It is the kind of love that we say is "blind." Does your partner have flaws? Of course, because—like you—she is only human. But adoration not only accepts those flaws, it celebrates them—because, along with everything else, they make her the unique creature she is. Even on those days when her flaws are most evident, your love must be steady and forgiving. It must be the kind of love that is known as *unconditional love*.

The more you let your woman know you adore her, the more she will see you as completely trustworthy. Having a trustworthy man by her side will make her feel safe and special. Like a flower growing in an ideal environment, she will then feel free to become her best and most complete self.

Tongue Teasers

Unconditional love refers to love without judgment. It isn't predicated on the fact that the object of one's love always act or look a certain way. It only requires that they exist.

T Is for Talking

One kind of book that women buy most is the genre that addresses communication in relationships. In fact, many such books are aimed specifically at women. It just goes to show how much women value—and really want to improve—the quality of talking and listening that goes on between them and their partners.

Women truly believe that a lack of communication endangers a relationship. Statistics bear out their belief. When divorce and break-ups occur, many couples admit that poor communication was a primary cause.

Your woman considers it nurturing to her when you are genuinely interested in what she is saying without worrying about what you're going to say next or rushing in with advice when all she really wants is your ear. But she also considers it nurturing to the relationship when you are open with her and willing to share your own vulnerabilities. No, she doesn't want you to whine, she just wants you to confide.

E Is for Esteem

Aretha Franklin sang about wanting R-E-S-P-E-C-T and women everywhere related to her plea. "Find out what it means to me," she said. Okay, so what does respecting her, and holding her in high esteem, mean to your woman?

For one thing, it means that you value her opinions and appreciate her intelligence. By intelligence, I mean more than just her accumulated knowledge—though it may be substantial indeed. Women are touted as having "intuition." What they really have is a wealth of creativity combined with common sense. Every woman is a wise woman, and when you acknowledge your woman's wisdom she feels esteemed and understood.

In addition, women want to be appreciated for their very femininity itself. Even if your woman operates a backhoe, fights fires, or runs a Fortune 500 company and has to be tough on the job, she wants you to see, and revel in, another side of her. She wants you to notice that although she is as capable as a man, she is, in fact, not a man. She is a gorgeous, one-of-kind creation.

R Is for Restoration

Is your woman a busy woman? If you answered no, look again. *All* women are busy, many exceptionally so. In addition to many of them holding jobs outside the home, they usually do more than their partners in areas such as housework and childcare. They also consider themselves the emotional guardians of their relationships with the men in their lives. To top it all off, they tend to spend a lot of time trying to stay in shape and look good—for you.

Every woman needs sustenance—in the form of adoring, faithful, respectful love—in order to follow through with her many responsibilities. She also needs you to notice how much she does, and to articulate your gratitude. But let's face it, she could also do with some practical hands-on assistance and, every now and then, a complete break.

He Says/She Says

"I love it when my husband thanks me for doing something around the house or for the family. I love it even more when he says, 'Hey, let me do that for a change.'"
—Bonnie, 37

To bring your woman's love to full fruition, remember to do whatever you can to restore her. Pitch in even more than you think you have to once in a while. Figure out some ingenious ways to give her some time off so she can be refreshed and re-invigorated.

Check Your Flower Power

So how are you doing with helping your flower grow? Take the following quiz and see. Be honest now. Obviously your intentions are good or you wouldn't be reading this book in the first place. The questions are meant to help you identify areas to work on in order to please your woman even more.

Am I Nurturing My Woman?

On a scale from 1 (strongly disagree) to 5 (strongly agree), rate how you feel about the following statements:

1. I still do some of the romantic things I did when we were courting.

    1 2 3 4 5

2. I never act like I take my woman for granted.

    1 2 3 4 5

3. I think the woman in my life is great just the way she is.

    1 2 3 4 5

4. I am easy-going and forgiving when it comes to my mate.

    1 2 3 4 5

5. I really listen to my partner when she talks.

    1 2 3 4 5

6. I confide in my woman and tell her things I tell no one else.

    1 2 3 4 5

7. I respect my lady's opinion and take it seriously.

    1 2 3 4 5

8.   I always notice and appreciate my lady's feminine side.

    1 2 3 4 5

9. I do things to help my partner out at home.

    1 2 3 4 5

10. I am conscious of how much my woman does for me and I tell her so.

    1 2 3 4 5

First, add up your score for an overview of how you're doing when it comes to pleasing your woman:

10–20   You need some step-by-step gardening lessons.

21–30   You mean well, but you need to put in some more time and effort to keep her pleasure growing.

31–40   You've got big-time "green thumb" potential.

41–50   Wow! Too bad you're already taken! (Just kidding.)

Now, let's break these questions down a little more closely:

The first two questions are meant to check your "wooing" power. If you circled numbers 1, 2, or 3 for either question, think of something you can do to recapture the magic of your early dating time. Then jot it down here.

_____

_____

_____

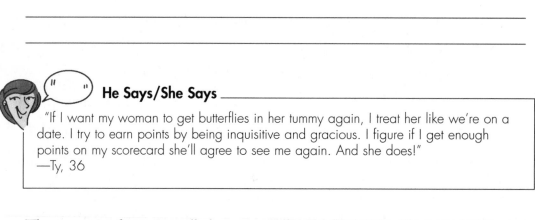

He Says/She Says

"If I want my woman to get butterflies in her tummy again, I treat her like we're on a date. I try to earn points by being inquisitive and gracious. I figure if I get enough points on my scorecard she'll agree to see me again. And she does!"
—Ty, 36

The next pair of questions allude to your "adoration" quotient. If you circled 3 or a number below it for either question, your woman probably needs to be reassured that she is your emotional focal point. What can you do to make her understand this?

_____

_____

_____

The fifth and sixth questions refer to the quality of your communication with your partner. Again, if your numbers were 3 or below, you can do better. Think of something you can do to enhance the quality of talk in your relationship.

_____

_____

_____

Questions 7 and 8 speak to your ability to let your woman know how much you hold her in high esteem. Ideas for improvement?

_____

_____

_____

The final pair of questions has to do with your willingness to pitch in and help your woman with her many tasks and responsibilities, as well as your expression of thanks for all she does. What more can you do?

_____

_____

_____

If you can't think of any practical strategies for nurturing your woman right now, have no fear. The point of this book is to offer lots of ideas and inspiration to help you along your way. Keep on reading and refer back to these pages at any time to update your responses.

The Dragon Slayer

Having a man who is loving and caring is important to women. But hold on a minute! If you think that is all there is to pleasing her, think again. Yes, a woman wants a man who is sensitive, but she also wants a man who will step up to the plate and be her bold champion when the situation warrants it. Sometimes she even needs him to stand up to her—because being sensitive does not equate with being subservient.

There's a reason why so many fairy tales included scenarios of men slaying dragons and battling ogres, demons, and assorted other unsavory characters in order to protect and defend their ladies. That reason has to do with some evolutionary realities. Since women have always been the one to bear children, and the ones primarily responsible for the care of little ones, there have been times when they were indisposed and men were called upon to save women and children from an outside threat, be it a rival tribe or a threatening storm on the horizon. Instinctively,

Mood Makers

Sometimes even a small gesture can make your woman feel protected. Along those lines, keep an umbrella in your car at all times. Have it at the ready so, in case of a sudden cloudburst, she won't get wet—and her hair won't frizz.

women were drawn to men who they felt could rise to such occasions without undue hesitation.

Contemporary realities may be somewhat altered, but threats of various kinds will always loom—and instincts have remained unchanged. If your woman is in trouble, protect her. If she feels endangered, put your arm around her and take a stand. Sensitivity to your woman also means being sensitive to her need to have you be a real man. Don't be hesitant—be strong and be *there* when she needs you.

Along these same lines, women love a man with a plan. That means women love men with goals and ambitions—men who know exactly what their strengths are and how to play them. A woman's ideal man knows where he's taking her tonight, what he's doing tomorrow, and what he wants to accomplish with the rest of his life. Certainly he might experience setbacks, but his attitude and self-respect is such that his confidence and resilience will prevail.

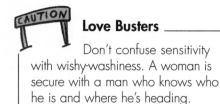

Love Busters

Don't confuse sensitivity with wishy-washiness. A woman is secure with a man who knows who he is and where he's heading.

Your ability to plan ahead and envision a life for the two of you will provide your woman with a sense of security. She will know that if she becomes sick, you will be there for her, and that when you both grow old, you will still be able to provide for yourselves. Again, this is about being able to rely on your strength of character.

Your Yang and Her Yin

When it comes to social, political, and economic equations, men and women are—or should be—on an equal footing. But on a physical, emotional, and spiritual level, the dynamic is not so much about equality but about being perfectly complementary.

Tongue Teasers

Yin and yang are words from the Chinese Taoist tradition. Yang energy, which represents the male aspect of universe, is necessary to balance and complete yin energy, which represents the female aspect of creation.

An ancient Chinese philosophy—still widely referred to today—describes this concept as *yin* and *yang*. According to this philosophy, everything in the entire world is comprised of female and male energies. The combination of yin and yang makes for harmony in the universe. The two balance each other absolutely, like night (yin) and day (yang), and have a mutually dependent relationship.

Oriental sages used the yin-yang concept to illuminate some important features of the relationships between opposites. They recognized that the normal, healthy existence of everything in nature depends upon the interaction of opposite forces—hot and cold, light and dark, growth and diminishment. They also noticed that yang attracts, nourishes, and sustains yin, and vice versa. The greater the degree of difference, the more powerful the attraction.

When it comes to man and woman, the implications of yin and yang are clear. The two genders are different—physically and emotionally—but the unity of their opposites is a sacred thing.

You and your woman are alike in some ways, but magnificently unalike in other, more profound ways. That's how it is and how it should be. Try to understand your woman's reality, but at the same time, do not lose sight of your male reality and your masculine instincts. Achieving this balance will help you achieve harmony with the woman you love.

The Least You Need to Know

- Confusion about women's wants is rampant—in her public life, a woman may want no differentiating treatment, but in her private life she wants to feel special.

- Every relationship needs one flower and one gardener—she's the former, you're the latter.

- A woman will blossom when her man woos her, adores her, talks with her, respects her, and helps her out so that her energy may be renewed.

- No matter how tough and self-sufficient a woman can be, she also appreciates it when her man is her champion.

- You and your woman are alike in some ways, but gloriously unalike in others—harmony prevails when your "yang" male energy balances and completes her "yin" female energy.

Chapter 2

What Women Don't Want

In This Chapter

- ◆ Why women joke about men
- ◆ How men can self-modify their behavior
- ◆ Five male types that make women crazy
- ◆ When it's okay to be "bad"

Do women ever complain about men? Hey, do bears live in the woods? Sometimes it seems like each gender complaining about the other is a national pastime. It certainly provides plenty of fodder for television sit-coms.

Some complaints by women about the males of the species are really just bemused, loving commentaries. Beneath their surface lies a true fondness for the male—even his idiosyncrasies. But *some* women *sometimes* have some *serious* complaints. Of course, you're allowed to be imperfect, but if you want to please your woman you're not allowed to act like a jerk. This chapter will help you understand the difference.

Is This What Men Are Like?

Women have probably joked about men since the beginning of domestic life itself. It's a great coping mechanism. Humor helps them commiserate with the sisterhood of other women.

With the advent of the Internet, of course, they can share their humorous observations more quickly and spread them more widely. Want to know some typical jokes that women are circulating?

◆ Men are like chocolate bars—sweet, smooth, and they usually head right for your hips.

◆ Men are like department stores—their clothes are always ½ off.

◆ Men are like mascara—they usually run at the first sign of emotion.

◆ Men are like government bonds—they take soooooooo long to mature.

◆ Men are like the weather—nothing can be done to change them.

What do these jokes say—in a general sense—about men? Well, they say that you're somewhat sex-obsessed (can't argue with that one, can you?), a bit untidy (ditto), less inclined than women to delve into discussions of feelings (still no big argument from you, right?), and that you take longer to ripen than the female of the species (yup).

He Says/She Says

"My friends and I swap jokes about men all the time. I think it's a great, harmless catharsis. It allows us to blow off steam about our frustrations with a good laugh."
—Kayce, 27

All in all, they're exaggerated comments about foibles that are forgivable—some even rather adorable in their own way. Even if you protest that all or some of these generalizations don't apply to you individually, I'll bet you can see the humor and the truth in them.

But what about that last joke? Is it true that nothing can be done to change you? Well, yes—in the sense that no woman will be able to wave a magic wand and alter your behavior. But every man is capable of changing *himself* if he has the right incentive.

Good Men Are No Joke

Any guy can revamp some of his attitudes and behaviors if he so chooses. Often, finding the right woman will compel him to do so. But where does he start?

To answer that question, let's look at an old fable—the story of The Princess and the Troll.

Once upon a time there was a troll who fell in love with a beautiful princess. Like many trolls, he was a bit rough around the edges. So he donned a mask and masqueraded as a gallant prince. The two wed, and the princess treated her husband with love and kindness. The troll came to act the role of a noble, generous, and gracious prince with greater and greater ability.

The princess and her husband lived happily, until one day a traveler from the troll's home village came to the court and recognized him. He told the princess her husband's true identity. "You are wrong, sir," said the princess. But the troll felt he could hide no longer. He took off his mask and underneath was ... a genuine handsome, noble, and gracious prince.

The lessons of this fable? One: the love of a good woman, and the urge to please her, are powerful incentives for smoothing over one's rough spots. Two: the best way to change an aspect of yourself is to act as if it is already changed—as an old proverb has it, "As a man acts, so shall he become."

So don't hesitate to jump in and brush up your pleasing behaviors. There's no time like the present. Once you start, the positive reinforcement you get from your woman will keep you on the right track.

Romance Dampers

Every man—just like every woman—could undoubtedly use a bit of self-improvement. But just how far should you go in your attempt to please your mate? Well, that all depends on where you're starting from.

A few rough spots are one thing, but read on to see if you fit any of the categories of males that really, really irk the ladies. These types of guys can give all of you a bad name!

If you see yourself reflected in any of the following portraits, give your woman a great big hug for putting up with you so far. Better yet, give her a medal—made of diamonds. Then get your act together, and stop being a troll—for both your sakes.

Mood Makers

Self-awareness is the first step on the road to self-improvement. Be honest with yourself about your habits and you can break out of any romance-dampening pattern.

Mr. Potato Head

The kind of guy I call Mr. Potato Head takes his name from two sources. One is the kid's toy of the same name, a blank head onto which you can stick facial features like a nose, eyes, a mustache, and so on. No matter how many times you stick things into Mr. Potato Head's head, he doesn't flinch, and his essential nature doesn't change. He's an oblivious lump.

This type of guy also owes the inspiration for his name to the phrase "couch potato." The couch potato, as you doubtless know, enjoys nothing so much as sitting around (preferably in a torn undershirt) and vegging out in front of the television set (preferably the large screen kind, complete with surround sound). No matter what else is happening around him—babies crying, phones ringing, dogs barking to be let out, a spouse futilely attempting to clean up—he is entranced by the tube.

Okay, maybe it's not fair to say that a Mr. Potato Head type is always watching T.V. Sometimes he gets up to get a snack. Sometimes he actually turns the T.V. off and peruses a sports or car magazine. But whatever he does, you have to admire his focus. Nothing seems to disturb him or impede on his potato-ness.

Although Mr. Potato Head can tell you what's on any of a hundred or so cable channels at any given moment, there are many things he has no knowledge of at all. These things include:

◆ How the house somehow miraculously gets cleaned

◆ Where food comes from and how it gets into the fridge so he can take it out

◆ What his kids' school and activities schedules are

◆ Who—let alone where—their pediatrician is

◆ When anyone's birthday is/when his anniversary is

◆ How to pack a school lunch

◆ Where the household bills are kept

◆ What social functions he and his partner need to attend

◆ When—or why—company is coming and what to do with them when they get there

Mr. Potato Head does not care to know any of these things, because he assumes someone else will take

Love Busters

It's a turn-off for a woman to be "shushed" by her man so he can hear what they're saying on *CSI Miami*. If conversation is interfering with your T.V. watching, think how much T.V. watching is interfering with conversation.

care of them. And someone (guess who) usually does. That's because his woman has probably given up trying to get through to him. How can she when she's always drowned out by the T.V.?

Mr. Potato Head is a somewhat extreme case. Nevertheless, if any of his behaviors seem to be hitting a little too close to home, consider that you just may have a *few* Mr. Potato Head tendencies. If so, you'll want to address them—because, needless to say, Mr. Potato Head is no lady-pleaser.

If you're prone to potato-hood, you might want to turn off the T.V. set once in a while and tune into your woman instead. In your case, every turn off will be a turn on.

His Highness, The Prince

His Highness the Prince is a male type that has a lot in common with Mr. Potato Head—but he's even more self-involved. He not only expects to be left to his own amusements; he also expects to be waited on while he is preoccupied. Where Mr. Potato Head occasionally rouses himself from his preoccupations to fetch a bowl of pretzels, for example, His Highness sits right where he is and says, "Hey, Honey, do we still have any of those great sourdough pretzels?" Translation: get me some pretzels.

His Highness the Prince is pretty clever in getting his woman to do his bidding. Note that he calls her "honey" and not "hey, you." Notice also that he gives his woman a peripheral compliment in alluding to the fact that she was smart enough to buy those "great sourdough pretzels." In the most clever move of all, His Highness the Prince gets what he wants by feigning helplessness. By asking "Do we have any of those pretzels," he intimates that he is clueless. If the pretzels exist, that must be top-secret information known only to his partner.

Some variations on the pretzel question often voiced by His Highness, include:

- Hey Sweetie, what happened to the butter?

- Now where did those sunglasses get to?

- Have you seen my tennis racket? You always know where to find things, babe!

- Oh, I thought we had *real* maple syrup—oh, we do? You're the best!

- Did we run out of the dark beer already? You'll pick some up? Wow, I don't deserve you.

If you have a bent for His Highness the Prince-type behavior, you may say you don't deserve special treatment, but you really think you do. In fairness to you, this may be because you learned to think this way under the influence of another very important woman in your life: your mother. If you were spoiled by your mother, you might expect that all women live to dote on you. It's time to readjust those expectations.

Mood Makers

Want to re-train yourself to do unto others? The next time you have the urge to ask your partner to bring you something, take a different tack. Get up and get it yourself, and then ask what you can bring *her* while you're up.

Should your woman do little things to pamper you from time to time? Yes. But give her a chance to do so spontaneously, as opposed to presenting her with a list of demands (it doesn't matter how prettily those demands are presented).

In addition, it's important to remember that such gestures of affection work both ways. She does for you and you do for her. Though a daily tally needn't be kept, over time, things should more or less even out. Come to think of it, in your case, maybe you should keep a daily tally for a while to help you develop the habit of doing for others.

Mr. "Yes, Dear"

Many women complain about a male type whose default answer to any comment or question is, "Yes, dear." This is such a familiar male mode that it has been the subject of numerous comic strips. Typically, men are shown hiding behind the sports page of the newspaper, replying "Yes, dear" to whatever their partner says. But despite their seeming agreeability, you can be sure that whatever they're agreeing to will never be attended to. The technical term for this type of behavior is *passive aggressive*.

The term passive aggressive was introduced in a 1945 U.S. war department technical bulletin, describing soldiers who weren't openly insubordinate but shirked duty through procrastination, willful incompetence, and so on. After the war, the term found its way into the *Diagnostic and Statistical Manual*, the bible of the American psychology field. According to the revised third edition (DSM-III-R, 1987), someone had "passive aggressive personality disorder" if he engaged in a number of task-dodging actions such as procrastination, working inefficiently on tasks, and "forgetting" obligations.

But was passive aggression really so serious and intractable as to be termed a personality disorder? Many argued it as just a strategy for eluding unpleasant chores while avoiding confrontation. Recognizing that the definition as then formulated wasn't working, the compilers of DSM-IV (1994) relegated passive aggression to an appendix.

The truth is that most everyone—yes, women, too—can be passive aggressive sometimes. It's a rational self-protective mechanism—sometimes it's just easier to say "yes" even when you mean "no." In fact, we may congratulate ourselves for cleverly evading a bit of work that we really find objectionable.

But when passive aggression is habitual, it can do a great deal of damage to relationships. A woman continually met with her man's passive aggressive resistance may well be tempted to explode at him, but that will just make matters worse. Mr. Yes, Dear hates confrontation so much that he will just retreat further into his chosen defensive stand. A vicious cycle ensues and frustration builds.

 He Says/She Says

"My wife complained that I just 'yessed her along' to keep her quiet. I finally told her she was right. If I said 'no' I was afraid she'd holler at me. She said, "But I'm hollering at you *now!*" I figured she had a point. Now, even though we don't always agree on what needs to get done, let alone when it needs to get done, at least I am more honest, and she is calmer." —Jack, 49

If you find yourself frequently "yes, dear-ing" when you know in your heart you should be saying "no way, dear," it's a good idea to ask yourself just what *would* be so wrong with confrontation. If you're being asked to do something you have good reason not to want to do, go ahead and say so. You may have to enter into some negotiations and reach some kind of compromise, but you'll both survive. In the long run, your woman will not be as put off by an honest objection as she will by a pattern of meaningless placation.

Mr. Never-Around

He's staying late at the office, he's out to dinner with clients or co-workers, he's on a business trip, or off to a golf tournament, or off playing softball or ice hockey, or gone fishing, or hanging out with his pals at the Volunteer Fire Squad. He's Mr. Never-Around: the perennial absentee male.

Most women would agree that even a man who only wants to *sit* around is preferable to one who is *never* around. It's lonely as can be in a relationship with an empty chair and an empty bed.

Even when Mr. Never-Around is around in body, he is not around in spirit. He is always on his cell phone, or being beeped via his pager, or checking his e-mail on his

Mood Makers

Even when you can't be around in body, you can be around in spirit. If you need to work long hours from time to time, check in via phone, e-mail, or instant messaging. If you need to be out of town, send her a memento while you're on the road—and bring her back a thoughtful souvenir.

Blackberry. (Technology has been a great boon to the Never-Around type of guy, and a great bane to his woman—who feels she cannot compete with it.)

Why is Mr. Never-Around so unavailable? He may have a million rationalizations for his absence. He's working hard! He's networking! He's participating in the community! He just needs a little R&R because he's such a busy guy in the first place!

Does everyone in a relationship deserve some freedom and time to pursue his own interests? Absolutely. But everyone needs to show up for the relationship as well.

Mr. Never-Around can be especially irritating if it happens that when he *is* around, he throws in some His Highness the Prince-type behavior. This double-whammy type of guy drops in between his various excursions and activities expecting to find all his clothes freshly laundered and his bags packed so he can be off again without delay. He may also want some extra physical affection, just before it's time to say good-bye again. For a while, he may even get it, because his woman may believe this will keep him around more. But when it doesn't work out that way, she'll most likely give up on that no-win strategy. Eventually she and her partner will pass like proverbial ships in the night.

If you're never around, or rarely around, or around less than you know deep down you ought to be, the solution is simple. Assign time with your partner a greater priority. Do it today, before she stops missing you so much.

Mr. Little Black Book

Mr. Little Black Book has what is referred to in female parlance as "commitment issues." He may love his woman a great deal, but he is still reluctant to part with his bachelor ways. He continues to flirt seriously with other women, and is not as clear as he should be in sending the message that he is now unavailable. Of all the types of behavior that women find objectionable, this behavior is the most objectionable—because it's the most hurtful.

The single life, and the single attitude, can be hard to part with, to be sure. Every man in a committed relationship may have moments when he fondly recalls his days of playing the field. But daydreams and happy recollections are one thing—actions are another.

If you're not letting other women know you're already spoken for as clearly as you should, it's time to face the ramifications of what you're actually doing. Nothing will hurt your woman more than feeling as if she is not enough for you.

> **Mood Makers**
>
> If you're married, wear a wedding band and wear it consistently and proudly. The tradition of using a wedding ring to symbolize a never-ending circle of ever-lasting love dates back to the ancient Egyptians, who made the bands from rushes that grew along the banks of the Nile. Men's wedding rings have become increasingly common in America since the end of World War II, and are now considered very fashionable. Wives like to see their husbands wearing them not only for their fashion value, but also because they serve as keep-away signals to other women. They say, "This guy is off the market."

The Combo Guy

Perhaps you don't precisely recognize yourself in any one of the foregoing types, but you nevertheless have experienced some distant bells ringing as you read through a few of them. This might mean you're a Combo Guy: sometimes a little bit of this; sometimes a wee bit of that.

The Combo Guy can be, overall, a pretty fine pleaser. Yet he is occasionally off his game. Now and again, especially when he's under stress and preoccupied with other pressing matters, he can err on the side of self-centeredness, passive aggression, or plain old obliviousness.

Hey, anyone can have a bad day. Really. No need to hang your head. Still, if you have recognized bits and pieces of behaviors that your woman might find undesirable, you might just want to ask her, "Hey, honey, does this sound like me?" If she sighs a bit or rolls her eyes, you'll know you've hit a nerve. A few tweaks could well be in order. Remember, no matter what else is on your mind, save some space for her in that busy, overworked brain of yours.

The Occasional Caveman

Please don't feel like pleasing your woman means giving up all of your defenses, or all of your freedoms, or all of your fun. On the contrary: no reasonable woman expects her partner to be a poster boy for connubial bliss all of the time. After all, that would leave her without any good material for "guy jokes." Besides, it would mean you were boring and predictable. And she certainly doesn't want that.

There is some truth to the rumor that women are on some level attracted to men with a hint of the "bad boy" and a dash of the "caveman" about them. Breaking a rule now and again, being a bit unruly sometimes—these things can be kind of charming. Just don't make a daily habit of it.

Yes, it's important to be a gentleman and a thoughtful mate. But it's also important to be real, to be playful, to be you. It's all about striking a balance—and that's no joke.

The Least You Need to Know

- ◆ There's no truth to the rumor that men cannot change—but if you want to change you must take the initiative by acting as if the change has already taken place.

- ◆ Women may joke about typical male behaviors, but when those behaviors are taken to extremes, they're destructive to relationships.

- ◆ Male behaviors that truly irk women include being oblivious, being excessively demanding, being passive-aggressive, being unavailable, and being ambivalent about commitment.

- ◆ No reasonable woman expects a man to be perfect—so be real, and don't lose sight of your inherent maleness.

The Romance Dance

In This Chapter

- ◆ How women connect love and sex
- ◆ The importance of little gestures
- ◆ The occasional grand gesture
- ◆ The importance of time together
- ◆ Glorious girl gifts

Romance is the expression of enthusiasm and tender emotions toward one's partner. Are you a romantic guy? If you are, you're already well ahead of the game when it comes to pleasing your woman. This chapter will offer you some additional tips.

If you're a little hesitant or awkward when it comes to showing signs of your emotional connection, this chapter will get you started.

Love and Sex

You may have heard this before, and I hope you believed it—because it's true: women are less likely than men to separate loving emotions from sexual desire. Whereas guys may respond to a beautiful woman by immediately launching into a sexual fantasy about her, women will more likely respond to an attractive man by conjuring up a romantic emotional scenario in which she and he co-star.

Sex, for women, is the logical outgrowth of emotional attachment, coupled with physical desire. Sex without love, for her, is the proverbial "taking a shower with a raincoat on." If you want to strengthen the physical bond with your partner, be sure to romance her as your first step.

It's the Little Things

Don't be intimidated by the idea of romance. You don't need to ride in on a horse and sweep her off to a magic kingdom—well, unless it's a surprise weekend at Disney World. You don't need to toss rose petals as she walks down the street. You could be ticketed for littering. And for heaven's sake, don't pull a Sir Walter Raleigh and throw your coat across a puddle for her. She'll only get miffed about the cost of the dry cleaning bill.

Romance is, at the heart of it, an attitude that conveys, "I'm thinking of you." For the most part, it can be expressed in small, thoughtful gestures. Want a few ideas to get you started? Here they are, but notice I've left the last few spots blank. That's so you can come up with some of your own ideas, too.

- ◆ Fall asleep holding her hand.
- ◆ Send her a balloon bouquet.
- ◆ Dance with her mother.
- ◆ Ask her father for some advice.
- ◆ Take her car through the car wash.
- ◆ Get her her own remote control.
- ◆ "Ooh" and "ahh" over her baby pictures.
- ◆ Talk her out of the Botox.
- ◆ Be nice to her pets.
- ◆ Let her pick the lottery numbers.
- ◆ Pick her up at the airport.
- ◆ Be on time.

- Stop the car when she needs to "go."

- Help her find her lost earring/contact lens.

- Always leave her the last cookie.

- Get up with the kids and let her sleep in.

- Help her with chores without being asked.

- Peck her on the cheek.

- Call your radio station and dedicate a song.

- Water her plants.

- Give her a locket with your photo.

- Waltz her around the kitchen.

- Say something in Italian—anything!

- _____

- _____

- _____

- _____

- _____

How did you do in filling in those blanks?

If you've come up with your own ideas, don't neglect to implement them. If you're still stumped, come back to this page as ideas occur to you—as they certainly will.

A Grand Surprise

While little things really do matter most, every once in a while it's extremely romantic—and particularly pleasing—to arrange a grander gesture as a testament to your enduring affections. Arranging for a more elaborate romantic surprise is not something you'll do once a week, or even once a month. But every now and again, this makes for a magnificent relationship resuscitation.

What kind of grand surprise gestures am I talking about? Perhaps you dreamed one up when you proposed to your wife. Maybe you took her to a top tier restaurant—the kind it takes months to get a reservation for—and had her ring hidden in a specially pre-ordered dish of Beluga caviar. Maybe you had "Will you marry me?" flashed on a screen during a seventh inning ballgame stretch. Maybe you were one of those clever guys who hung around the outdoor set of a nationwide morning T.V. show and managed to get the weatherman to let you pop the question live. Even if you weren't one of those guys, I'll bet you thought up something special. But ask yourself: was that the last time you went to such lengths of planning?

As a rare and special romantic event, consider the following:

◆ **A surprise getaway.** Arrange for childcare, pet care, and whatever other kind of care you need to hold down the home front. Take her out for what she thinks is dinner, but instead drive to the charming inn where you've reserved a room with a view. Pull the bag you've pre-packed for her out of the trunk and tell her she has carte blanche to buy whatever else it is she needs.

Love Busters

Some women love being the center of attention, others are more reticent. Know and respect your woman's style, so you don't risk embarrassing her.

Mood Makers

Every woman wants to look extra fabulous when she's the center of attention. To make sure your lady's surprise party is the right kind of surprise, ask her to dress for a special night out—but offer misleading details about exactly what she'll be doing once she gets there. Never have a crowd yell "surprise" when she's wearing a sweat suit, sneakers, and no make-up.

◆ **A public testimonial.** Arrange for a skywriting plane to inscribe "I Love You" and her name above a beach where you'll both be lying. Or make a brief home movie declaring your love and arrange to have it shown at a small local theatre during the coming attractions. Or place a small ad in your local paper declaring your affections (use nicknames if you want to keep this public act private).

◆ **A surprise party.** Arrange to celebrate her birthday or your anniversary in grand style with family and friends. Choose entertainment she'll enjoy and a menu she'll relish.

You have to be pretty good at keeping secrets to pull off a grand surprise. There's no doubt they do take a good bit of effort. That, of course, is the whole point. Your woman will be thrilled by your surprise, not only for the event itself but even more so because she will understand the immense amount of resourcefulness and work that went into it. Along with the memory of what you did, she'll cherish that for years to come.

It's About Time

Of course, it's hard to be romantic in small or extravagant ways unless you factor in one crucial ingredient: time. When you were first getting together with your woman you made it a priority to spend time with her. It wasn't something you felt obligated to do—it was just fun. Somehow, everything else in your hectic life got accomplished *even though* you devoted hours to doing things with and for your love.

I'll bet your life is even busier and more complicated now that you two have became a couple and started building a life together. Even so, making time for a little romance will always pay off.

Do you have any idea how much time you do—or don't—spend with your lady, and what the two of you do with the time you spend? Use the following chart to help you keep track for a week.

Day	Hours You Spent Together	What You Did
Monday	_____	_____
Tuesday	_____	_____
Wednesday	_____	_____
Thursday	_____	_____
Friday	_____	_____
Saturday	_____	_____
Sunday	_____	_____

Add up your joint waking hours. Now, deduct from those hours when you were actually thinking about work. Come on, be honest. Now deduct those hours when you were both actually obsessing on your kids. The time remaining counts as quality couple time. You may find that it is a shockingly minute amount. Now it's time to do something about it.

Work Worries

Work is important for all sorts of reasons. As a practical matter, it generates income. That's good, because every couple needs revenue to turn their dreams into reality.

But work also makes people feel useful and valuable. Any job well done can be a source of personal fulfillment and pride.

But all of this makes it much too easy to blame work for not spending time with your partner. Some men—and women, too—can actually become addicted to work, the way they can to a drug. Since our society strongly values the work ethic, it's sometimes difficult to recognize this for the problem it is.

Even if neither of you is a workaholic, balancing work with private life is becoming increasingly difficult. Technology is causing the whole world to speed up. It also allows communications from the workplace to intrude more and more into the realm of personal life. Even if you are not literally taking your work home, you may still be bringing home leftover emotional baggage from the workday. This negative spillover can be intensely consuming.

Love Busters

How do you know if you're in danger of turning into a workaholic? If you find it difficult *not* to work, and sometimes use work as an escape from other parts of your life, this could be the start of addiction. Monitor yourself to avoid slipping further into workaholism. Be sure to create no-work time periods and no-work zones in your home.

If work or work-related thoughts are sapping quality time from you and your partner, ask yourself this question:

Exactly what is it you're working for?

When all's said and done, no one has ever devoted their dying words to the wish that they had spent more time working.

What About the Kids?

For both moms and dads, caring for children is an eight-day-a-week commitment. But kids have not yet learned about setting limits, so adults have to. If you and your partner have rarely been alone since children became a part of your lives, here's a word you need to add to your vocabulary: *baby-sitter*.

Baby-sitters don't have to be an expensive indulgence. If you're lucky enough to live near either set of grandparents, bear in mind how thrilled they will be to spend quality time with their grandchildren. If there's no family nearby, try kid-swapping with other couples in the same boat as you. Trade off a few hours once a week, and make four adults really happy. You'll make the kids happy, too, because they'll enjoy being together. In fact, you can build on this swapping idea with another magic word: *sleepover*. It's a party when kids get to spend the whole night at a friend's house. The following week you and your family can reciprocate. In the meantime, you and your lady can have a party for two.

Feeling too uneasy to leave them with a stranger? If your kids are very small, consider having a sitter come in after they fall asleep. If your children are older, hire a sitter who enjoys doing the things they like to do—be it playing video games, chess, or tag.

It's all too easy to say you feel guilty about leaving the kids. But, as a responsible parent, try to take a larger view about what's genuinely in the kids' best interests. When you and your mate are happy and satisfied, they will flourish.

Gift Your Girl

Now we come to another important way to be romantic: gift giving. When is the right time to give your woman a gift? What time is it now?

Sure, gifts should be given for birthdays and anniversaries—and I strongly suggest putting reminders for these dates in your calendar or programming them into your PDA at the start of each year. Then there's Valentine's Day, of course, and Christmas or Chanukah. Oh, and if you have kids you'll certainly want to help them keep an eye out for Mother's Day (it's the second Sunday in May).

But the element of surprise can also be introduced in gift giving. If you can't think of an occasion, make one up (Happy Recycling Center Day), or feel free to borrow holidays from other cultures (there's always Bastille Day and Cinco de Mayo). The old "Just Because I Love You Day" is always a good one, too.

If you can't think what to get her, read on for ideas and inspiration.

 Mood Makers

Incorporate a three-week lead time when noting birthday and anniversaries dates in your calendar or PDA. Longer than that and you'll procrastinate and then forget anyway; shorter than that and you may not have time to find just the right thing.

Jewelry

Women are easier to buy gifts for than men, and jewelry is one of the big reasons why. Can a woman ever have too much jewelry? Let me put it this way: no.

Be thoughtful, though, when you are selecting just the right piece, be it a necklace, bracelet, earrings, or a new watch. Many women have a distinct preference for yellow gold, white gold, platinum, or silver jewelry. Observe what she wears most and try to get her something that fits in with her theme. Some women also have a preference for certain gemstones, like diamonds, emeralds, or sapphires. When in doubt, consider her birthstone. Use the following list if you aren't sure what her birthstone is.

January	Garnet
February	Amethyst
March	Aquamarine
April	Diamond
May	Emerald
June	Pearl
July	Ruby
August	Peridot
September	Sapphire
October	Opal
November	Topaz
December	Turquoise

If this sounds too rich for your blood, the good news is that costume jewelry is really in vogue these days. It's okay to go fake as long as the fakes are fashionable. Hint: if you're really desperate for ideas, try perusing her fashion magazines for ideas when she's out of the house.

Chocolate

Chocolate: she's got to love it. I mean she really has *got* to. This highly popular substance actually does have measurable effects on human behavior—and research shows it has a greater impact on females than on males.

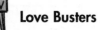

Love Busters

If she's really, really on a weight loss diet and specifically asks you not to get her chocolate, respect her wishes. If she indulges in spite of herself and blames you, it won't be pretty. Along those lines, sugar-free or low-fat chocolate is never a good idea. Yuck.

Chocolate contains *phenylethylamine* and *serotonin*, both of which are mood-lifting agents that occur naturally in the human brain. The release of these chemicals into the nervous system causes rapid mood change, a rise in blood pressure, and an increasing heart rate. In short, chocolate can create a substantial temporary energy boost as well as induce feelings of well-being usually associated with being in love or in lust.

As far as your lady is concerned, all chocolate may not be created equal. Find out if she prefers dark or milk chocolate. She might like fillings, or she might be a purist. When in doubt, buy a sampler assortment. Maybe she'll share—then again, maybe not.

Flowers

It may sound corny, but you really can always say it with flowers. There's nothing like a festive arrangement delivered to her door to make her swoon. Send them to her workplace if you want to double her pleasure by allowing her friends and co-workers to see what a great guy she has.

Are there any wrong kinds of flowers? Only the ones that she's allergic to.

Books

Does your woman lament the fact that she just doesn't have as much time to read as she used to? Don't let that stop you from buying her books. Reading is an inspirational activity: we hope to get to all those books one day. It's comforting to have a trove of books by the bedside and atop the coffee table, even if she knows she may not get to all of them until the kids are grown and she retires.

If she has favorite authors, seek out their newest work. If she has favorite categories or subjects—for example, biographies, natural history, travel books, or gardening books—browse through a bookstore, or search an online one, to see what's come out on the topic. When in doubt, a gift certificate will do, but a book you picked out yourself exhibits a bit more of that all-important romantic attitude and thoughtfulness.

Music

Keep an eye out for releases from her favorite artists. You can buy her CDs or even a gift card to download tunes from a website. If she's technologically inclined, think about an iPod or MP3 player as well. In addition, watch for her favorite artist performing locally. Take her to their concerts.

Gardening Goodies

If your woman is a gardener, or would like to be one, there is no end to the wonderful creative gifts you can conjure up for her. Beyond the basics—tools, gloves, and plantings—nurseries and specialized catalogues offer everything from waterproof Wellington boots to whimsical garden statuary to exotic planters and fountains.

Like reading, this may be an activity she would like to have more time for than she actually does. Nevertheless, having the right accessories may inspire her to find more time.

High-End Housewares

No, don't buy her a new iron or a hand-held vacuum as a present. Gifts should never be that practical or that boring. But do consider items that add a touch of elegance to the home, such as pottery, tableware, glassware, fine linens, candles, and wall hangings. Candles, in interesting shapes and scintillating scents, can also be a truly luxurious and sensual item.

If she likes to cook—and I mean genuinely likes it—think about gourmet food prep items like Cuisinarts, Le Creuset pots, and assorted restaurant grade griddles, double boilers, and so on.

If you genuinely feel lost in an elegant housewares shop, ask a female friend or relative to accompany you and enlighten you. Or find a salesperson who's willing to show you mercy.

Clothes and Lingerie

As much as most women like getting and wearing new clothes, I admit that in this area we are tricky to buy for. The reason has to do partly with style—we are very picky about which trends we embrace and which we think make us look silly—but also with sizing.

What size does your woman take in a dress, in a coat, in pants, or in a bathing suit? Of course you don't know, because half the time we don't know either. Manufacturers vary widely in how they size items. This has always been a problem but is an even more pronounced one lately as *vanity sizing* becomes a more common practice. When in doubt—which will be most of the time—get her a gift certificate. Then she gets the fun of getting the gift and the extra fun of shopping. (You can also offer to go shopping with her, if she'd like your company. She might say no, but she'll be thrilled you thought to ask.)

As for lingerie, if you dare to pick it out yourself, an important thing to remember is that you are buying the lingerie to please her—not you. Don't think "centerfold." Think about *your* woman and what makes her feel comfortable and sensual.

Tongue Teasers

Vanity sizing is the practice of resizing clothing so that customers feel like they are thinner than they used to be—miraculously so, without shedding a pound. Manufacturers might take a dress that used to be a size 12 and reclassify it as a size 10, a 10 as an 8, and so on. This practice is becoming more and more popular as the majority of the population ages and waist sizes expand along with the number of birthdays under one's belt.

The Write Stuff

Want a luscious love note? Get her the right supplies. Women love stationery, note cards, and elegant writing implements. A host of specialty stores and catalogues cater to this penchant. Many are happy to personalize her gifts, although this does call for some advance planning on your part. (By the way, you can always borrow some of her stationery to pen your own love missive.)

Leather Goods

Ah, the aroma of high quality leather—just about every woman adores it. Whether it's a briefcase, business card holder, wallet, or handbag, she'll relish it for years to come. If you're planning a special getaway, think about enhancing her trip with a fine leather carry-all.

Spa Days

Your woman needs a break. How do I know? Because all women need one.

If there's no time for a full-fledged getaway, an hour or two at a day spa may just do the trick. Treat her to a gift certificate redeemable for a facial, a massage, a pedicure, or a more exotic treatment like a full body exfoliating salt scrub (from which she'll be smooth as silk afterward). Many day spas also offer half- and full-day packages that include a potpourri of services and a light, nutritious lunch.

He Says/She Says

"One of the coolest things my husband ever did was to get a spa day package for me *and* my sister. That was so sweet because I think it is so much more fun to go to the spa with someone. It was really an emotionally generous gift."
—Nancy, 33

Perfume

If you know her favorite scent, pamper her with perfume—or one of its variants. Confused about what's what? Most perfumes are complex combinations of natural materials, such as essential oils from plants, and synthetic products that heighten the smell and increase their staying power. Alcohol is used as a liquid base for perfume, and the ratio of alcohol to scented perfume concentrates determines how the final concoction is labeled.

From highest concentration of scent to least, the different forms of perfume are:

- **Perfume, also called extract or *extrait* perfume.** This is the purest form of a scented product and, as a result, the most expensive. It can include 15 to 40 percent perfume concentrates.

- **Eau de parfum.** The most popular and common form of perfume, this concentration provides long-lasting fragrance and usually doesn't cost as much as extract perfume. It contains about 7 to 15 percent perfume concentrates.

- **Eau de toilette.** This has about 1 to 6 percent perfume concentrates, making for a lighter scent that doesn't linger as long as the more intense versions. *Eau de toilette* was originally intended to be a refreshing body splash that helped women wake up in the morning.

- **Eau de cologne.** This term is sometimes used interchangeably with the term *eau de toilette*. However, the concoction began as the name of a light fragrance mixed with citrus oils—made popular by Napoleon. Some perfumers today have a version of this called *eau fraiche*.

While these are the main classes of perfume, numerous other products are scented with perfume concentrates as well. Your lady might enjoy a variety of such lotions, creams, powders, body splashes, soaps, and other cosmetic products that contain small amounts of fragrance.

By the way, if you don't know your partner's favorite scent, or if she expresses a desire to try a new perfume, consider accompanying her on a sampling safari. She can try different fragrances and you can tell her which ones make her smell the most delicious. Be sure to let them soak into her skin for a minute. If you sniff too soon all you'll smell is alcohol.

Athletic Gear

For outdoor types, consider quality hiking, biking, or cycling gear—or whatever ties in with her favorite activity. These days it's possible to appear stylish even while rock climbing or hang-gliding. But always remember—safety first. Go for state-of-the-art items that will protect her, even if they sell at a premium.

For indoor athletic types, consider yoga and dance accessories, as well as workout tapes or DVDs.

Tickets

Treat her to tickets to some of her favorite events: theatre, concerts, ballet, and so on. She'll not only enjoy getting the tickets, but will also have the pleasure of looking forward to an evening out with her man. If she's really interested in the arts, consider buying a seasonal subscription.

The Least You Need to Know

- ◆ Women are less apt than men to separate loving emotions from sexual desire.

- ◆ Romance is an attitude that conveys tender emotions—it can often be expressed in small, thoughtful gestures.

- ◆ Now and again, a surprise grand gesture is welcome—your woman will most appreciate the effort behind it.

- ◆ In order to romance your lady, you need time—arrange your priorities to make the most of this valuable commodity.

- ◆ Anytime is the right time to get your lady a gift—special occasions call for gifts, but any day you give her a gift becomes special.

Chapter **4**

Adore Her Gorgeousness

In This Chapter

- ◆ Why your woman caught your eye
- ◆ Women and self-image
- ◆ Help her feel more gorgeous
- ◆ Some things you should never say
- ◆ Help her glow outside and inside
- ◆ Pregnant women are extra gorgeous

Men are visual creatures. You are programmed to be absorbed by what you see. There's no question that part of what attracted you to your woman in the first place was her appearance.

Your appreciation of her face, her figure, her eyes, her skin, and her smile made her even prettier. As a result of your attentions, she glowed from the inside. She also probably did many things to make sure she kept looking her most appealing on the outside. She had a good time doing so, too, because it's fun to look great for a guy who appreciates you.

But when's the last time you made her feel gorgeous? If you can't remember, it was too long ago. This chapter will offer some advice on seeing your woman once again through the eyes of a new love—and letting her know it.

The Eye of the Beholder

To a lover in the throes of initial attraction, the object of his affection is the most beautiful sight in the world. No, make that the universe. Though he might still objectively appreciate the pleasure of looking at other attractive women (he's only human after all), they leave him emotionally cold by comparison. There's just something about *this particular woman* … even though he might not be able to articulate exactly what it is.

So what is it?

Many studies have been done that attempt to quantify what precisely it is about another person's appearance that draws us in. Some research suggests that men and women both are attracted to mates with *facial symmetry*. Even babies, it turns out, will spend more time staring at photographs of people whose facial features are symmetrical. Of course, many famous people who are generally considered very attractive have asymmetrical faces, some with very quirky features. But symmetry connotes "normalcy"—which studies show is another desirable trait for a prospective mate.

Tongue Teasers

Facial symmetry means that the left and right sides of the face match up, appearing perfectly balanced.

Additional research studies show that males are generally attracted to females with a small waist to hip ratio, or what is more commonly known as an "hour glass figure." When men are asked to rank female body types, they consistently give high rankings to women whose waist to hip ratio is about .70—meaning the width of the waist is about two thirds the width of the hips.

Interestingly, the actual weight of the woman's body has little to do with the attraction. One study compiled the measurements of Playboy centerfolds and Miss America winners from 1923 to 1990. Their bodies got slimmer and leaner over the decades, yet their waist-hip ratios stayed within the narrow range of .68 to .72. Marilyn Monroe personified this ratio, and so did Sophia Loren and the Venus de Milo—but, then again, so did Twiggy and Kate Moss. Why the preference? From a biological standpoint, it is probably because women with such proportions are perceived as being—and in fact are—highly fertile.

But if you were attracted to your partner for such minutely measurable reasons, it's unlikely you knew—or if you did it's unlikely you would have cared. It's more likely that you could have named some particular features that you admired. In general, men say they like women with large eyes, long eyelashes and dark eyebrows, high cheekbones, full lips, voluminous shiny hair, and a well-defined jaw line. Oh, and great legs.

Ah, but was any of that what really caught your eye? A good deal of research says that although such features are admired, what most men—and most women for that matter—are drawn to are average-looking mates. Averageness signals "normal" and "healthy." Again, from an evolutionary perspective, a predilection for normality makes sense. We want "normal genes" to merge with our own.

So where does that leave us? Why did your woman draw you in more than any other? Why was it that she turned you on? It is, as the French say, that *je ne sais quoi*—an indefinable yet palpable *something*.

He Says/She Says

"What physical attributes attracted me to my wife? It's difficult to say, but one thing—as silly as it sounds—is this way she has of crinkling her nose when she laughs. Oh, and I also love the curve of her neck, and her delicate hands. I guess it's the little things, or the way all the little things combine into one adorable package."
—George, 46

But one thing is for sure, no matter what your lady looks like, your liking of her appearance raised her above the crowd in your estimation. Beauty, as they say, is in the eye of the beholder. And it is your appreciative beholding of her that makes your woman feel truly special.

Women and Self-Image

For many women, feeling beautiful in a relationship is a welcome change. Sadly, they may have spent a great deal of their lives believing that their looks were inadequate. This dynamic can apply even to the very women that most males and females would objectively rate as highly attractive.

Many factors contribute to a woman's potential for negative self-evaluation. From childhood, the images of "ideal women" to which she is exposed can be exceedingly unrealistic. It can be hard to feel good-looking when the perceived ideal is beyond attainment. It's not too surprising, then, that some studies suggest up to 90 percent of women would like to change something about their appearance.

Barbie's Plastic Proportions

For many girls, getting their first "Barbie" is a very special event. Now they have a doll to dress up in high fashion, to accessorize, and to act out "grown-up" scenarios with. Over the years, Barbie has evolved into quite a career girl, becoming a doctor, surgical nurse, ballerina, flight attendant, Olympic skier, gymnast, and skater. She has even run for president. But one thing that hasn't changed is that Barbie's bodily proportions are out of the range of most mere mortals.

If the doll that was originally marketed in 1959 were human-sized, her measurements would have been 39" 18" 33". Needless to say, these measurements were not based on actual human metrics. (We'd tip over if we were built like that!) In response to criticism, the doll's manufacturer later adjusted Barbie's chest measurement down and waist measurement up, but her proportions are still uncharacteristic of most females.

The Barbie ideal is culturally pervasive—the doll is a 1.9 billion dollar a year industry, and two Barbies are purchased every second. Does her impact still influence women who have grown out of the play-with-dolls phase? Well, one woman has admitted to having over 40 plastic surgeries in order to emulate Barbie. That's an extreme case, to be sure; nevertheless, many grown women still find the doll's impact on their formative years hard to shake off.

The Supermodel and Star Syndrome

Supermodels and movie stars are also held up as paragons of the "perfect" woman. No woman can turn on her television set, flip through a magazine or catalog, or go to a movie without facing the tall, excessively thin, perfectly coiffed, wrinkle-free pinnacle of womanhood as presented by the media. To varying degrees, women may devote an exorbitant amount of time and money trying to recreate themselves in these images. But no matter how much effort and how many resources a woman expends, she finds she still doesn't look quite like the superstars do.

The truth is—as supermodels and actresses would be the first to admit—*they* don't look like that either *in real life*. Are they lovely women? Yes. But lighting experts, brilliant photographers, makeup artists, fashion consultants, hairstylists, and colorists are also part of the reason that they look completely flawless. Why does a "regular" woman never look like a model looks, even if she weighs the same and is wearing identical clothing? Because models are lit and photographed perfectly—and even pinned and sewn into clothes—so that they offer up the illusion of perfection.

Besides, models and actresses consider staying in shape, watching their weight, partaking in rigorous beauty treatments, and sometimes even having surgery, part of their job description. They devote hours to their beauty regime each day.

Many women understand all of this intellectually, but emotions sometimes don't obey the rational mind. Many women still long to attain an unattainable goal when it comes to their appearance. They compare themselves with a fantasy. When they cannot achieve the fantasy, they may feel unhappy with themselves, regardless of how lovely they are.

How Gorgeous Does Your Woman Feel?

Does your woman feel less beautiful than you think she should and wish she would? You know the answer is yes if she is often critical of her own physical characteristics. See if any of these behaviors ring a bell:

- Does she repeatedly complain about and sigh over her body weight—even if she only wants to lose 5 to 10 pounds?

- Does she lament her wrinkles and laugh lines?

- Is she continually voicing disapproval of hair that simply will not do as she bids it?

- Does she often wonder aloud if she should alter her looks with surgical or quasi-surgical procedures? (The later category could include Botox injections, laser skin treatments, and so on.)

- Does she complain about looking older?

If so, her discontent is pretty obvious. But some women are much more inscrutable when it comes to revealing how they feel about their looks. You might think a woman who has given up on maintaining her looks has happily resigned herself to "just being who she is." But she might feel dejected—as if it's all a lost cause. Conversely, you might think a woman who spends an inordinate amount of time on her appearance is vain, but she may be extremely insecure.

Now don't get me wrong. A certain amount of primping is fun for most of us, and fully the entitlement of the female gender. But overdoing it—or taking the opposite approach and paying no attention to her appearance—may well mean your woman's self-esteem could use a boost.

Even if she's not prone to extreme behavior, give your lady a boost anyhow. We could all use one sometimes.

Let Her Know She's a Beauty

Almost all of us fall prey to negative self-talk now and again. We remind ourselves about what's wrong with us much more often than we remind ourselves what's right. Our self-talk will become more positive if those we love give us positive reinforcement. Along those lines, there are a number of things a man can do to let his woman know he still finds her attractive.

♦ **Be observant.** When's the last time you commented on a new outfit she was wearing, or a new hairdo, or on how aglow her face looked in a particular light? You can't comment on something you don't notice! Open your eyes and appreciate what you've got.

♦ **Offer a specific compliment.** Let her know you like what you see by telling her why you like it. For example, "Wow, that's a great blouse. I love you in blue. It brings out the color in your eyes."

♦ **Offer general praise.** When's the last time you greeted your lady with a salutation like, "Hey, gorgeous" or "Hello, beautiful"? It may seem like a little thing, but as you already know, little things mean a lot.

♦ **Give her the once-over.** Let your eyes take in your woman's body. Then cast them, in turn, on her eyes, her lips, and her eyes once again. This says, "I wish I was touching you and kissing you right now."

♦ **Give her a wink.** Winking is a very clear flirting signal. Winking is especially fun and effective in public situations because it can be used to broadcast a secret, private signal across a crowded room. Next time you're at a party or other public event with your lady, catch her eye and give her a quick one. You may hear later how it actually gave her goose bumps.

♦ **Let out a wolf whistle.** You know what I mean: *whooh, whooh*.

♦ **Flash an appraisal smile.** Look her over from head to toe, nod with approval, and then flash her a slow, approving grin.

♦ **Give her an over-the-shoulder smile.** Look over your shoulder … and give her a swift, subtle smile. This asymmetrical position signals that you find her intriguing.

Love Busters

Never fake a smile. Do it when you feel it. Most people can intuitively sense when we're truly smiling, as opposed to faking it. That's because a simulated smile doesn't involve the muscles round the eyes in the way a genuine one does.

The wonderful thing about communicating your continuing attraction to your partner is that doing so will make her even more attractive. When a woman is self-confident, she feels beautiful. When a woman feels beautiful, she looks beautiful.

What Not to Say

Just as positive messages about a woman's appearance have beneficial effects, negative messages have harmful ones. As agreeable a guy as you are, there are some times you should never, ever agree with your woman. Those are the times when she is getting down on herself.

See the following for correct and incorrect responses to such situations.

She says: I need to lose five pounds.

You say: I like you as you are.

You don't say: Great, when will you start?

_____

She says: I look old.

You say: To me, you look like the day we met.

You don't say: Well, you're getting older.

_____

She says: I look as tired as I feel.

You say: If you feel tired, let me give you a massage.

You don't say: Well, why don't you get some rest?

_____

She says: I'm not as pretty as _____.

You say: No, you're prettier.

You don't say: Yeah, she's something else.

_____

What if you think she has something of a point? Forget it. Little white lies are a necessary part of most healthy relationships. They're not called white lies for nothing: the term is used to signify their noble intent.

Help Her Glow on the Outside

Another way to adore your woman's gorgeousness is to do things that help her stay gorgeous. To keep her looking lovely on the outside, you can of course, gift her with items that enhance her appearance, like jewelry, clothes, and gift certificates to day spas, as mentioned in Chapter 3. (See Appendix A for lots of specifics, too.)

You can also help her stay in great shape physically by joining her in some exercise. Exercise has a myriad of benefits for health and appearance (and an added benefit is that aerobic exercise may increase sexual desire) but many find it daunting to undertake alone. Happily, there are lots of fun ways to stay fit as a couple.

Bicycle Buds

Remember how exhilarated you felt when you first learned to ride a bike? Even for grown-ups, bikes still conjure up associations with freedom, fresh air, and fun. Biking is also an incredibly healthy pastime that tones muscles without impact, and cultivates overall fitness.

People of all shapes, sizes, and ages can enjoy bicycle riding, so it's a great way to start getting fit together. If you don't own bikes, try renting some for starters. If you really enjoy it, check out Chapter 11 for information on cycling vacations.

Slimming with Swimming

Swimming is one of the best forms of exercise there is. It promotes strength, stamina, and mobility, and is especially great for upper-body tone. The more you swim, the better you'll both look in your bathing suits.

The thought of swimming together may have never crossed your mind if you don't even know where to gain access to a pool. But access is more available than you might think. Try your local YMCA, and explore the possibilities of municipal pools. In summer, explore nearby beaches, lakes, or ponds. Hiking to a secluded swimming venue can offer exercise as excellent as the swim itself.

Don't know how to swim? Take lessons together and enjoy a great sense of accomplishment along with the benefits of shaping up.

Walkabouts

If your lady is intimidated by cycling or water sports or hard-core gym offerings, don't give up. Experts say that one of the best exercises of all is one of the most basic:

walking. Walking is easy and it's free. You and your woman can do it anywhere, anytime—enjoying the opportunity to be alone together, take in the scenery, and do yourselves a world of good.

Mood Makers _____

Simply walking at a brisk three-to-four-mile-an-hour pace for ten minutes or so five or six days a week can do a tremendous amount of good for the body—and the soul. Experts say that nothing is as apt to cheer up one's attitude in a hurry as a good, vigorous walk.

Help Her Glow from Within

Making certain your woman eats good food is one way to keep her healthy on the inside. There's much truth to the adage "we are what we eat." When her diet is healthy and nutritious, her skin, hair, and her eyes will show it—as well as her body. (See Chapter 13 on preparing food for your lady.)

Also, help her develop good eating habits by developing some yourself. When the two of you got together you formed an *eating unit*—so your eating behaviors influence hers. Avoid keeping junk food in the house. Don't keep food in any room of the house other than the kitchen. Keep lots of fresh fruit and vegetables around. Eat slowly, enjoy your food. Never eat on the run, and try not to eat in front of the TV, either.

You can also charge up your woman's inner glow by joining her in a calming daily routine such as 15 or 20 minutes of yoga, t'ai chi, or some form of meditation. (See Chapter 6 for more on this.) Performing such activities on a daily basis over time will have an amazing cumulative effect on inner serenity that also reflects itself outwardly.

Tongue Teasers _____

When a couple joins together, they form what nutritional sociologists call an **eating unit**. The food choices and eating and exercise habits of each individual affect those of the other. Couples who support each other in eating healthfully and exercising regularly will contribute to the health of one another and to the health of their relationship.

Finally—and here's a suggestion you'll really like—having a really great sex life can help your woman feel more beautiful. She'll feel this way not only because she knows you desire her, but because the hormones that are released during sexual arousal and orgasm are great for one's overall well being.

When She's Pregnant

It's worth mentioning that when a woman is carrying a child, she is likely to have many mixed feelings about her appearance. It's true that pregnancy can make some women feel beautiful and desirable, but starting at about the fourth month, when a pregnancy starts to show, it's not unusual for a woman to begin feeling a bit ungainly. Her clothes no longer fit due not only to weight gain but also due to the fact that she may be experiencing some bloating.

As the pregnancy progresses, her weight gain increases. In some cases, her mobility is compromised. She no longer feels agile and flexible. In some cases, too, a woman's hands and feet may become swollen. Even her face may take on a different shape.

The result of all of this is that a woman, even when thrilled to be having a baby, hardly recognizes herself during pregnancy. When she looks in the mirror she doesn't know who she sees. When she gets dressed in maternity clothes, she wonders if she'll ever fit into her pre-pregnancy wardrobe again.

He Says/She Says

"When I was pregnant I used to joke that I was so full of gas and water that I felt like a pubic utility. Or sometimes I described myself as a helium balloon with legs. But, really, it was no joke to me. Underneath my laughter, I couldn't imagine ever looking or feeling 'normal' again. Fortunately, my husband was very reassuring. Every time I said something negative about myself he hugged me and called me beautiful. I knew that, to him, it was true."
—Eileen, 28

Ironically, a woman's pregnancy is the time when a woman's partner may find her more attractive than ever. A man is often enraptured by the appearance of a woman who is carrying his child. Men are often heard to say that pregnant women look "sexy," "adorable," and "glowing."

Guys, this is the time to step up to the plate and tell your pregnant partner exactly how magnificent she looks. Reassure her, too, that she'll look again as she did before—but don't let that overshadow the message that she looks wonderful right now, in the midst of her pregnancy.

This is a situation where a husband's adoration can really have an exceptionally important impact. Never make a joke about her pregnant appearance at her expense, even if she is joking herself. Right now what she needs to know most is that you are as adoring and loyal as ever. No, make that more so.

The Least You Need to Know

◆ Visual attraction played a significant role in what drew you to your woman—
to a man in the grips of initial attraction, his woman is the most beautiful
person in the world.

◆ Women's self-image with regard to their appearance can be compromised
by cultural images of perfection.

◆ You can help your lady feel—and look—more beautiful by communicating,
verbally and nonverbally, how attractive you still find her.

◆ Giving your woman beauty-related gifts and exercising with her are some of
the things you can do to help keep her looking gorgeous on the outside.

◆ Sharing healthy food with your lady, joining her in relaxation techniques, and
even having great sex with her are some of the things you can do to give her an
inner glow that reflects outwardly.

◆ Pregnant women may have many mixed feelings about their appearance—this
is an important time to reinforce your woman's sense of personal attractiveness.

Part **2**

Intimate Companions

You've heard that women like to talk things over. It's true. They also like being genuinely listened to. This part of the book will help you talk the talk of love and relate to your woman better than you ever have before. It will offer advice for strengthening the friendship that underpins your bond by laughing and playing together. Finally, it will help you navigate though life's occasionally choppy waters and emerge a stronger couple.

5

Relation-Talk

In This Chapter

- ◆ What women get out of talking
- ◆ Tips for talking to your woman
- ◆ Avoiding communication pitfalls
- ◆ The art of listening
- ◆ Reading female body language

Conventional wisdom has it that when it comes to talking to one another, most men and women are communication-challenged. This is a case where conventional wisdom is absolutely correct. Men and women may not exactly speak different languages, but they often have different goals in speaking and different ways of communicating. They also tend to interpret some of the same words and phrases in different ways.

Perhaps in an ideal world, every man would come equipped with a "universal translator" device—just like they have on Star Trek—so that he would know exactly what his woman means and how best to respond to her. But since that still falls into the realm of science fiction, you'll want to read this chapter to help you and your partner better relate.

Sweet Talk, Serious Talk

As you already know from the previous two chapters, a man who wants to please his woman will be romantic and complimentary. Part of being this way is, of course, to offer a certain amount of sweet-talk. Sweet-talk consists of overt declarations of love as well as subtle flirtation and praise. It's evident in the affectionate nicknames you bestow on your love, be they generic ("sweetie," "honey," "darling," "pumpkin," "pookie") or specific ones that make sense in a private way only to the two of you.

All women want some sweet-talk from their man, and if you're not peppering your conversation with such loving pleasantries, today would be an excellent day to start. But I'm sorry to say that's actually the easy part of communicating with your woman. Matters can get a bit more convoluted when the talk turns to serious subjects. Okay, they can get a lot more convoluted.

The Goals of Woman-Talk

The first thing you should know is that women's talk often has different goals than men's talk. Sure, everyone talks to communicate basic information—"It's raining outside"; "We're running low on milk"; "I'll meet you at six o'clock in front of the coffee shop." But when it comes to talking, women don't necessarily need a particular concrete subject or purpose. Sometimes, women like to talk to those they love in order to create a connection and keep it going.

To a woman, exchanging words is exchanging affection and exchanging energy. It is a kind of give-and-take—almost a way of *making love*, although not in the bodily sense. Females see talking as bridging a gap between the inner worlds of two individuals. If your woman asks, "Hey, want to just talk for a while?" don't assume she has an ulterior motive. Take it at face value. Often, it's the same as your saying, "Hey, wanna fool around?"

Woman also sometimes talk in order to process their feelings. Typically, a man might mull something over in his mind, decide what he thinks about it or what he wants to do about it, and then state the outcome of his internal deliberations. Many women, on the other hand, like to "think out loud."

Hearing a woman think out loud can be confusing to men. They might assume that someone who is airing opinions on both sides of a situation is just plain mixed-up. But for women, talking is a way of becoming unmixed-up. Through hearing herself say things aloud, she can then feel better equipped to make up her mind. This is all part of her natural way of processing information and weighing things from many different angles.

Women also tend to talk in order to relieve tension and anxiety. This, too, is a behavior that tends to be diametrically opposed to that of most men. Men who are nervous or stressed often withdraw into silence. This could be because they do not want their vulnerability to show.

Not so with women. Many women find that externalizing their fears, doubts, and worries actually makes them less upset. This venting allows them to blow off steam and calm down. Sometimes this can take a while. A woman may even say the same sorts of things over and over again, perhaps in slightly different words or with slight variations on the theme, before she comes to grips with what's bothering her.

He Says/She Says

"When I was trying to deal with something and figure it out by going over it a few times, my husband used to say I was 'obsessing.' I finally convinced him that I was doing the opposite. By going over something out loud, I was desensitizing myself to emotions that made the problem too tough for me to handle initially. It's when I don't say anything that I am probably silently obsessing."
—Christine, 45

When a Woman Is Silent

Some men might wish that women were not as talkative as they are. But if wishing made things so, you'd already have a Ferrari. Besides, you ought to be careful what you wish for. In most cases, a woman who is inordinately, uncharacteristically silent is sending out a sign that there's something not-so-good going on.

Of course, everyone feels like being quiet sometimes. That's fine. There is nothing wrong with mutual silence between two people. In fact, one of the joys of long-term companionship is that a man and a woman are sometimes able to share low-key, tranquil moments when both are in "kick-back" mode.

That said, if your partner has suddenly turned from a communicative woman into an uncommunicative one, you'd do well to keep an eye on her overall emotional demeanor and on the state of the relationship itself. A suddenly silent woman could well be a woman who is feeling hopeless or even seriously depressed. She may also be harboring serious hurts or grievances. In fact, she may be so upset about a problem—perhaps about the state of your bond—that she feels the issue is now "beyond words."

Mood Makers

If the woman in your life is uncharacteristically silent, it might be because she feels that you don't want to hear from her. This in turn will make her feel very rejected. Ask her if there's anything on her mind that she'd like to talk with you about.

These are certainly scenarios where silence is anything but golden. They are usually indicative of communication difficulties that have endured in a relationship for far too long. The reality is, it's best to keep the lines of communication not only open, but abuzz.

How to Talk to a Woman

Talking to women in a productive way is probably not as hard as you think it is. But it's quite possible that no one ever let you in on a few little secrets that are bound to come in handy. There are many little things that you can do to keep communication thriving and to get it back on the right track should it ever start to derail.

Ask for and Offer Details

Women are very detail-oriented in their talk. They like to paint pictures with words. When we recount a conversation, for example, we don't simply recount the gist of it. We tell how others looked when they spoke to us—what their facial expressions were, what their gestures were. We do the same when we recount our end of the conversation. We can tell you exactly where something happened, and when. More than likely, we'll also be able to tell you what everyone was wearing, and what we thought about their choice of ensemble.

When you're conversing with your partner, don't ask her to rush to the bottom line. She will undoubtedly get to it sooner or later. Remember, she's trying to create a connection between the two of you by giving you an accurate glimpse into her world, her reality. When you ask her to rush her story along, or give her nonverbal cues to that effect—like sighing, or tapping your fingers impatiently—she feels as though you don't really care about her perspective.

Women also like to ask for lots of details. If you tell us you went out for a lunch with your boss, we want to know what you said, and what your boss said. We want to know what you thought your boss meant when they said such-and-such, and how you felt about that. But we also want to know what everybody ordered, and whether or not the food was good. Was it a new restaurant you tried, or someplace familiar? Was it crowded? Who else was there? Anyone we know?

If your partner presses you for specifics, she's not trying to give you the third degree. She's genuinely interested in understanding what the experience was like for you. Try offering up those details before she has to press you for them. Now you're talking!

Assign a Word to the Feeling

If you are conversing about feelings, be as specific as possible about naming your emotions. The English language is full of words that describe primary feelings. Each of them can help your partner better understand your mood and your take on situations that you are reacting to.

Try expanding your vocabulary in the area of descriptive emotions. This applies whether the feeling you are having is a difficult, vulnerable feeling or a welcome, positive feeling. See the following table for some starter suggestions.

Vulnerable Feelings	Positive Feelings
Afraid	Confident
Anxious	Calm
Dejected	Hopeful
Embarrassed	Proud
Defeated	Resilient
Threatened	Secure
Reluctant	Eager
Unsympathetic	Compassionate
Isolated	Involved
Dissatisfied	Fulfilled
Awkward	Comfortable

Please note that the table does not refer to "negative" feelings. As far as females are concerned, all feelings are valid feelings that are worthy of expression. The only thing that's negative is glossing over feelings or keeping them bottled up inside until they overflow in a volcanic eruption.

Accept Her Lack of Editing

Sometimes you may feel as if your woman is saying too much without thinking first. Frankly, you may be right. When a woman is in a state of high emotion, self-editing may not be a skill she's employing in the moment as well as she might.

But try not to let it throw you too much. If she's repeating herself, remember that this is part of her way of ultimately calming herself down. If she's exaggerating to make a point, try not to take what she says literally. Allow for a little dramatic license. As the eighteenth century feminist Mary Wollstonecraft wrote, "Surely we women have a gene—in addition to those saucy, but ill-mannered hormones—for theatrics, so frequently do they puncture our inner lives and decorate our outer ones in operatic robes."

Pointing out that a woman is "ranting" when she's in the midst of venting will only rev her up more. If she says something personally hurtful to you during such times, you have every right to let her know that it upsets you—and so you should. But, if you can, try waiting until she has let off some of her excess emotional energy.

Initiate Conversation

Is it always your partner who asks, "How was your day?" or "What's new?" Would you ever volunteer this information if she didn't ask for it? Try switching roles and getting the ball rolling for a change. Make a concerted effort to ask her how things are going for her.

You certainly don't have to limit your conversation openers to subjective topics. If you read something interesting in the paper, ask her what she thinks about it. She'll be delighted to be asked her opinion on topics that interest you and that you consider relevant.

Respect Her Opinion

Once your woman does offer an opinion, respect it. Couples will not always agree—either on personal matters or on interpretations of events in the outside world. But even if you two disagree, don't shut your partner down by explaining her "faulty" logic to her or by clamming up and abruptly terminating the discussion.

Agreeing to disagree is a skill successful couples embrace. The two of you can go off to the polls on election day, for example, vote for two different candidates, and still make love that night. Just ask James Carville and Mary Matalin, two famous political consultants and commentators who are, respectively, a Democrat and a Republican. A good relationship is strong enough to accommodate differing points of view.

Mood Makers

Expand your domestic conversation to include nondomestic topics—like community and world news. Women want to know you value their input on more than items related to the family dinner menu and the kids' antics.

How Not To Talk To a Woman

As always, knowing what *not* to do is as important as knowing pointers for what *to* do. There are some communication behaviors that many men are prone to that just so happen to drive a lot of women crazy. Persist in doing them at your own peril! Or, better yet, don't persist. Read on to find out what behaviors to best avoid if woman-pleasing communication is your goal.

Don't Rush In with Suggestions

Advice can be nice—when it is solicited. If your woman asks you what you think she ought to do about a particular problem or situation, by all means offer up your opinion. But do not opine in the absence of her direct invitation.

Remember, men are very goal-oriented when they communicate, whereas women are process-oriented. Before a woman decides what to do—if she's going to do anything at all—she may air a number of options aloud to see how each of them feels to her. It's like trying on lots of different shoes. Although you may feel as though you are chomping at the bit to propose the "obvious" answer to her quandary, remember that she may not be ready to arrive at any answer yet, and when she does she may need to come to it all on her own.

Although you may only have the best intentions, a woman might perceive your offering of premature or unasked-for advice as the equivalent of ordering her around. This serves to make her feel treated like a scolded child, which of course she will resent. Even if your suggestion is offered delicately, she might still react negatively and defensively if she is in a heightened emotional state.

Don't Make Fun of Her Feelings

Whatever you do, never mock or joke about the feelings your partner is expressing. Shared humor is a very beneficial part of relationships (see more on this in Chapter 6), however sarcasm at her expense is definitely *not* appreciated—especially when she is already upset.

Why would a man be sarcastic when his woman is obviously in the grips of a difficult emotion? Not because he's cruel, but because he just doesn't want or know how to deal with what he considers an unpleasant situation. Sadly, his attempt to deflect unpleasantness by misusing "humor" will only make his partner more upset because she will feel disrespected. She has gotten a message from her man that says, "You're ridiculous."

Don't Fib

Another common way that men have of avoiding what they consider an unpleasant conversation—especially when it's a confrontation—is to tell a fib. They might say, for example …

- That they've taken care of something they've been asked to do—even if they haven't quite gotten to it yet.

- That they have to work late while their mother-in-law is visiting, when in fact they plan to stay late and more or less kill time until the unwanted guest has gone home.

- That they *have* to go golfing for business reasons, when in fact they mostly want to get out of doing the yard work they promised they'd do.

There may be grains of truth in these fibs. Sure, they might plan to get to their un-done chore later. And they might actually do some work while they're hanging out at the office. And they might talk about a bit of business between the 17th and 18th hole of the golf course. But, technically, they're still telling untruths. When your woman knows you've deliberately misled her—and she will, because remember, she knows you well *and* she's very intuitive—she will likely be *more* upset than if you'd simply leveled with her to begin with. The fib has only compounded the initial problem.

Women feel extremely insecure when they catch their man in a fib because it leads them to suspect there may be many more things he's fibbing about. It's better to face the music than to sow seeds of doubt and suspicion. Trust is the bedrock of a relation-ship as far as women are concerned.

Don't Pop Your Cork

Many times men bottle up their anger over a period of time, only to release it in a big blowout. A volatile man can be very intimidating to a woman. He can also say things he doesn't mean and wishes he could take back later.

Better to air your grievances one at a time in the calmest way possible by owning up to your feelings as they occur. You might briefly feel better after you explode, but she won't.

Don't Walk Out

Of all the things you can do to offend a woman who wants to communicate with you, walking out in the middle of a discussion may be the worst of all. This behavior is perceived as more than a rude act: it is perceived as abandonment. As such, it is extremely hurtful.

It is understandable that sometimes you have just reached your limit and exhausted your tolerance for a particular topic in the moment. This can be especially true if your partner has committed breaches of communication propriety herself, such as prolonging a discussion for hours on end, or harshly criticizing you with her words. At such times—and especially when you feel you might be about to "lose it" and explode in anger—it is perfectly fair to call a time out. But do explain that although you wish to call a temporary halt to the discussion in order to think things through, or to regain your equanimity, you are willing to continue talking about this subject at another, more appropriate time. Ideally you should pre-arrange such a time, so she won't feel as if she's been left hanging.

To Love Is to Listen

What women want most out of communication with their man is to feel understood. The only way you can understand what someone is saying is to listen to them. It may sound simplistic to say, "listen when your woman speaks"—but you know how easy it is to simply feign listening while someone's words go "in one ear and out the other."

All of us, women too, are guilty at times of not paying enough attention when someone is talking to us. Sometimes it's because we've just got so many things on our minds that competing concerns are throwing up a lot of static. Sometimes it's because we deliberately tune someone out rather than deal with what they're saying. Most often, it's probably because we're thinking about how it is we're going to respond. We're so busy trying to be one step ahead that we actually miss a significant bit of information.

One useful strategy when it comes to improving listening skills is to slow down the pace of conversation. Your partner does not need a lightening fast response from you, and she does not need you to impress her with your cleverness. She needs to know that you *heard what she said.*

An excellent way to show her that you did in fact hear her, and that you understand her needs, is to take what she has said and reflect her own message back to her. This is known as the art of *paraphrasing*.

Tongue Teasers

Paraphrasing is a way of letting a speaker know they're being heard by restating their message, as well as the emotion behind their words, and then reflecting it back to them.

You may have heard of paraphrasing before, especially if you've taken any kind of communication or management training course at your place of work. The technique has been around for quite some time. Still, a lot of people are uncertain about how best to do it.

The trick of the paraphrasing technique is not to be "technique-y." Paraphrasing must be done with sincerity and sensitivity. Even if the message you are hearing is a criticism of you, you must reflect it in a nondefensive way. Paraphrasing should also match the emotional intensity, as well as the literal message of the person to whom you've been listening.

Imagine your partner says, "I get so angry when you forget to write things in the checkbook. Then I don't know how much money is in the bank and I end up feeling like an idiot when I overdraw the account."

Now imagine you respond with, "So I hear you saying you're angry."

That's probably not going to get you anywhere because it's overly simplistic. She already knows she's angry. But she's not convinced that you understand that she also feels humiliated when she overdraws the checking account, nor that you understand the role you are playing in her upset.

Now imagine instead that you said something like, "Wow. Here you go to all the trouble of balancing our books and keeping an eye on our money. Then I forget to keep track and put you in a really awkward position."

Much better! Now she is apt to feel that you understand *why* she is angry and what she would like you to do about it. She feels, above all, that you were paying attention and taking her seriously. Such is the power of listening and paraphrasing.

Female Body Language

Communication, of course, is not only about the spoken word, but also about what is unspoken. Learning to interpret your woman's stances and gestures will help you with knowing how to time your more important conversations with her, as well as knowing when she is or is not "in the mood" for love. Reading body cues will be especially useful in terms of knowing when she is in an open, expansive frame of mind or temporarily closed off. Doing so will also help you notice when she is feeling insecure or more confident about herself.

There is probably a part of you that has been responding to these signs already, albeit on a subliminal level. But once you become consciously aware of them, you can use your knowledge to improve all kinds of communication with your partner.

The following table will clue you in to some key body language shorthand.

When She Does This	Her Message Is ...
Crosses her arms over her chest.	I'm nervous, agitated, or defensive and closed off.
Crinkles her brow.	I'm confused or tense, or both.
Rolls her eyes.	You're embarrassing me.
Taps finger.	I'm bored.
Taps toes.	I'm restless.
Crosses her arms and legs (knee pointing away from you).	You're in trouble.
Leaning back (away from you).	Go away—at least for now.
Shoulders hunched forward.	I'm feeling insecure.
Tosses hair and stretches neck.	Notice that I'm attractive.
Exposes her wrists and palms.	I'm open to suggestion, we'll do it your way.
Shoulders pointed toward you.	I'm totally into you.
Touches you on forearm while she's talking to you and leaning in toward you.	Ditto.
Remains very still.	I'm very interested in what you're saying.

Naturally, many things can affect a person's body language in the moment. If her gestures are closed off, don't always personalize what she's doing; she could be having a bad day. Test the waters and see.

Also keep in mind that you can sometimes actually change your partner's body language—and her underlying mood—simply by making eye contact, smiling, and nodding. Then, of course, there's always the greatest body language communication of all: give her a hug.

Love Busters

Keep your body language interpretation skills to yourself. Never tell your woman, "Hey, I know how you're feeling by the way you're holding your arms." All you'll do is make her self-conscious.

The Least You Need to Know

- ◆ Women need some sweet-talking, but they also need a certain amount of serious relationship-oriented talk.

- ◆ Women often talk in order to forge intimate connections, to process their feelings, and to relieve tension.

- ◆ To successfully talk with their partners, men can try being more oriented toward details and toward feelings—they can also initiate conversation and make it known they respect their woman's opinion.

- ◆ Among the things many men do wrong in speaking with women are giving unsolicited advice, being sarcastic, fibbing, erupting in anger, and walking out on a conversation.

- ◆ Women long to feel understood—listening to and paraphrasing what she says will help her to know her message has been heard and her emotion has been registered.

- ◆ Learning to read your partner's body language can help with reading her mood and timing other kinds of communications.

Chapter **6**

Be a Pal

In This Chapter

- The role of friendship in love
- The high comfort level of friendship
- Learning and playing together
- Exploring spiritual interests together
- The role of laughter in love

How many times have you heard a woman rhapsodize that her man is not only her partner and her lover, but also her best friend? This is truly a woman's ideal. Women place a very high value on friendship, having formed close social and emotional affiliations with others since they were little girls.

A woman wants to feel like her man is one of her closest pals. This chapter will explore how being your woman's friend is one of the special ways you can please her.

Friends First

Sometimes lovers start out as friends. They enjoy one another's company, have a good time together, and one day—wow!—they both realize there's even more to their relationship than they'd imagined. Sometimes a powerful physical attraction—so-called "love at first sight"—occurs before a friendly bond later forms between a couple. But if that latter bond fails to cement, love at first sight will soon give way to a feeling of "what the heck was I thinking?"

Whichever way the progression happens, friendship is a cornerstone of any loving relationship between a man and a woman. This makes perfect sense when you think about the various characteristics that define the nature of friendship itself.

- **Friends have common interests.** When you were a boy you probably were friends with other boys who liked to do the same kinds of things you liked to do, whether those activities included playing ball, participating in Boy Scouts, or performing skateboard feats. As you grew, your male friendships were probably also rooted in common interests, whether it was playing golf, talking politics, or restoring antique cars. Chances are you were thrilled to find, near the start of your relationship with your woman, that you and she also shared a penchant for certain undertakings. Maybe you discovered that you both liked to scuba dive, or play tennis, or hike, or play bridge. Having common interests was reassuring because it gave you the sense that the two of you would never run out of fun things to do together.

- **Friends have common preferences.** Were you over the moon when you found out your woman loved anchovies (but hated mushrooms) on her pizza as much as you did, that she loved listening to *Car Talk*, and that her favorite rock band was the same as yours? It almost seemed like it was too good to be true, didn't it? Sharing common likes and dislikes is another thing that brings friends together. Having someone that agrees with us—even about certain likes and dislikes that others might consider quirky—makes us feel, "Aha, we were right all along!"

- **Friends share common traits.** Friends come in all shapes and sizes, but studies show they do tend to have similar levels of intellect and similar levels of emotional intelligence (such as the capacity for empathy). They also share a similar sense of humor. Finding a new friend will certainly not give you the sense that you are gazing into a mirror, but it will give you the comfortable sense of encountering someone who is somehow already familiar.

♦ **Friends admire one another's different traits.** Good friends also embody a certain number of differences. If they didn't, they would soon bore us. We are intrigued by the things our friends can master that we are not so good at. We are impressed with their unique talents.

♦ **Friends forgive each other's flaws.** Are our friends perfect? Ha! No more than we ourselves are perfect. But we put up with them and they put up with us—even when one of us is being annoying. That's the implicit bargain underlying a sound friendship. Both people get to irritate the other from time to time, with relatively little negative fallout.

Mood Makers

Never underestimate the value of friendship. Studies show that confiding friends lessens our perception and experience of stress. This reduces our level of stress hormones, which has a far-reaching positive effect on our health.

♦ **Friends trust one another.** Friends are loyal. Friends keep one another's confidences. They defend one another in the face of criticism. They may like to gossip between themselves, but the unspoken deal is that they never gossip about one another to anyone else (well, at least not much).

♦ **Friends encourage and inspire one another.** They back one another up when each of them needs support and understanding. They are each other's cheerleaders—always ready with a pep talk.

♦ **Friends socialize together and apart.** Friends like to be friendly together, and often expand their circle to include other people. They enjoy socializing with other individuals and groups as a twosome. They each also, however, feel free to do things with others. Friendship is one thing; being joined at the hip quite another.

What all of this adds up to is a very high comfort level. Friends know that in one another's company they can be themselves. They don't have to put on any kind of pretense. They can be as silly as they like, or as smart as they want to be. They can feel free to suggest, "Hey, let's do something" or, conversely, "Hey, let's just do nothing." No wonder lovers who are also friends really do seem to have it all!

Are You Pals With Your Gal?

There's little doubt that friendly feelings toward your woman played a role in your decision to make a long-term commitment to her. But is your friendship as solid now as it was once upon a time? Take this quiz and see:

Find Your Pal Quotient

On a scale from 1 (not at all) to 5 (very strongly agree) describe how you feel about each of the following statements:

1. My woman and I participate in many recreational activities together.

   1 2 3 4 5

2. We like or dislike a lot of the same things—including new things we try.

   1 2 3 4 5

3. We seem to react the same way in a lot of social situations.

   1 2 3 4 5

4. We often have the same "take" on things intellectually.

   1 2 3 4 5

5. We often have the same emotional responses to things (e.g. something might make us both angry, or sad, or happy).

   1 2 3 4 5

6. We tend to find the same things humorous.

   1 2 3 4 5

7. We can easily make one another laugh.

   1 2 3 4 5

8. We enjoy socializing with others as a twosome, but we also do things with others individually.

   1 2 3 4 5

9. We cheer one another on.

   1 2 3 4 5

10. We say good things about one another.

    1 2 3 4 5

11. We keep each other's confidences.

    1 2 3 4 5

12. We admire one another's strengths and underplay one another's flaws.

    1 2 3 4 5

How did you do?

12–24 You two have let the friendship fade somewhat. Other aspects of your relationship may be satisfying, but they'll be enhanced when you bring this one up to par.

25–48 You're availing yourself of some of the benefits of friendship with your partner, but you can do even more to enhance your mutual camaraderie and your enjoyment of one another.

 Love Busters

Can you be too friendly with your lover, at the expense of love? The two should go hand in hand. Friendship should complement romance, not replace it. It's all about balance.

49–60 You're great pals, and your relationship will be all the better for it. You'll never be bored—or boring. And you'll almost always feel comfortable and natural in each other's company.

Reinvigorating the friendship quotient in a relationship where it already helped form the foundation isn't as hard as you might think. Many times friends find that a bit of distance has arisen between them. But when they put a little effort into getting their friendly relationship going again, things usually get back on track in short order.

Learning and Playing Together

Most people can think of dozens of excuses why they and their partners don't engage in as many of the recreational or intellectual activities they used to enjoy participating in together. There's no time, there are too many other obligations, the kids come first. As you read in Chapter 3, making time together is possible with some forethought, and is one of the most important things you can do to please your woman. In fact, if you add one quality hour a week of time with your woman, that adds up to 52 hours per year—the equivalent of over two full days and nights.

But solving the time problem does not always solve some couples' resistance to doing the fun things they used to do. They say they're rusty, out of practice. They're no longer so sure of their learned skill and innate abilities as they used to be. Fair enough—so it's time to do something about it.

Learning new skills, or brushing up on old ones, in any area in which you both have an interest is a great way to renew your friendship, and to enrich both your lives. Adult education is booming and courses in practically everything you can think of are readily available through local community colleges, YMCAs, park systems, churches, synagogues, and all kinds of private learning centers. A look through a few catalogs will leave you with a plethora of mind-boggling choices. You can take lessons in everything from perfecting your golf swing to writing detective fiction to painting with watercolors to making homemade sushi. You can brush up on your tennis serve, your martial arts technique, or the foreign language you studied in high school.

If you like, you can even explore online courses, or courses given via videotape or audio CD. But these lack the social advantage you'll gain by showing up and taking in-person lessons: meeting other couples that enjoy doing what you two enjoy. Meeting like-minded men and women will motivate you both to keep at what you're doing and afford you lots of social opportunities. Remember, friends like to expand their circle of friendship.

 He Says/She Says

"My wife and I loved to hike and camp. We did this all the time when we were first together. In fact, we used to fantasize about hiking the Appalachian Trail together one day. Then life got busy, as you would expect. We hiked and camped less often, and then found we hadn't done it for years. One night we watched a TV special on the Appalachian Trail, and got inspired. But we both felt daunted about getting back into that kind of shape. We ended up joining an orienteering course given by a local parks system. We soon made friends who egged us on to join them for some pretty arduous hikes. We had, and continue to have, a great time. And now we are seriously planning ahead for our big trek when our last kid leaves for college in a year."
—Joe, 48

It's Okay to Take a Break

But wait a minute! Do you and your woman have to do everything together? What about your time pursuing things on your own, or your time hanging out with the guys? For that matter, what about her time to hang out with her girlfriends?

It's all okay. Remember, being friends doesn't mean being welded together. Friends know how to give one another breathing room. Togetherness is great, but separateness has its place in a long-term relationship, too. Seeking out new adventures together should be complemented by seeking out new adventures as individuals. If you discover a new aspect of your self, you will be able to share that more energized and interesting self with your lover. You will also be able to learn from each other and appreciate one another's accomplishments.

One of the myths we have about long-term relationships is that couples have to be compatible in *all* ways, and like to do *all* of the same things. But think back to when you first fell for your woman. Weren't you really intrigued by the ways in which you and your woman were different? There is no reason to let such differences recede into the background of your lives once you decide to share those lives. Let her exercise those traits you found so appealing and exciting, and you do the same.

There's no need to worry that the two of you pursuing some new experiences on your own will detract from your relationship—so long as you remember to do two important things. First, don't neglect to pursue *some* new experiences as a couple. Second, always take the time to update your knowledge of your partner. Show an interest in what she's been pursuing and be sure to let her know what it is about *your* activities that excites you.

Don't ever worry, by the way, about what other people say. Sometimes other couples—especially ones that might be insecure about their own relationships—see a man and a woman pursuing separate hobbies and decide they are "going their separate ways." But true compatibility is born not of always *acting* alike, but of *interacting* well.

Mood Makers

Encourage your lady to do things with "the girls." Then ask her about her activities. She'll be thrilled that you're interested. What's more, she'll be more likely to want you to feel free to spend time with the guys.

Exploring the Spiritual Side

Another factor that sometimes plays a role in a couple coming together is a similar religious background, or similar spiritual interests. Sometimes, even if this did not play an initial role, partners find they become more interested in the spiritual side of life as they grow older. Pursuing spiritual activities together is another way to strengthen your relationship, and—equally important—a way to strengthen both of you as individuals.

If you and your woman share a religious tradition, but have moved away from it to a degree as life became more complex and over-scheduled, you might want to broach the subject of getting more involved again. If you're not sure how to go about it, simply attending some services at your community place of worship will probably give you all kinds of ideas. Read the newsletters and other handouts that are available before and after the service, and take a look at what's listed on any bulletin boards. You will likely find all kinds of classes you can take, study groups you can join, and community projects in which you can both take part. You can also talk to your pastor, priest, or rabbi about how to start dipping your toes into spiritual waters again.

Although many couples take nourishment from the faith in which they were raised, you may be among a growing number who might describe themselves as being more "spiritual" than "religious" per se. Many in such situations are creating their own collage of spiritual beliefs, often by drawing on beliefs and practices from various religious faiths or philosophic traditions. Pursuing this kind of spiritual quest with your partner can be enlightening and gratifying if you both feel committed to the exploration. Chances are that you will find that your spiritual beliefs, however unconventionally defined, will begin to guide and influence your everyday actions in an ethical and moral sense. They will probably also bring the two of you closer together as partners in the spirit.

Even if you and your partner do not necessarily consider yourselves religious *or* spiritual, you might find that introducing a time into your relationship when you can both experience moments of calm reflection will ground you. You might wish to explore a yoga or meditation practice, or you may simply want to try a secular relaxation technique, such as the "relaxation response"—in which you find just 20 minutes a day to sit in a quiet room, find a point of auditory focus (a special word or phrase, such as "one" or "peace"), and silently repeat that word as you breathe calmly. As your thoughts wander—which they most certainly will, especially as you train yourself to do this practice—simply guide your attention back to your focus word.

This method, and a variety of similar ones, have been definitively proven to be stress-reducers and, as such, beneficial to both physical and mental health. However, in addition to these benefits, many who practice quiet reflection on a regular basis find that they gradually become more open to life's spiritual aspects as well.

Love and Laughter

Finally, let's look more closely at one of the things that I mentioned draws friends and lovers together in the first place: a shared sense of humor. The value of humor and its result—laughter—simply cannot be underestimated. In a multitude of ways, this unique form of expression is a beneficial force.

Mood Makers

Laughter is a mild form of aerobic exercise. Share a laugh and burn calories together.

Some studies suggest that humor can cure everything from the common cold to much more severe ailments. Laughter has been shown to boost antibody levels and immune system functions. Humor has also been shown, according to some researchers, to boost creativity, and to lift depression. Even the Bible tells us—in Proverbs 17:22—"A merry heart doeth good like a medicine."

But what role can humor play in your relationship and how can you and your woman share more laughs?

The Laughing Bond

If you look through the personal ads on the Internet (just as an academic exercise, mind you) you'll notice how often the singles that place them say they are looking for a mate who is "witty" or "funny" or who "has a good sense of humor." Sometimes the ad placer simply stipulates that they want someone "to laugh with."

Why? For one thing, having a sense of humor correlates with what we think of as a good personality. Funny people are fun to be with. Their conversation is engaging, and they also tend to be smart. In fact, while not all intelligent people are necessarily funny, I think it's fair to say that all people who are funny are intelligent.

However, there's another reason so many people are looking for laughter in their relationship. Whether they consciously realize it or not, laughter creates an emotional bond between people. In fact, some speculate that this may be—in the broadest evolutionary sense—why laughter has evolved.

If you think about it, you'll realize that we almost never laugh when we are strictly alone—even what we think of as solitary laughter usually results from interacting with some sort of media, such as watching television. Laughter is, by and large, a shared social activity.

Laughter can be, quite literally, contagious. It can spread among people at lightening speed. It's hard to be somber when someone near you is giggling, cackling, or hooting with hilarity. In fact, sometimes despite your best intent to remain serious, you find yourself embarking on a laughing jag. Few things feel better. Sharing an infectious laugh with someone you love is almost as good as having simultaneous orgasms. Some might say just as good!

Another reason love-seekers want a humorous rapport with a partner is that many understand that humor is a wonderful coping mechanism. Being able to laugh in a difficult, frustrating, or confusing situation relieves stress and tension. Couples who can laugh at the world's ironies and contradictions, and even at their own behaviors, are apt to have a resilient attitude and, therefore, a more satisfied and sanguine existence overall.

But now let's get back to the personal ads for a moment. Here's a piece of very interesting news: A study of nearly 4,000 personal ads conducted by Robert R. Provine, world-renowned humor researcher and author of *Laughter: A Scientific Investigation* (Penguin Books, 2001), revealed that women are 62 percent more likely than men to stipulate a sense of humor as a requirement for a prospective partner. Additional studies reported by Provine show that females laugh more than males, but males are the leading laugh-getters. The reasons for this are not clear, but it all adds up to one thing you should know: a man who wants to please his woman will try to keep her laughing.

More Laughs In Her Life

Laugh enhancement is a gratifying task to assign yourself. Daily life can be much more fun when you approach it as material for humorous observations and as an opportunity to share levity. Besides, making someone laugh is great for one's ego. That's why stand-up comics talk about the thrill of having an audience in "the palm of their hand."

I realize you might not consider yourself the stand-up comic type, so relax—I am not going to suggest that you quit your day job and take a valise full of jokes on the road. I also realize that humor is a very subjective concept—a matter of personal taste. What makes one person laugh might not strike another person as particularly funny. But while the content of your humor is yours alone to craft, I am going to suggest some ways that you can introduce more humor into your lady's life—and, therefore, your own.

♦ **Adopt a laugh-seeking attitude.** Our expectations of any situation contribute to its outcome. This is what's known as a self-fulfilling prophecy. This means go not only to social events prepared to laugh and have a good time, but also go to work, to your kid's soccer game, or to the grocery store, always ready to find amusement in everyday absurdities. Think of it as keeping your own personal laugh track geared up to run. With the right attitude, you'll almost always be able to come home with a funny anecdote to recount.

Love Busters

One type of humor that probably will not make your woman laugh is sardonic humor—humor that is scornful and contemptuous of others. Sardonic humor is bitter. It gets its name from an herb that grows on the island of Sardinia. The herb, when eaten, allegedly paralyzes one's face in a grimace resembling a bitter smile.

♦ **Socialize with light-hearted people.** Seek out the company of those who are also ready, willing, and able to laugh. Avoid grumps, complainers, and curmudgeons.

♦ **Socialize in large groups.** Remember, laugher is contagious—it creates more laughter. Studies show that an enlargement in group size facilitates laughter. You're more likely to "catch" some laughter in a big group, just as you're more likely to catch the flu in a big group—but, hey, we won't think about that, will we?

- **Create occasions to reminisce.** Reunions—of classmates, co-workers, neighbors, or even people who met on a vacation—tend to generate a lot of laughter. The context of the occasion is such that everyone has a funny memory to share—and, of course, one thing leads to another ....

- **Keep humorous materials around.** What makes your lady break into serious gales of laughter? Maybe it's Monty Python; maybe it's the Marx Brothers. Start collecting a video or DVD library you can always turn to for a surefire guffaw. Have humorous written materials—perhaps books of *New Yorker* cartoons or collections of Dave Barry essays—around the house, especially in spots where she can dip into them quickly and conveniently—such as on the coffee table and by the bedside. (Okay, you can keep them in the bathroom too, although guys tend to do more reading in there than women.) Having humor-stimulating materials readily available can be a powerful antidote for those times when your lady begins to feel a bit down in the dumps.

- **Surprise her with a laugh.** Send her a funny card, forward a funny e-mail, or do something else impromptu to create an unexpected laugh in her day.

- **Help her to be less inhibited.** Do you love to hear your lady laugh? Does it really turn you on to see her smile? Tell her so. Sometimes women are disinclined to laugh too boisterously because they have been socialized to believe it is unladylike. Nonsense! Tell her how sexy she is when she is laughing.

When all else fails, here's something no one can do to make your women laugh except for you: tickle her. Tickling is a powerful, ancient laugh stimulus, and if anyone should know where her ticklish spots are, it's you. Tickling needs to be done judiciously. When it's overdone it can be an irritant rather than a pleasure. But when it's done right, under the right intimate circumstances, it can elicit a type of laugh reaction that is intensely deep and primal. By the way, everyone needs someone else to tickle them. It's impossible to tickle yourself!

The Least You Need to Know

- Feelings of friendship form part of the basis for long-term love.

- Friends have a lot in common, but also celebrate each other's differences— what they share most is a high comfort level in one another's company.

- If you've stopped pursuing the recreational and intellectual activities you used to pursue with your woman, find an opportunity to take some refresher courses— or to learn some new skills.

◆ Exploring the spiritual side of life together—either in a formal religious tradition or via more informal and varied spiritual pursuits—can nourish you as a couple and as individuals.

◆ Laughter reinforces emotional bonds—introducing more opportunities for humor in your lives will increase your level of overall satisfaction and improve your outlook on life.

7

Riding the Rough Spots

In This Chapter

- ◆ Why some conflict is natural and normal
- ◆ The art of fighting fair
- ◆ Offering apologies
- ◆ Dealing with setbacks and challenges

Did you ever run into one of those couples that tell you they have never exchanged a harsh word or had a moment of disagreement between them? There is a word for people like that: we call them liars.

The course of true love, as the saying goes, never runs smoothly. This chapter will tell you how to handle things when you and your woman run into a rough patch.

Why We Don't Always See Eye to Eye

Robert Louis Stevenson wrote "Marriage is one long conversation, checkered by disputes." This may be a bit of an exaggeration, but the truth is that all couples in long-term committed relationships argue from time to time.

Why? Because you are two individuals, each with your own tastes, temperaments, and backgrounds. Sure, you were attracted to one another, in part, because of your similarities. But you were also attracted because aspects of you were opposite.

Opposite tendencies in any aspect of personality can sometimes manifest as opposite priorities.

Mood Makers

Most people in relationships would probably agree that they love 95 percent of everything about their mate, and are irritated by the remaining 5 percent. But, over time and with the right attitude, it can actually be that five percent that ends up making them all the more endearing. These are the things you might grow not only to accept but to love about the person.

Another reason couples fight is to assert their territoriality in a relationship. Both men and women might sometimes feel that the power balance in the relationship is out of whack, with one partner taking charge of most decisions. Arguments can be by-products of attempts to shift the balance.

Another reason couples might occasionally quarrel is that both people might just be in bad moods at the same time. Sometimes, even if we're not especially mad at the person we love, we take our frustrations out on them. It's not a commendable behavior, but everyone is guilty of it now and again.

Fair Fights

Just because you occasionally disagree, however, is no reason to abandon your resolve to please your woman. Even during a disagreement, you can choose to act out your more noble instincts as opposed to your worst. To choose the latter, fight fair. Doing so will help you keep from turning a minor skirmish into a major battle, and a more serious fight into "the beginning of the end."

It is possible to argue and to verbalize angry feelings without going overboard and damaging your partner's ego and your own self-esteem. But in order to do this, it's a good idea to understand some fundamental ground rules that can keep a healthy conflict of interest from deteriorating into a mutually destructive exchange.

You might contend that if you're going to obey these ground rules, your woman should also. And you are quite right. But since you're the one reading this book right now, you can be the first to set a good example by taking the high road. You can also take the opportunity at some point to share these ground rules with your partner and get her buy-in so that you both will be aware of the proactive choices you can make to clear the air without doing a lot of collateral damage to your relationship.

Remember The "I's"

I'm sure your woman is perfect for you. But once in a while she may *do* something imperfect. No need to make a big deal out of it—except when it's something you truly feel you can't overlook. But even when that happens, you can offer criticism in a non-destructive manner.

Couples therapists and communication experts generally agree that the kindest, most effective way to deliver a critical appraisal is to begin your statements with the pronoun *I*. Steer clear of the word *you* as much as possible.

Consider the difference between these two statements:

Statement # 1: You left the sunroof on the car open again. You didn't park in the garage either. If it had rained last night you would have caused a lot of damage. You better not do that again.

Statement # 2: I noticed the sunroof on the car was open and the car was in the driveway. I get really concerned that a rainstorm could cause a lot of damage. I think it's safer to close it or to park in the garage.

If you were the sunroof culprit, which message would you rather hear? The *you* statement is provocative because it sounds blatantly accusatory. If your partner heard that she'd doubtless feel extremely defensive. The second statement still might not make them smile, but it is easier to take in.

Beginning your statements with *I*, on the other hand, is a way of reporting what's on your mind and suggesting solutions to a problem without making your partner feel badgered.

In the heat of an argument, our tendency is to cast blame—"you do this to me" and "you do that to me." But this is when it is most important to remember to stick with *I* messages. Statements of blame tend to lead to rebuttal. "*Oh, yes? Well, you do this and that.*" That's the way vicious cycles begin.

Stay In the Now

A specific disagreement can turn into a globalized dispute if you dredge up past incidents and behavior. If you have a legitimate grievance about something your partner has done, stick with the topic at hand. Don't dig up ancient history and throw in every wrongdoing you think she's ever committed.

 Love Busters

Reminding someone of past misbehavior is not only hurtful, but also futile. Unless you're prepared to provide your partner with a time machine, she can't go back and undo what's been done.

Some phrases you never want to utter are:

- ◆ You always _____.

- ◆ You never _____.

- ◆ What about the time you _____.

This kind of "everything but the kitchen sink" approach detracts from your woman's underlying sense of security in the relationship and her trust in you. She is likely to feel as though you've been keeping a list and checking it twice.

Consider Your Timing

If you have something to say, it's up to you to choose the moment to say it. It's unwise to introduce a sensitive issue just before a group of dinner guests is about to descend. You don't want to do it just as your woman comes in from a long day at work, or just after she's gotten some grief from the kids.

What you want is a period of time when both of you are in fairly unencumbered frames of mind. It's also wise to choose a time when the two of you will be ensured some prolonged privacy.

How can you be certain it's a reasonable time for a serious discussion? Ask her. Tell her you have something you'd like to talk with her about: is this a good time? Being a woman, she will probably be eager to talk to you, and if it isn't a good time she will suggest one that is better.

While you're waiting for the right time to talk, use the breathing room to plan how you will present what you have to say in a nonaccusatory way. Practice using "I's" and staying grounded in the present.

Hands Off Her Hot Buttons

Every woman has her emotional hot buttons. When certain subjects are touched upon, she may react in a way that seems disproportionately emotional. Often these buttons correlate with triggers that have been pulled all too often throughout her life. They have some historical significance for her.

Let's say, for example, that you gently chastise your woman for taking too much time in the bathroom when she gets ready to go out. Instead of bantering with you and laughing it off, as she usually might, she becomes defensive and starts recounting, at the top of her voice, all the times you keep her waiting. The she bursts into tears.

Whoops! What's going on here? Could be that if you talk with her about it later you'll discover that fighting over time in front of the bathroom mirror is something she and her sister did for years when she was growing up.

If you push sensitive buttons during an argument, you might as well abandon hope that your conflict will have a rational resolution. But how do you know exactly what her sensitive emotional areas are?

First, be observant. Noticing how your partner interacts with her own family members can provide you with some valuable clues. Does she flinch when her father jokes about her "two left feet" in the third grade ballet recital? Here's a woman that has no need for you to criticize her inability to follow your lead on the dance floor. Does she tense up when her mother asks her if she's put on a little weight lately? Oh-oh. There's an area you'll want to avoid.

Tongue Teasers

The ancient story of Achilles tells of a great warrior immune to all moral wounds except in the heel area that was untouched by the magic waters that protected the rest of him. Every person has an emotional **Achilles' heel**—a vulnerable spot that can cause him or her undue hurt.

Also, learn to rely on your own experience. The longer the two of you are together, the more you'll know there are simply some places you shouldn't go. So don't go there. Just don't.

Remember, sore spots are always sore for a reason. Even if you're not exactly sure of the reason, steer clear of them. After all, you wouldn't step on her *Achilles' heel*, would you?

Don't "Lose It" Simultaneously

Regardless of how hard couples try to fight fair and to find constructive ways of expressing displeasure, there will be times when one person or another just plain "loses it"—and lets loose an uncensored tirade. If the partner at whom the diatribe is aimed responds by losing it as well, the high-decibel result won't do anything except pique the curiosity of the neighbors. It certainly will not solve any problems.

He Says/She Says

"My wife and I have an agreement. Only one of us is allowed to go crazy at a time. It really works, so long as you both get your chance.
—Louis, 36

It may be a natural inclination to respond to yelling with yelling. However, if one partner can overcome their instincts, they can keep the situation from escalating.

How can you respond to a temper tantrum without throwing one of your own?

◆ Refrain from responding quickly—think before you react.

◆ Take at least three deep inhalations and exhalations before you say anything.

◆ Buy time by saying "I need time to think about that, so can we please talk later?"

I know you've got your grievances, too. But now is not the time to air them. Think of it this way: a child who is in the throes of a temper tantrum is, whether he is aware of it or not, counting on his parents not to throw one in kind. Somebody has to be the rational one.

Don't Make Threats

It's a mistake to threaten to end a relationship or to threaten any other drastic measures while in the heat of an argument. It is also unreasonable to issue ultimatums. Chances are you will not mean what you say, but you never know how seriously your partner will take it.

Without meaning to, you could easily create a "you can't fire me—I quit" response. Your partner may be so upset with being threatened that she will make a snap decision that she would rather be the deserter than the one being deserted. Even if you both come to your senses, things have been said which are hard to forget and hard to ignore.

Threats and ultimatums are reminiscent of fights you might have had back on the playground when you were in grade school. But remember, here and now the stakes are much higher.

Resist Interpretations

Never tell your woman what she's "really trying to say" during the course of a quarrel. Even if you're right on the money with your interpretation, she'll feel exposed and embarrassed.

You may be very psychologically astute, but that doesn't change things. Keep your insights to yourself unless you are asked to share them. Your lady wants you to be her friend and lover, but not her shrink.

Keep It Between You

Never fight in front of others. Making a scene in front of strangers is bad enough. Doing so in front of friends, relatives, or neighbors is even worse.

There isn't a person on Earth who does not feel awkward when a couple starts arguing in front of them. No one knows quite what to do with themselves, except to wish that they could disappear.

Love Busters

Never drag a third party into an argument or ask them to take sides. This will not only embarrass your partner, but will also make innocent bystanders incredibly uncomfortable.

The Art of Apology

In June of 2005, a British couple—Percy Arrowsmith, 105, and his 100-year-old wife, Florence—achieved the Guinness World Record of the world's longest-married couple. On the occasion of their 80th (!) wedding anniversary, everyone wanted to know their secret. The Arrowsmiths revealed that it was "never sleeping on an argument." They maintained that no matter what had transpired between them, they always shared a kiss and held hands before going to bed.

As their love tip circulated around the world, a number of people said they weren't quite sure they believed this couple. They were so old, a number of late night comics joked, that they had probably just forgotten what really happened.

No doubt you have probably heard the advice to kiss and make up before bed. Is it good advice? Yes. But, it may not always be realistic. Most happily committed couples confess to an occasional night of restlessness as they nurse leftover residue from a quarrel.

So how about this? If you can't make up before bed, or in bed, or even before breakfast, at least never let more than 24 hours go by without making peace. When hurt feelings are clung to, you risk setting your own and your partner's negative feelings in stone and creating a chasm between you that will be harder to bridge later on. It is certainly not true that "love means never having to say you're sorry." In fact, just the opposite is the case.

A committed relationship is no place to hold a grudge. That defies the very nature of commitment. Making up after an argument is a wonderful way to re-establish the depth of your devotion and dedication to one another—rough patches or not.

Does it matter who started the argument? Does the person who started it have to be the one to initiate an apology? No. Just as it takes two to make love, it takes two to quarrel.

Acknowledge your role in what occurred and remind your woman of your regard and love for her. If you don't want to accept specific blame, you don't have to. You can simply say something like, "I'm sorry we quarreled. You know how much I love you."

As I hope you already know, making up can be a lot of fun.

And there are many inventive, endearing ways of augmenting a verbal apology. You can:

◆ Send a loving note or card.

◆ Serve a food or wine she considers special.

◆ Rent a chick flick she's wanted to see and watch it with her.

◆ Find a way to make her laugh.

◆ Have some good make-up loving, with some extra-long foreplay.

Don't dwell on your own guilt, or assign blame. If you do, the argument might just start all over again. Above all, of course, be sincere and authentic. You would not have chosen this woman if your love and admiration for her didn't transcend day-to-day irritants. And you would not be so adoring and devoted to her if even the bigger, deeper issues did not pale alongside your abiding, underlying affection. Apologize from your heart, and enjoy making up with all your parts.

A Woman's Setbacks and Challenges

Individual quarrels are certainly not the only things that can strain a relationship. There are times in everyone's life when they experience disappointments and setbacks that can create a difficult emotional climate. It is at such times that your partner will require extra sensitivity and support from you.

Men and women experience many of the same life challenges. Like you, a woman might become distraught over work-related problems, problems related to physical illness, and problems related to the well-being of one's children or one's aging parents.

But you should also be aware of some times in life when women in particular need some extra support, understanding, and tender loving care.

The Ups and Downs of Pregnancy

No matter how much a woman has looked forward to being pregnant and becoming a mother, pregnancy is a highly stressful time. As discussed in Chapter 4, a pregnant woman's body undergoes all sorts of changes. In addition to these, she undergoes many perfectly natural—but nevertheless challenging—fears and doubts. Will her baby be healthy? Will she be a good parent? How will this new baby impact her daily life, her work life, and her life with you? The only thing she knows for certain is that life, as she knows it, is definitely about to undergo huge changes.

To complicate matters, a drastic hormonal shift begins to take place in a woman's body—emanating from her own glands and from the developing placenta—from the time she conceives a child. These hormones can have not only physiological but also psychological effects. While it wouldn't be quite correct to say that hormones manufacture emotions from out of the blue, they certainly exacerbate emotions. A small stroke of insecurity, awash in hormones, can sometimes evolve into a vast canvas of self-doubt.

Another thing that happens during pregnancy is that a woman's senses become extra sensitive. Scents that you hardly notice can overwhelm her. Tastes she once found pleasing can be abhorrent, and foods she once found displeasing can be the ones she craves. Sex drive? She might have a higher one than ever before, or very little, or none at various junctures.

What else could possibly disturb her during this time? Well, there are pressures from her family members, not to mention yours, with regard to every aspect of how the baby will be raised. There could be serious pregnancy one-upmanship games played out between her and other women who are in the same situation. (I'll bet you never knew the choice of the "right" stroller could take on such immense social significance.) There might be on-the-job pressures as to when to reveal her condition and how it will impact her career. That's a lot to deal with for any woman, no matter how serene she might usually be.

It may feel to you that living with a pregnant woman is like living with Dr. Jekyll and Mr. Hyde simultaneously. If it does, I can only say that you have the appropriate feeling. Certainly, you'll be going through lots of changes yourself during this period, and grappling with how your own life and relationship with your woman will alter. There's no doubt you need to look after yourself, but don't

Mood Makers

For a helpful, funny guide through your wife's pregnancy, see *Pregnancy Sucks for Men* by Joanne and Jeff Kimes (Adams Media, 2004).

neglect to give her all the extra attention and thoughtfulness you possibly can. Your patience and understanding during her fluctuating moods will be the best gift you can give not only her but also to your developing baby.

A pregnant woman may not want to be treated any differently on the job, but at home she simply cannot be too pampered. Whether you're giving her physical support, in the form of a pillow to rest her lumbar against, or emotional support in the form of encouragement, forbearance, and understanding, support is what your role is all about during this important transition.

The Passage of Menopause

Menopause is another time when a woman's emotions may be particularly vulnerable. As in pregnancy, a woman's body is changing and her hormones are fluctuating. During this passage, a woman may be beset with worries about growing older and facing her own mortality.

That said, every woman experiences menopause differently. Some have intense reactions; some have reactions that are quite minimal. But this is another time when your support and reassurance will be invaluable.

One thing that might stand in the way of your being supportive, however, is a lack of information, or a lot of misinformation, about menopause itself. If you are oblivious to the process, or unduly anxious about it, it will be hard for you to be an understanding companion. The following myths and facts about menopause will provide you with some valuable information on a process you may simply never have learned much about.

Myth # 1: All women lose interest in sex while in menopause.

Fact: Sex drive does not automatically wane, let alone vanish, during menopause. At least 50 percent of women in menopause report no drop in sexual interest. Fewer than 20 percent report any marked lack of interest. Some menopausal women report an increase in desire (which may be in part hormonal and part practical—there is no concern about birth control, and the kids might be out of the house).

Myth #2: All menopausal women experience symptoms such as hot flashes, mood swings, insomnia, and depression for years.

Fact: Research indicates that at least 15 percent of women are symptom-free during menopause. Many others have few or no symptoms, except for hot flashes.

Myth # 3: Menopause always causes weight gain.

Fact: Just as some women never experience hot flashes during menopause, some women never gain weight at this time. In fact, some women lose weight during menopause.

Myth # 4: Women in menopause are apt to become hysterical.

Fact: They will most likely become hysterical only if you treat them as if they're hysterical.

Most important, menopause is a natural process and not a disease. If you and your woman are approximately the same age, you will be going through your own mid-life process at around the same time she is going through hers.

Mid-life can be a time when the two of you try each other's patience now and then, but it can also be a time of renewal, when you both discover what you most want to do with the second half of your lives, and how much you are looking forward to spending those years together.

The Least You Need to Know

- ◆ All couples argue sometimes because it's only natural—anyone who says they don't is lying.

- ◆ The trick is not to never fight, but to fight fair.

- ◆ Fighting fair involves many strategies, including framing your comments in the first-person, staying with the subject at hand, avoiding times that are already stressful, and steering clear of your woman's emotional hot buttons.

- ◆ Apologies should be offered within 24 hours of an argument, regardless of what it was about or who started it—embellishing your verbal apology with a thoughtful gesture is a nice touch.

- ◆ Women and men can experience similar setbacks and challenges in life, but she experiences unique challenges during pregnancy and menopause—all challenges call for your support.

Part 3

Mr. Wonderful

Want to know some little-known, but very hot, forms of foreplay? Be neat and sweet. Pick up a vacuum cleaner and straighten up around the house. Be polite and respectful not only to your lady but also to her friends and family. Spruce up your attire and clean under your fingernails. This part of the book will show you how to be the kind of guy that will make his woman proud to say, "This is a guy who *gets it*. He doesn't take me for granted and he always makes an effort."

Chapter **8**

Lend a Helping Hand

In This Chapter

- Why you should do more around the house
- Evaluating how much you do
- The art of the clean-up
- When—and when not to—be her handyman
- Helping out with the kids

Want to know about a really great sex toy? It's got a long hose, lots of fancy attachments, and makes a kind of humming noise. When you turn it on, your woman will get turned on, too. It's called a vacuum cleaner!

No kidding. If you want to endear yourself to your partner, pitch in around the house. Remember she's a fair maiden, not a maid. This chapter will give you a clue—or two.

Doing Your Fair Share

Once upon a time, the majority of men went to work and the majority of women stayed home and tended the house and kids. Men did far less than women when it came to household chores. Then social and economic realities changed, and both men and women worked outside the home in a far greater number of households. Did men begin to take on a greater share of the housework? Yes (and good for you!). But still, women are doing a far greater share than their male partners.

American men are doing about 16 hours of housework a week, up from 12 hours in 1965, according to a study by the University of Michigan Institute for Social Research. Yet, women are still doing about 27 hours of housework a week. The findings are part of a study of time-use trends. Researchers analyzed data from time-diaries and supplemental data from questionnaires asking men and women to recall how much time they spent on housework in an average week, including cooking, cleaning, and doing other chores around the house.

While the number of hours men reported spending on such work rose steadily from 1965 to 1985, the increase subsequently stalled. Guys, it's time to get with the program and help your ladies out so that things are more equitable.

Pitching in to a greater degree has many clear advantages for you. If you take some more of the burden off your woman …

♦ The amount of leisure time you will have to spend together will increase.

♦ She'll have more time to renew and refresh herself—thus being a more content, energetic companion.

♦ She'll think you're a great guy—which, indeed you will be—and that will please her to no end.

 **Mood Makers**

The positive impact of helping your woman out around the house is a proven scientific fact. At the University of Washington's "Love Lab," psychologist John M. Gottman conducted a study where couples interact in a household setting under the eyes of researchers. He found that the more men participate in housework, the more their women report increased feelings of satisfaction and sexual intimacy.

Granted, doing housework and related chores don't rank high on anyone's list of preferred ways to spend their time. Some joke that it falls into the "I'd rather have a root canal" category. Perhaps you can relate. Nevertheless, it's time to suck it up, both literally and figuratively. A little more of your attention given to the vacuum cleaner will mean a lot more of your lady's attention given to you.

How Much Do You Do?

Maybe you think you do a lot already. And perhaps you do. But do you do as much as your partner? Take this quiz and see.

Who Does What Around the House?

For the following list of chores, circle the phrase that describes which of you does more. If you're really not sure, keep a diary for a week. Hint: If something's getting done around the house and you're not doing it, chances are she is—unless you have a housekeeper or a magic house elf.

1. Cleaning the kitchen after each meal.

   I do more / She does more / We do the same amount

2. Straightening up general living space, e.g. the living room and family room.

   I do more / She does more / We do the same amount

3. Cleaning the bathrooms.

   I do more / She does more / We do the same amount

4. Vacuuming and dusting.

   I do more / She does more / We do the same amount

5. Doing the laundry.

   I do more / She does more / We do the same amount

6. Taking out the trash.

   I do more / She does more / We do the same amount

7. Cleaning out the refrigerator.

   I do more / She does more / We do the same amount

8. Changing sheets.

   I do more / She does more / We do the same amount

9. Straightening up the bedroom.

   I do more / She does more / We do the same amount

10. Cleaning out closets.

    I do more / She does more / We do the same amount

11. Picking up after the kids/pets (if applicable).

    I do more / She does more / We do the same amount

How did you do? If you scored even, or answered that you do more, then kudos to you … as long as this is how your woman would evaluate the situation as well.

If you circled more of the "she does more" categories than any other it's time to even the score, so to speak. Read on for some suggestions as to how to begin.

Mr. Clean

Remember when you turned in a paper at school? Even if your teacher didn't say so explicitly, you knew that neatness counted. Even if your woman has never overtly expressed the desire for you to pitch in more around the house, you know in your heart how much she'll appreciate it.

But perhaps you're like a lot of guys in that no one ever really told you or showed you what to do when it comes to housework. Your mom may have thrown up her hands and given up on you when you were an adolescent, telling herself it was easier to pick up your socks than to argue with you about your not having done so. Your college roommates may have been as bad as you were, being content to wallow in Animal House ambience until someone's girlfriend took pity on all of you. Sadly, everyone would have been better off if any of these merciful ladies had handed you a mop, a bucket, and a pep talk.

Love Busters

It's too late for procrastination. Don't save for tomorrow the things you can clean today. They will only get dirtier and harder to deal with. Besides, your woman might feel she has to jump in and take care of it herself—and then she might get harder to deal with as well.

But, hey, you're a smart guy. And housecleaning is not exactly rocket science or neurosurgery. Attack the housework challenge man-style, with a strategic plan and some muscle.

Cool Tools for Cleaning Fools

Any job goes more smoothly with good tools. Familiarizing yourself with the tools and products necessary to do a job, and adding any that may be missing is a great way to get into the spirit of housecleaning, and of ensuring that any task you take on can be done efficiently. While cleaning is important, there's no sense spending more time on it than you have to, right?

Here are some fundamentals that you'll need:

♦ **Vacuum cleaner(s).** Upright models work best if you have lots of carpeting; canisters work better on wood and tile flooring. Every house should also have at least one cordless hand-held vac for quick spot clean-ups.

♦ **Broom(s).** A stand-up broom with flexible bristles is good for indoor floors; a push broom with heavier bristles works best in the garage, in the driveway, and on decks. Hand-held whiskbrooms are great for tiny jobs (like cat litter trails).

♦ **Cleaning cloths.** You can purchase packs of them at hardware stores, but cotton rags work just great. This is a wonderful use for your old T-shirts. Paper towels work in a pinch, but they're wasteful. Save a tree and use them sparingly.

Mood Makers

Impress your lady with your household health smarts. Sponges need cleaning too, or they'll collect and spread germs. Run kitchen sponges through a dishwasher cycle on a weekly basis. Toss them when they start to tatter.

♦ **Sponges.** Get large cellulose sponges to attack large surfaces and keep a ready supply of smaller ones for kitchen counter clean-ups.

♦ **Plastic buckets.** Keep one to haul cleaning products in, another couple for mixing water and cleaning liquids.

♦ **All-purpose disinfectant/liquid cleaner.** With one product you can get rid of lots of dirt, grime, and "cooties." Refill sprayer bottles from larger refill bottles and save money.

♦ **Glass cleaner.** This is great for windows, glass tables, mirrors, and so on. Obey the refill bottle principle noted above.

♦ **Spray-on rug cleaner.** A must-have for those incidents when you get more salsa on your carpet than on your chips. Keep some handy when you're watching "the big game" on T.V.

Mood Makers

Shower squeegees help keep the water spot build-up to a minimum. Keep one handy. They're no trouble at all to use.

♦ **Spray-shower cleaner.** Mold and mildew and soap scum won't require scrubbing if you use this kind of product with regularity.

♦ **Baking soda.** This cheap, basic product deodorizes just about anything—dishwasher, litter box, drains, cutting boards. Its classic use is in the fridge, but don't forget to change the open box monthly.

♦ **White vinegar.** Great for quick, light clean-ups of food prep areas—like range tops, counters, and the inside of microwaves—especially if you don't want to use chemicals in these spots.

There are lots of specialty tools and cleaners as well, but these items ought to give you a good start. Don't go rushing off on a shopping spree, though, until you inventory what you already have. If you don't know where your lady keeps the stuff (tsk, tsk), just ask.

Kitchen Detail

Once you've got the proper tools and supplies, the kitchen is a great place to start using them. That's because most people spend more time in the kitchen than any other room in the house. Not only do you prepare meals there, but you hang out there, too—even when you have guests, right? The kitchen is the heart of the home—and as such deserves extra tender loving care.

The best advice when it comes to cleaning the kitchen is not to get it too dirty in the first place. Minimize the mount of stuff you keep on the countertops—e.g., small appliances, dishware, and food canisters—so they won't get dusty or covered with food. When you cook, clean as you go, putting ingredients away after you use them. Put dirty dishes immediately into the dishwasher (note: this requires actually emptying the dishwasher at the end of a cycle instead of waiting for "somebody else" to do it).

He Says/She Says

"My husband once asked me why the oven was dirty if we had a self-cleaning oven. I pointed out that in order for the oven to self-clean, someone had to turn it on to the self-clean setting. It was a true revelation. He actually did it from then on!"
—Madison, 35

When it's your turn for kitchen cleanup—and sometimes when it's not your turn, but just to be nice—wipe down all surfaces after a meal. Also, give the floor a quick sweep or once-over with a hand-held vacuum. Empty the trash bin if necessary.

Once a week *somebody* ought to go through the fridge and throw out any food that looks suspect or that you just know, in your bones, that no one is ever actually going to finish. Wipe down the inside of the refrigerator once a week, too, along with the inside and outside of other appliances. Wash the floor on a weekly basis, and clean the oven monthly.

Battling the Bathroom

If you and your wife have separate bathrooms, you are both lucky, and I predict a long and happy relationship. Although you should clean yours and keep it relatively tidy, a *little* slacking now and then isn't likely to cause a ruckus. If you share a bathroom, you're beholden to do your part with greater regularity.

I know, I know—she has more stuff in the bathroom than you do. I apologize on behalf of women everywhere, but that's the way it is. Both of you should keep as much of your stuff as possible off of outer surfaces. The best idea for keeping a bathroom neat is to get lots of organizers and arrange toiletry items in closets and in cabinets under sinks.

According to University of Washington sociologist Julie E. Brines, cleaning the bathroom falls "at the bottom of the task hierarchy." Nevertheless, it's highly necessary—and can be simpler if you don't put it off. If "clean as you go" is a slogan for the kitchen, "clean after you go" is the right one for the bathroom. Use a toilet brush (the stand-up kind kept right by the side of the commode) to clean the inside of the toilet bowl and keep wet wipes handy to wipe seat surfaces as needed. Wipe down the sink after use as well. Use spray shower cleaners daily, and leave the shower door slightly ajar after use to prevent mildew build-up. Change the towels at least twice a week. Clean the mirrors and wash the floor weekly. Once a month, clean out the medicine cabinet.

Love Busters

It doesn't matter if you hang the toilet paper so that it pulls over or under. What matters is that you hang it at all. If you finish a roll, don't leave the cardboard tube on the spindle. Replace it with a fresh roll.

Bedroom Basics

The bedroom is—or should be—a peaceful, private place where you and your lover can block out the world. When it's messy or just plain unclean it's hard to feel restful, let alone amorous.

Since the bed is the centerpiece, it's a good idea to tend to it daily. For women, bed making is the household task tended to most often. According to *USA Today*, 67 percent of women in America say they make the bed daily. So how about you guys taking a turn once in a while? Don't be half-hearted about it either—pull up the sheets, fold over the top, and tuck them in. Fluff the pillows and smooth out the bedspread or comforter. The whole point is to make the bed look like something she'll be longing to get back into. Along these lines, change the sheets weekly and toss the pillowcases into the laundry as frequently as possible.

Mood Makers

Turn the mattress every two or three months, to keep the bed more comfy for sleeping—as well as other activities. Unless you turn the mattress on occasion, permanent indentations can occur.

In the grand scheme of things, bedroom cleaning is pretty simple, so long as you don't let too much clutter build up. Vacuum, dust, and Windex the mirrors weekly. When you pick up the dry-cleaning, put it away, as opposed to leaving plastic bags hanging from the doorknobs. Likewise, when you take off your clothes, hang them up immediately—unless you're in the throes of passion, in which case hang them up afterward.

Shared Space, Sacred Space

Every household has a number of rooms that all household members consider common ground. To keep the living room livable and the family room fit for family use, clutter busting is key. Clutter—in the form of old newspaper and magazine piles, unwashed cups and glasses, unhung jackets and strewn-about shoes, and sheer knick-knack build-up—has a way of sneaking up on you if you're not vigilant.

Anti-clutter solutions are actually relatively simple to enact. First, have adequate storage space. Second, actually use the storage space to store stuff. Third, don't keep anything around that you're already done with. Since everyone contributes to clutter, everyone needs to participate in these activities—and that, of course, includes you.

Now we come to the issue of those sacred household "guy spaces" that you consider your rightful domain. You know the ones I mean. Men have always felt comfortable on the periphery of the home turf, perhaps because it's in your nature to stand guard between your kin and the outside world. In the days of antiquity, while women tended the fires, men looked afar to see what was on the horizon. In medieval times, while women sat near the hearth and made a home, men mounted turrets and looked to defend the outskirts of their land. In modern times, men still tend to have dominion over the outer edges of the home in the form of the garage, the basement, and the backyard.

It's fine with us if you continue caring for these realms, and as a rule we're not as particular about their appearance as we are about the rest of our dwelling place. These are areas where you are perfectly entitled to spread out to a reasonable degree. But please, do clean them out once in a while, discarding those cans of paint with nothing left but a few dried up drops of semi-gloss and those prehistoric Flintstones lawn-mowers you've long since replaced with newer models.

In a perfect world, we'd like to be able to park our car in the garage, as opposed to the driveway, and we'd like to be able to walk across the basement without having to circumnavigate a tools-and-spare-parts inventory that would make the Home Depot pale by comparison. In exchange for this small courtesy, we promise not to make you lacey curtains for the garage windows and doilies for your hammers and saws.

As for the yard, please note that it has a tendency to become junglelike if not attended to regularly. If mowing, trimming, and pruning are not your favorite activities, consider desert-style landscaping, brick pavers, or even "fake" grass that looks great and requires no maintenance.

Love Your Laundry

Another task that seems to fall mainly to the womenfolk is that of doing the laundry. One thing you can say about laundry: you can only put it off so long—unless you have an endless stream of revenue to spend on replacement underwear. *Somebody's* got to do it. Once in a while, why not give it a whirl?

Like cleaning up and de-cluttering, laundry requires no advanced degree of any kind. In fact, today's fabrics are, for the most part, relatively durable, colorfast, and wrinkle-resistant. So your worst nightmares of extracting a pathetic load of shrunken, crumpled, suddenly–pink clothing from the washer or dryer are unlikely to come true.

Unlikely—but not impossible. There are a few rules you do need to keep in mind when tackling the laundry:

- **Psyching out stains.** The longer a stain sits, the harder it is to get out. Wash stained items as soon as possible, but if an immediate wash is not practical, pre-soak the item before you throw it in the washer at a later time. Check out special products made for pre-soaking purposes.

- **Getting into hot water.** Hot water is best for getting things really clean, but it can shrink some garments, such as those made of all natural fibers. Also, not all garments are color safe, so some sorting may be required. If you're unsure whether a garment is at risk, read the washing instructions on the label sewn inside.

- **Kid stuff.** If your kids' clothes are caked with loose dirt, scrape as much of it off as possible before you put the clothes into the washer—otherwise it remains in the water during the wash.

- **Hold onto your socks.** Put a dozen socks into the laundry and eleven come out. Nobody knows why this metaphysical mystery occurs, but it does. The only way to prevent socks disappearing into a black hole—or wherever it is they go—is to put them all in a pillowcase and safety pin the end. Even better, buy a mesh sock bag made for this purpose. (By the way, socks go in right-side out or at least turn them right-side-out when folding them.)

♦ **Drying out.** Generally, items that are safe for machine washing are safe for tumble-drying, but check the label anyway. Also pay attention to the different dryer temperature settings. When the dryer cycle is done, remove clothes as soon as possible to prevent wrinkling.

♦ **Doing a thorough job.** Doing only your laundry doesn't count as "doing the laundry." Also, doing the laundry, but not folding it or putting it away is not "complete."

Last but not least, don't do anything to your woman's jeans without explicitly checking with her first. She may or may not want them washed in hot water, whatever the label says. She may or may not want them to fade (turn them inside out to prevent it). Better yet, just leave the jeans to her and take a crack at the rest of the laundry. That will likely be the pleasing solution of all.

Mr. Fix It

Speaking of tools, it's only fair to note that statistics prove you guys tend to do more of the repair work and do-it-yourself type building projects at home. Do women appreciate you efforts in these areas? You bet we do. It's not that we're genetically incapable of wielding a hammer or manipulating a screwdriver—no more so than you're genetically incapable of doing the laundry—but, social influences being what they are, many of us were never trained in the home repair arts. Since you seem to enjoy fixing and constructing things so much, and given everything else we have to do, we're often delighted to delegate.

But here's the thing: despite your very good intentions to "do it yourself," we notice that you often don't have the time to do it—or to finish it if you start it. We understand, and we sympathize. That's why *sometimes* we try to convince you to call in a pro.

Oh, and we also tend to urge you to enlist a professional if it appears you've bitten off more than you can chew in terms of specific expertise. Like that time you were standing in the kitchen knee deep in water and your lady tried to get you to finally give in and call a plumber—or a deep sea diver. Or that time she got a little bit antsy about all the sparks coming out of the new outlet you installed and asked if *maybe* you didn't want to check with an electrician.

So here are some general guidelines. Do it yourself only if …

- ◆ You know what you're doing, or at least have an inkling. (Hint: watching a *This Old House* segment does not count if you fall asleep during it.)

- ◆ You can finish it in a reasonable amount of time. (Hint: it is not reasonable to finish fixing air conditioner over New Years.)

- ◆ You can do it without causing bodily harm to yourself or others. (Hint: we will stop you when we smell charred flesh or notice a gushing head wound.)

We all understand that it is hard for men to admit they need help, especially when it comes to allegedly "manly pursuits." In general, support-seeking behavior is more a female thing than a guy thing. But no woman will think less of you if you include the Yellow Pages as part of your handyman arsenal. Yes, we want the stuff done. But sometimes we don't want you to overtax yourself, let alone kill yourself, playing with high voltage. We love you too much for that.

Mr. Mom

According to a report issued by the Bureau of Labor Statistics in 2004, women in dual-income households still spend an hour a day more than men tending to young children. With older children, these same women spend six hours a day in "secondary care," like chauffeuring kids and shopping with them in tow. Men spent only four hours in providing secondary care.

Are you seeing a pattern here similar to that of housework? Very observant! But there's good news too: dads today are definitely spending more time with their kids than they used to—and that's great. If you can arrange to spend even more, their mom will thank you and they will, too, because kids really enjoy their quality dad time.

In general, moms tend to be the more nurturing parent, and the one who exhibits more protective behavior. They nurse the kids' wounds, both physical and emotional. They bake more of the cookies. They do more of the tucking in and the comforting in the middle of the night when monsters lurk beneath the bed. They're also the ones reminding the little ones to "put on a jacket or you'll catch your death" and "stop running with that stick or you'll poke out your eye out."

What do dads do? They show more of what developmental psychologists call *affiliative behavior.*

Kids often think of dad time as fun time. They look forward to those times you can toss a ball or a Frisbee with them, take them to a movie or the zoo, or just go to the park and maybe get an ice cream. But to tell the truth it wouldn't hurt your relationship with them—or their mom—one bit if you were also to spend some time …

Tongue Teasers

Affiliative behavior is behavior that indicates friendly intent, such as smiling, laughing, and engaging in pleasant shared pastimes. With regard to parenting, it is sometimes used in contrast to attachment behaviors, which foster a complex, more emotionally charged bond.

- Doing homework with them or helping them study for tests.

- Taking them to their dentist and optometrist appointments.

- Taking them clothes shopping.

- Driving them to and from birthday parties, sports matches, and piano lessons.

They'd probably still think it was a rocking good time to have some extra moments with you. Not incidentally, those would also be a few extra moments that mom could use to catch her breath. In the end, the entire family would benefit from a more equitable division of labor when it comes to childcare. You know what they say about families, don't you? "If mama's not happy, ain't nobody happy." On the other hand, when mama is happy, all's right with the world.

The Least You Need to Know

- Studies show women do more housework than men, even when both partners work outside the home.

- The more men participate in housework, the more their women report increased feelings of satisfaction and sexual intimacy.

- Cleaning up isn't rocket science—all you need is good tools, good products, and a good attitude.

- Men do tend to do more home repair and building projects than women—but please "do it yourself" only if you have the time and the know-how to follow through.

- Men generally spend less time with their kids than women do, even when both mom and dad have jobs—make the time to pitch in and pal around with your children.

Chapter 9

Mind Your Manly Manners

In This Chapter

- ◆ Why manners mustn't fade
- ◆ Things a woman shouldn't see or hear
- ◆ Respecting her friends and family
- ◆ Bedroom etiquette
- ◆ The golden rule of manners

In the initial phase of courtship every man and woman is on their best behavior. We know better than to let it all hang out—physically, verbally, or emotionally. Even if we're feeling grumpy or tired, we are still conscious of being gracious toward our partner. It makes good sense. After all, our relationship is new and tenuous, and we don't want to scare our lover off.

Then some time passes, familiarity sets in, and things start to slip. We are not nearly as courteous and considerate of our partner. In fact, we regularly commit breaches of etiquette. Our partners may pretend not to notice … but they do. And they're most assuredly not pleased.

This chapter will help you to restore your early level of consideration to your relationship. It will remind you what being a real gentleman is all about.

Don't Forget Etiquette

Good manners and a respectful attitude are among the most underestimated tools when it comes to keeping relationships on track and romance thriving. When they are absent, however, things can deteriorate pretty quickly. To understand the difference, consider these two scenarios.

Scenario Number 1: A man is heading home from work, after having had a stressful, hectic day. He's not in the best mood. To make things worse, the traffic en route is awful. While he's driving, his wife calls him on his cell phone. She reminds him she's hosting a historical preservation committee meeting at their house after dinner. There will be seven other women there. Since she's had a busy workday as well, she asks if he'd mind stopping by the local gourmet shop, which is on his way home, and picking up an order she's placed so the group can have some refreshments. He grunts unintelligibly into the phone and hangs up.

He picks up the order, drops it on the kitchen counter, and then sulks through dinner. The last thing he wants is a bunch of company coming over. When his wife's associates arrive, he ignores them. He sets up camp in the den, adjacent to the room in which they're meeting, and blares the T.V.

Scenario Number 2: A man is heading home from work. He's had a stressful day. While he's sitting in traffic, his wife calls him on his cell and reminds him she's hosting a historical preservation committee meeting at their house after dinner. Seven other women will be there. She asks if he'd mind stopping by the gourmet store on his way home to pick up an order of refreshments. He says, "I'm glad you found time to place that order. I'll bet your day was as crazy as mine."

He picks up the order, and while he's at it he decides to surprise his wife by picking up a take-out dinner as well. As they eat dinner, he inquires about what the historical preservation committee is working on. He does this even though it's not of paramount interest to him. In truth, the last thing he wants is a bunch of company coming over. Nevertheless, when his wife's associates arrive, he greets them cheerfully and exchanges a few pleasantries. He then excuses himself, sets up camp in the den, closes the door and turns the T.V. on low volume so as not to create a disturbance.

Think of the differences between what happened in the first and second scenarios. Now try jotting some of them down:

1. _____
   _____

2. _____
   _____

3. _____
   _____

4. _____
   _____

5. _____
   _____

Did you notice that in the second scenario, the man talked pleasantly with his wife on the phone, despite his bad mood? Did you notice his empathic communication with her, in which he acknowledged that she too had a long, hard day?

In addition to this, he was considerate enough to pick up dinner, and thoughtful enough to inquire about his wife's meeting. When her committee members showed up he was appropriately polite and, later, unobtrusive.

Which man do you think made his woman happier? And which woman do you think made him happier later that night? It's a no-brainer. Good manners also offer an instant pay-off in the form of instant reciprocity. It's hard not to be nice to someone who is being nice to you.

Some Things Your Woman Should Never See

When it comes to etiquette between men and women, one of the main things to keep in mind is that there are certain things a woman should never see you do. Ever. This is true no matter how long you two have been together.

Subjecting a lady to certain sights will turn her off. It will also lead her to think of you as just plain rude. Here are the top visual taboos—activities a man should never pursue in the sight of his girlfriend or wife:

1. Don't use the toilet in front of her. Closing the bathroom door only takes a second. It's well worth the investment of your time. They don't call it "the privy" for nothing.

2. Don't leave the toilet seat up. I know it seems irrational, even unfair, and maybe it is. But women find it unsightly.

3. Don't use anything as a toilet that isn't one. You guys are lucky in that it is logistically easier for you to relieve yourselves than it is for us. We understand that, as a practical matter, you may feel compelled to do some impromptu relieving out in the wild, say when you are hiking in the woods. Nevertheless, it's still polite to excuse yourself and seek out a shrub for cover if your partner is hiking with you. If you're not in the wild, please find a lavatory.

4. Don't wear undergarments with tears and holes in them. This is unbecoming and sends the message that you don't think enough of your mate to mend your ways. (See Chapter 10 on the benefits of a yearly underwear purge.)

5. Don't tug on your underwear. If you have a wedgie, excuse yourself for some quick repair work.

6. Don't leave your jock straps lying around. We're glad you're protecting yourself, but we don't need to know too much.

7. Don't walk around the house naked. Well, except at appropriate moments. If you're not sure if it's an appropriate moment, it's not.

8. Don't eat or drink straight from containers or jars. Use silverware, plates, and glasses. Having the occasional "cold one" straight from the bottle is acceptable on a hot day when you're working outdoors. But it's unsightly and unsanitary to chug milk or scrape Heavenly Hash from the carton.

9. Don't "flip the bird" in traffic. We know it's tempting to express yourself when some other guy cuts you off or does something else dumb or dangerous. But rude gestures can't lead to anything except road rage. Who needs it?

He Says/She Says

"My husband is a pretty well-mannered guy, but he used to turn into Attila the Hun behind the wheel. It seemed like his middle finger was constantly in motion. When the kids started imitating him and he saw them in the rear view mirror, he finally realized it was time to stop acting like a Barbarian."
—Claire, 42

10. Don't roll your eyes when she makes a comment. Even if your partner says or does something objectionable (she's not perfect, nor is anyone), don't compound the problem. Also, take note: as impolite as this behavior is in private, making a face behind her back in public is even worse.

11. Don't gape at another woman. Sure, it's okay to look. It means you're alive and well. But an appreciative glance is different than a slack-jawed, drooling stare.

Look over this list and see how many of these mannerly infractions you may be guilty of. If you can eliminate even one per month until they're all extinguished, you will be amazed how much goodwill you'll generate. A little civility goes a long way.

Some Things Your Woman Should Never Hear

If you want to make yourself agreeable to all of your woman's senses, you should know that just as there are things she should never see, there are things she ought never to hear. These are the top aural taboos of which to steer clear:

1. Don't belch. You may argue that sometimes this behavior just can't be controlled. Yet somehow you managed to control it during courtship. You also manage to control it when you're giving a presentation at work, don't you? I rest my case. If you know there are foods that make you gassy, limit them or take an anti-gas food enzyme before you eat them. It also helps to eat slowly, so don't shovel food in. It's true that in some cultures it is considered polite to indulge in a loud, satisfied belch at the end of a meal—but ours is not one of those cultures.

2. Don't berate "the help." Your woman will cringe if you are disrespectful to cab drivers, store clerks, waiters, bellhops, valets, or anyone who is performing a service for you. These are difficult, stressful jobs and even if the service is less than perfect it will help the situation if you're empathic rather than obnoxious. (Please note, there is one exception to this: if someone is deliberately rude to your woman, you should defend her.)

3. Don't be sarcastic. Always resist the temptation to be clever at someone else's expense, especially your woman's.

4. Don't use foul language. There's nothing manly about a mouth full of swear words. All cursing does is make it seem as though you have a very limited vocabulary.

5. Don't tell dirty jokes. They're usually not that funny anyway.

Love Busters

Substitute fine language for foul. According to *Aggravating Circumstances: A Status Report on Rudeness in America*, a nationwide study prepared by the nonprofit organization Public Agenda, 44 percent of over 2,000 adults polled said they heard crude language often and 56 percent said they were bothered a lot when they heard it.

6. Don't yell. It's scary. The old adage about counting to 10 also works well for a quick calm-down. A nice embellishment of this technique is to close your eyes and picture a birthday cake with 10 candles. Count backward from 10 to 1 and as you do, mentally picture yourself blowing out each candle. As each candle is extinguished, feel your stress, anger, and frustration dissipate.

If you're guilty of any of these breaches in etiquette, begin to edit yourself. Granted, it's certainly not easy to summon up the self-control needed to change what may have become an ingrained habit. However, if you remain mindful you will reach your goal little by little.

Manners with Her Friends

Since girlhood, members of the female sex enjoy huddling with their girlfriends, sharing feelings and exchanging confidences. The importance of what our girlfriends think is important to us when we are 9 years old, and 19, and 29, and forever after. If they approve of the men in our lives, that's considered a big plus. If they envy us just a tad, that's even better.

Naturally enough, every woman wants her friends to think that the man she landed is a treasure. Since you are a treasure, you might assume she's all set. But no. The truth is that you need to do some ongoing self-marketing to keep her friends mindful of your many wonderful attributes. If this isn't enough incentive, there's also the fact that your woman's friends are to some extent an extension of her. Being gracious toward them is being respectful of her.

With friends you like, and whose company you enjoy, this can be relatively easy. Surely you always remember to:

- Look presentable when you're in their compan.
- Greet them by name.
- Favor them with one of your most charming smiles.
- Exchange pleasantries and a bit of banter.
- Inquire after their families.
- Ask about their work.
- Compliment them on their families and their work.
- Compliment their appearance.

Now, what about the friends you're not so fond of? What about the one that's an incorrigible gossip, or the one that always seems to be on her high horse about some cause or other? What about the ones who are a little wealthier, a little more socially connected—and who will never let you forget it? What about the one that always seems to be in a bad mood? How should you treat them? And how should you treat the husbands and boyfriends who come with the friends—even if they're not the kinds of guys you'd normally pal around with?

The answer, of course, is that you treat them exactly the same as those friends whose company you genuinely enjoy. In fact, for those you don't like you need to go that extra mile and turn up the charm just a notch. If it's difficult, just pretend you're at work dealing with managers or customers that might not exactly be your kind of folks but in front of whom it's necessary to be on your best behavior. You have nothing to lose and everything to gain by being gracious.

Mood Makers

Praising your woman and showing some signs of affection toward her so that her friends will see and hear will win you bonus points in the pleasing department.

Bear in mind though, that there is a fine line between graciousness and obsequiousness. However you feel about your wife's friends, don't go over the top. This is especially true when it comes to complimenting the women. You don't want your attentions to be mistaken as flirtation.

Of course not all the things your partner does with her friends will include you. It's easy to feel a bit resentful when activities she plans with others cut into your time together. But it's best to hold your tongue in such matters. Learn to enjoy the time you spend on your own. Offer to take charge of the kids, if you have kids, so that she can get some serious girl time in. A relationship is all that much stronger when neither partner is the other's sole means of a social life.

Manners with Her Family

Making a commitment to your woman also means making a commitment to her family. In some cases—if your partner's family is warm, accepting, and easy to get along with—this is a simple commitment to uphold. But, let's face it, almost every family comes with its share of annoying members. It seems that Mother Nature must have doled them out this way to keep things more or less even across the universe. Nevertheless, any member of your wife's family deserves your forbearance. This applies especially to your partner's parents. Remember, she wouldn't be here if it weren't for them.

Granted, sometimes a woman's parents can get very territorial with regard to her affections. She's their "little girl" and they may have mixed feelings about sharing her with someone else. Underneath it all, they feel insecure, and they may act out this insecurity by violating certain boundaries. For example they may call or visit too often and stay too long when they do visit. They may try to interfere in your life, offering unsolicited advice at the drop of a hat.

It's important to delineate the boundaries between the private relationship that you and your partner share and the relationship you and she share with her parents. It is necessary, for instance, to stipulate what is and isn't a convenient time for the two of you to have them visit. But there are still properly polite ways to state your needs. It's one thing to say, "You can't come over tomorrow. We're too busy to deal with you"; it's another to say, "Gosh, we're all tied up tomorrow, but we'd love to have an early lunch with you next Saturday before we run our afternoon errands." The second communication spares their feelings, offers an alternative that works for you, and sets a time parameter on your next encounter.

Of course parents are not the only members of your wife's family that you may find irksome. Setting boundaries politely is a good strategy to use with them all. Another is to ready yourself to interact with them by finding something praiseworthy about each one of them and also on planning out ahead of time a noncontroversial topic you can talk with them about—an interest you share, an item from a newspaper or magazine, sports talk, or car talk. What the heck: there's always the weather. Having these plans in your back pocket—perhaps literally on a note card there—will help you to overlook their more challenging characteristics. Try filling out this list for practice:

Family Member	Positive Trait	Something to Talk About
Mother	_____	_____
Father	_____	_____
Brother	_____	_____
Sister	_____	_____
Uncle	_____	_____
Aunt	_____	_____
Cousin	_____	_____
Grandmother	_____	_____
Grandfather	_____	_____

Having neutral topics for discussion will also prevent you from fueling a family boundary violation by revealing too much personal information. Never divulge too much of what's going on between the two of you, or within your own nuclear family. Being polite does not necessitate spilling your guts. Keep your problems to yourselves.

If you think it is just too hard to grin and bear the company of your in-laws, extend the circle of company. Invite some fun friends over to join the festivities when your partner's family is around. Make sure these are friends both you and your lady agree are the entertaining, easygoing sort. These added guests can create the perfect *buffer zone*, taking some of the pressure off you and allowing you to feel more relaxed and, thus, be more cheerful and polite.

Finally, if your wife or girlfriend wants to vent about her own family, let her do so and be supportive. But resist the temptation to join in. For one thing, it will only add fuel to the fire. For another thing, she may take offense to what you say even if she is angry at them. She is free to criticize her family; you are not.

Tongue Teasers

In military terms, a **buffer zone** is a neutral area that lies between hostile forces and reduces the risk of conflict between them. More colloquially, it refers to any means designed to form a barrier that prevents potential conflict or harmful contact. Socially skilled friends make a wonderful buffer zone when challenging family members visit.

Bediquette

Another kind of etiquette lapse that all too often occurs in long-term relationships is a lack of manners in the bedroom. In fact, lack of consideration when it comes to sex can be one of the main reasons that some couples begin to lose interest in their sex life altogether.

Do you know the score when it comes to "bediquette?" Answer these questions and see:

◆ Have you ever compared your partner unfavorably with a previous lover?
Often / Sometimes / Never

◆ Have you ever critiqued your partner's body flaws during lovemaking?
Often / Sometimes / Never

◆ Have you ever asked "What the heck are you doing?" or "Where'd you get that one?" when your lover tries something new?
Often / Sometimes / Never

◆ Do you give her orders or make demands instead of seductively asking for what you want?
Often / Sometimes / Never

◆ Do you ever stop sexual activity if you climax before she does?
Often / Sometimes / Never

◆ Have you ever refused to use a condom when she asked you to?
Often / Sometimes / Never

◆ Have you ever expressed disapproval if she doesn't want sex during her "time of the month?"
Often / Sometimes / Never

◆ Have you ever told her you discuss your sex life with other people?
Often / Sometimes / Never

If you've answered "Often" to or even "Sometimes" to any of these questions, it's time to refurbish your sexual etiquette. You can't undo what's been done, but you can stop such *faux pas* from happening ever again.

Putting your partner down by making unfavorable comparisons or criticizing her body is inexcusably rude. It's almost as bad as calling her by someone else's name in the throes of passion. Such gaffes are also completely counter-productive. They'll badly puncture her self-esteem and her sex drive.

Love Busters

Other than teenagers, it's women in their forties who experience the greatest number of unplanned pregnancies. Any woman who is still menstruating can get pregnant; never assume otherwise. The best strategy is to discuss birth control options with your partner before the crucial moment.

The same goes for discouraging your woman's sexual curiosity and creativity. If you embarrass her when she tries new things, she never will again. Always praise her for attempting something new, even if it's not exactly something you want to try again.

Harshly correcting her technique during lovemaking will similarly undermine her confidence. If her technique is off, gently guide her. Likewise, being selfish about your gratification is a surefire way to get her to lose interest.

As for birth control, be a sport. Birth control is never the sole responsibility of one partner.

With regard to your woman's time of the month, please be sensitive to her preferences. Some women simply do not wish to engage in any sexual activity in this time. If you cool your jets for a few days instead of sulking, rewards will be forthcoming.

Finally, discussing your sex life with others—unless it's a therapist or counselor with whom you've both agreed to speak—will embarrass your lover and make her self-conscious.

Manners work as well between the sheets as they do anywhere else. Be considerate of your partner's feelings. Be aware of her needs. And while you're at it, don't neglect to say please and thank you.

The Golden Rule of Etiquette

Ultimately what relationship etiquette all boils down to is one thing: do unto the woman in your life as you would have her do unto you. If that sounds familiar, it should. They don't call this the golden rule for nothing.

Of course, the catch to the golden rule is that it's often easier articulated than enforced. So here's a useful trick: if you're having any difficulty being gracious in your relationship, pretend that your wife or girlfriend is someone you met only recently. We usually think twice about what we say and do in the company of new acquaintances. You can't go wrong if you extend the same courtesy to your partner.

The Least You Need to Know

- Familiarity may tend to breed discourtesy—make an effort to sustain good manners past courtship.

- Edit what you say and do—some things should not be seen or heard.

- Friends and family are an extension of your woman—always treat them with respect.

- Bad manners in bed can cause women to lose interest in sex—so behave yourself.

- When in doubt, just do unto your woman as you would have her do unto you.

Chapter **10**

Handsome for Your Honey

In This Chapter

- ◆ Why look great for your girl?
- ◆ Clothes closet basics
- ◆ Colors and patterns for men
- ◆ Care for your hair and skin
- ◆ The "man"icure and pedicure
- ◆ The hair "down there"

In the animal kingdom, males of the species often show off their physical characteristics to attract a mate. The peacock spreads his lustrous, elegant tail; the frigate bird puffs out his brilliant red chest. Throughout the centuries men have done many things to better their appearance in order to attract women—dating back to the days when cavemen made a fashion statement, and a statement about their virility, by wearing loincloths made of skins of the prey they had felled.

Chances are that when you and your lady first met you made an effort to appeal to her by looking your best. But now—be honest—do you put as much thought into your appearance as you used to? Read on for some tips on pleasing your woman by giving her something hot and handsome to cast her loving eyes upon—and I don't mean a picture of George Clooney.

Be Her Arm Candy

When it comes to pleasing your woman, appearance counts. That's not because we're shallow creatures—not any more than you are. A pleasant-looking husband or boyfriend—well groomed, appropriately dressed, and beaming a winning smile—is a joy to behold for many reasons.

◆ He makes a statement about himself—that he is confident and secure.

◆ He makes a statement about us—that we rate a mate who takes pride in presenting himself well.

◆ He makes a statement about the relationship—looking presentable in the presence of one's partner is a sign of politeness and respect.

Besides, *arm candy* is sweet and delicious. How wonderful to be in the company of a mate that others think of as "yummy."

Tongue Teasers

Gossip and society columnists popularized the phrase **arm candy,** which at first referred to an attractive woman who was escorted by a gentleman so that others could eye her appreciatively. The term was first used to describe Marilyn Monroe in a walk-on role she played in a party scene in the 1950 film, *All About Eve.* Today, in the name of gender equality, men are sometimes referred to as arm candy (and I've never heard them complain).

It will also interest you to know that good grooming and a pleasant appearance correlate with worldly success and financial advantage. A review of experimental studies clearly shows that physical attractiveness is of considerable significance in the business world.

Overwhelmingly, attractive people fare better in terms of personal recommendations, perceived job qualifications, and predicted job success. In fact, appearance is often the factor that tips the scales in hiring situations. When two job applicants with similar experience and abilities compete, the one who wins is most often the one that decision makers agree makes a nicer appearance. So looking good can also help you earn more. What woman will be displeased with that?

Have You a Clue?

Of course, it's understandable if you are not sure how to enhance your appearance so that you look your most attractive and appealing. Unlike we females, you probably were not coached in the art of looking your best from an early age. Besides, in the past few decades—until just recently—men had relatively few fashion options. In addition, only a small number of appearance-enhancing products had been developed specifically with men in mind.

Tongue Teasers

The term **metrosexual** refers to an urban, heterosexual male who is fashion-conscious, has a strong aesthetic sense, and spends significant time and money on his appearance and lifestyle. He is the target audience of men's magazines. The term was coined in 1994 (along with the noun, *metrosexuality*) by British journalist Mark Simpson.

Happily, more and more fashion choices and grooming products are now available for the male. As part of what the media has termed the *metrosexual* trend, attitudes are changing, too, and many men are now openly more interested in looking good without feeling that such concerns are "unmanly."

But some men who have the desire to spiff up their appearance are not sure where to start. As with any endeavor, it's a good idea to benchmark your initial level of expertise at the start so you can figure out where to begin and what needs your attention. The following quiz will help you learn where you fit on the spectrum that spans a range from clueless to clued in.

1. The last time you had a haircut was …

    A. Last week

    B. Last month

    C. When I tripped over my hair

2. The last you shaved was …

    A. Today

    B. Yesterday

    C. After I kissed my woman and gave her severe lacerations

3. Your medicine cabinet contains …

    A. High quality hair styling products and skin creams

    B. Shampoo, shaving cream, floss

    C. Tums

4. The inside of your clothes closet is …

   A. Carefully arranged

   B. Helter skelter

   C. Gull of golf clubs—my clothes are on the floor

5. For an evening out you would normally wear …

   A. Khakis and a dressy sport shirt

   B. Jeans and a sweater

   C. Go out?

6. Your idea of fashionable footwear is …

   A. Italian leather loafers

   B. Sneakers

   C. Shower shoes

7. In general, my wardrobe is …

   A. Contemporary

   B. A bit dated

   C. Early Flintstones

8. My clothing color and pattern matching skills …

   A. Are beyond reproach

   B. Are based on trial and error

   C. Often cause my woman to take Dramamine

9. Your woman asks you to attend a black-tie dinner. You would …

   A. Happily agree

   B. Reluctantly agree

   C. Feign a heart attack

10. Your house catches fire and you can save one item of clothing. It is …

   A. A designer suit

   B. Your most comfortable khakis or jeans

   C. Your bowling shoes

11. Your overall opinion of your clothing and fashion sense is …

    A. I know I look good

    B. I guess I look sort of okay

    C. I'm sorry

If you answered mostly A's you are already interested in and skilled at looking your best. That's good. Of course, you're open to making a good thing even better.

If you answered mostly B's you are trying. You might not lack motivation, but need information and inspiration. With a little effort and the right attitude, you'll be looking fine in no time.

If you answered mostly C's you qualify for emergency assistance. You may never look like Leonardo de Caprio in black tie, but remember, a little improvement can go a long way toward making your woman smile. It's painless to improve on the "Animal House" look if you take things one step at a time.

The Clothes That You Know

The woman in your life probably thinks of shopping for clothing as a sport. We like to hunt for the perfect outfit at the perfect price. We'll take our time doing it because the chase is part of the thrill. For you, the same activity is most likely a chore, even a bore.

The reason that you always find the Men's Department on the first floor of department stores is that retailers know you want to get your clothes shopping over and done as quickly as possible. It's a hit and run endeavor. Run in, snag a pair of trousers and a shrink-wrapped shirt and hope that they fit you, more or less. Nevertheless, there's something behind that old adage that clothes make the man—meaning that what a man wears says a lot about his character. It's hardly a new belief. The original line "The apparel oft proclaims the man" dates back to Shakespeare's *Hamlet*.

You may be the kind of guy who has little in your closet except a few well-worn staples that you think of as old friends. If so, nothing will turn you into a fashion plate. But, face it, those old friends could use a little new company. In just a couple of shopping trips, you can expand your options and up your style quotient.

Some men seem to look well put-together all the time, without being pre-occupied with the matter or devoting an inordinate amount of time to it. What do they have that you might not have? Here are a few essentials that every man ought to have in his wardrobe:

1. Several well-fitted, solid-colored, fine cotton T-shirts

2. Three pullovers made of fine wool

3. Some polo-style knit shirts—in both short and long sleeves

3. A white dress shirt (a classic)

4. A black turtleneck (so sexy)

5. Two pairs of flat-front khaki pants (a putty or sand shade for spring and a warm gold or a brown shade for summer)

6. A couple pairs of well-fitting dress pants—at least one of them in navy and perhaps one in herringbone

7. A three-button navy gabardine jacket (goes with everything all year round)

8. A lightweight windbreaker

9. A leather jacket (makes you look rugged and manly)

10. A few silk ties in solid colors or understated patterns

11. One staple gray or navy suit (splurge on a classic that fits exceptionally well)

12. A pair of great-fitting jeans (please don't cuff them)

Afraid of shopping alone? You should be. A second opinion is something you should never leave home without. Besides, if you go alone, sometimes the clerks will encourage you to buy things that you don't need or that don't really look that great, just to make a sale.

Remember, chances are your wife or girlfriend loves to shop. Even if they're shopping for someone else, they will get a vicarious thrill. So ask her to come along as your wardrobe mistress.

He Says/She Says

"I was thrilled when my boyfriend asked me to take him clothes shopping, I actually did prep work by reading magazines like GQ and Cargo. I thought I'd break him in easy by going to one or two stores, but it ends up we made a day of it and had a blast. We devised a thumbs up/thumbs down system for whenever he came out of the dressing room. By the end of the afternoon, he was making really good picks and getting lots of thumbs up signs."
—Sandy 26

The Matching Game

One clothing issue that appears to stump a lot of men is the dilemma of colors and patterns. Your woman can probably go on, chapter and verse, about which colors flatter her skin tones and which do not. When prompted, she might go on about whether she is a "spring" or "winter" palette. This concept is probably about as alien to you as a discourse on quantum physics in a parallel universe.

Nevertheless, your skin tone does matter when selecting the right shades to wear. Colors that are too close your skin tone will give you a washed-out look without any interesting contrast. If you're naturally dark-skinned or sporting a tan, you'll look most handsome in whites and bright colors. If you're fair-skinned, pastels and Earth tones work well.

Mood Makers

When in doubt on what color to buy, get a shirt that matches your eyes. For some reason, men always look great in those!

Another color rule for men, more so than women, is to keep it simple. Yes, the rainbow look works well for peacocks, but a peacock you're not. If you're wearing one bright shade, always pair it with a neutral, like black, beige, or denim.

As for patterns, a good rule of thumb is one per outfit. For example, don't wear striped pants with a paisley shirt. In addition, if you're shopping for a sports coat or suit with a pattern, check to make sure that the pattern matches up where the seams meet (as you would if you were hanging wall paper). If the patterns don't match up, that's reason enough to suspect the quality of the garment.

What to Wear Under There

Here's something a woman never wants to see: a sexy man taking off his sexy clothes and revealing a stained undershirt and a pair of boxer shorts that look like they were chewed on by a Labrador retriever. Here's something else she never wants to see: her man in a silk leopard-print bikini brief. Granted, undergarments are clearly a very personal decision, but those are definite no's in the underwear category if you want to please the person who will actually be seeing you in your underwear.

Boxers and boxer briefs are nice, as are crewneck tees for under sweaters or sport shirts and V-neck tees for under dress shirts. I'd stick with white or gray—but not white that has turned gray. To that end, you'll want to be sure to do a yearly underwear purge. Empty out that dresser drawer and start over. If you think you are apt to forget, tie this activity to a special day like tax day, your wedding anniversary, or the Super Bowl.

Love Busters

Choose underwear made of cotton. Cotton breathes. Keep that air circulation flowing. Besides, when it's your turn to do the laundry you will find that it's easier to wash than any other material. Of course, the occasional pair of silk boxers, might feel nice and be pleasant for your woman to feel.

Shoe Biz

If clothes make the man, be aware that bad shoes can break even the most well dressed gentleman. Let me tell you a secret: many a woman who feels she's met a really neat guy will suddenly make a run for it if she notices that his footwear is of poor taste or quality. Others feel the same. Prospective employers, clients, business associates, virtually any new acquaintance can be instantly put off by the sight of inappropriate or beaten-up shoes. The thing about shoes is that they seem to have a way of indicating whether or not their wearer is a man with a high opinion of himself. And if he does not have a high opinion of himself, why should anyone else?

Every guy has his favorite pair of beat up sneakers. There's no sense in telling you to throw them out. We all know they're here to stay. Your woman will have to make peace with them and that's that. But if the occasion calls for anything more—and, like it or not, many do—you'll need a few pair of classic shoes to see you through.

Lucky for you, the matter of men's shoes is much less complex than that of female footwear. No strappy sandals and pumps in every color of the spectrum for you, my friend. In addition to your trusty sneakers, you'll want:

- **Fine-leather loafers.** These can be worn with jeans, with casual sportswear, and even with a sport coat.

- **Wingtips (sometimes called "brogues").** These are versatile and never ever go out of style. High-quality ones keep their shape indefinitely, so they're worth a splurge. (Keep them polished and you'll always look like you care about your appearance.)

- **Moccasins.** They go with everything and are great to throw on in a rush, like when you're getting the paper or walking the dog. They're comfortable for driving, too.

- **Tennis shoes.** Classic tennies in solid navy, or natural cotton shades provide a nice alternative to wearing beat-up sneakers everywhere.

What to wear with the shoes? The proper kind of socks. Athletic socks go with athletic shoes. Period. Dress shoes call for dress socks. Two times you shouldn't wear socks: When you're wearing flip-flops and when you're having sex.

No More Bad Hair

Come on, admit it: you men may not spend as much time worrying about your hair as women do, but this is one area where you come close to matching us. The top of your head can be your crowning glory, but troubled hair can be a thorn in the crown.

When it comes to your hair, you ought to consider taking a page from your partner's book. One thing your wife or girlfriend might do that you might not is to enlist quality professional help in the form of a hair stylist.

What's the difference between a barber and a stylist? It's somewhat like the difference between someone who mows lawns and someone who does landscaping. Barbershops are good for Basic Haircuts 101. Stylists are skilled at choosing a hairstyle that fits a client's face and hair type. If you have always gone to the barbershop, you might be amazed at what a good stylist can do for you.

I know you might be resistant to the notion of a hair stylist. Even the word—stylist—can give you the willies. You might consider hair styling an expensive indulgence. Besides, you're understandably loyal to your barber, with whom you've traded sports talk, jokes, and insights on the meaning of life throughout the years. Well, you won't have to suffer complete barbershop withdrawal. If you visit a good stylist (ask around for personal recommendations) a few times a year, your barber can handle the maintenance trims in between.

Just as seeing a hair stylist is now a perfectly acceptable male behavior, so is using an appropriate array of hair-care products. While you're in your stylist's chair, take the opportunity to ask for some guidance through the thicket of products that are currently available for men. At the very least you'll want a shampoo and a conditioner suited to your hair type (fine or thick, oily or dry). You'll probably also need a styling product, like gel or mousse.

If you have an especially stubborn cowlick, a rogue tuft growing in the wrong direction, your stylist can zap it with the kind of hair relaxer that's used to straighten curls. It only needs to be left on for 5 to 10 minutes, and reapplied every 3 months or so. While a cowlick can add to boyish charm, it can also wreck a perfectly good hairstyle.

Tongue Teasers _____

Androgenetic alopecia is the technical term for male pattern hair loss (MPHL). "Andro" refers to the androgens (testosterone, dihydrotestosterone) necessary to produce the condition, which usually begins with recession in the temporal areas.

Now I'm afraid it's time to address a tough issue: Suppose you have a lot less hair than you used to have? Hey, you are far from alone. An estimated 35 million men in the United States are affected by hair loss known as _androgenetic alopecia_.

Losing some hair is not as big a deal as you think it is. Honestly, we ladies don't mind it when you do. It doesn't correlate with the loss of any of your attractiveness. All of us can think of guys with little or no hair that turn us on: Bruce Willis, Ed Harris, Patrick Stewart, Gene Hackman, Sean Connery, and Vin Diesel to name a few.

The problem is that you guys often commit your worst hair bloopers when you begin to lose some of your locks. Bad comb-overs and ill-fitting toupees are not sexy, and they don't fool anyone. As a personal favor to your woman—and as a public service—give up either of these misguided strategies if you're currently using them. Instead, consult your stylist for better options. These include:

◆ Cutting your hair shorter and styling it more naturally.

◆ Adding some facial hair.

◆ Shaving it all off and showing off that shiny scalp.

Mood Makers _____

Some hairs you definitely ought to lose are any prevalent hairs in your nose. They tickle when you kiss us, and we don't want to be distracted! Buy a trimmer. And don't forget to trim your ear hair, too.

Although you may be initially reluctant to see it this way, often the secret of good hair is that less is more. I know you might well be emotionally wed to the hairstyle of your youth, but if it is no longer suitable it will only serve to date your look. With luck, your stylist will offer some tough love in this area.

By the way, if you are experiencing male pattern hair loss, don't blame your mother. A common myth is that this condition is inherited only from the mother's side. This is not true. The gene for MPHL can be inherited from either your mother or father's side.

Good Skin for Men

Framing your soulful eyes, your rugged chin, and your magnetic smile are about 30 square inches of epidermis. That's skin. And it requires some tender loving care. When your skin looks clear and fresh, it will automatically show the rest of your facial features off to their greatest advantage.

Your face is your visual calling card. A well cared for visage will mark you as an individual brimming with health and vigor. Make no mistake: skin care is not just for women. Unfortunately, skin care is one of those areas of knowledge to which most men have had little or no exposure. When girls grow up, their moms teach them not to wash their face with soap because it dries out the skin. When boys grow up, their mothers are happy if they use soap anywhere at all!

Even if you've never done anything to take care of your skin before, if you begin protecting it today you will soon see a noticeable difference.

Start slowly, with three skin care fundamentals:

1. A moisturizer will keep your face hydrated and give your razor a smooth surface to glide over.

2. A mild cleanser, unlike soap, will clean skin without stripping it of its natural oils.

3. Sunscreen, to protect your skin from damaging sunrays that cause premature aging and, in the worst case, skin cancer. (Even if your moisturizer has sunscreen in it, you need extra protection when spending time outdoors, like on the golf course.)

Like women, men may be prone to certain skin problems simply because they have skin that is naturally oily or dry. You might have special issues too, such as dermal dandruff—itchy, flaking, reds patches— because you poor guys have to take a razor to your faces every day.

In addition, certain skin problems may evolve as you age. An estimated 5 percent of men over 40 have rosacea. This is a condition where hyperactive blood vessels produce a red-faced effect. At first, the blush comes and goes. But if untreated, the blushes last longer, and bumps and pimples start to crop up.

 Love Busters

Put that back! Don't pilfer skin care products from your lady. Get your own, please, and make sure they're formulated for your skin type. For example, if your skin is oily, use an oil-free cleanser formulated to help prevent breakouts.

Simply taking better basic care of your skin—with good moisturizer, skin cleanser, sunscreen, and perhaps later a mild astringent to close the pores—can have a very positive initial impact on a number of mild conditions. A dermatologist can correctly diagnosis any of these conditions and recommend treatment. I know, you don't like doctors—but as medical exams go, a dermatological one is pretty noninvasive.

Put the "Man" in Manicure

Finally, if women could effect one simple change in the grooming habits of the men they love it might well be better nail care. There is nothing appealing about being stroked by a hand with caked dirt under the fingernails—especially if those fingernails are overly long or ragged from being bitten.

If you do nothing else about your nails, at least keep them trimmed and clean. Once in a while, it wouldn't hurt to get a professional manicure. Yes. Lots of guys are doing it. It's not about colored fingernail polish for you; it's about making yourself presentable right down to your extremities. Besides, it is the only time that your woman will let another woman hold your hand without getting her nose out of joint.

Sweet Feet

While we're talking "cures," let's not neglect pedicures. I am talking to all guys, but especially to you guys who like to wear sandals and flip-flops. Ungroomed feet—yours, that is—are a pet peeve of vast numbers of the ladies, some of whom have been heard to complain that most guy's feet look like they'd work better on hobbits.

A pedicurist will trim your toenails, so your woman won't yelp when you play footsie in the night. She—well, it is usually a "she"—will exfoliate dead skin from your soles (no, it doesn't hurt) and treat your feet with assorted balms, lotions, and potions to soothe and soften them from end to end.

While one foot is being worked on, the other is soaking in fragrant, swirling warm water in a kind of mini hot tub for your aching tootsies. What could possibly be bad about that?

Your Hair "Down There"

Last but not least, a word about that most delicate of grooming matters: your hair, er, down there. Once upon a time, both men and women never gave pubic hair much of a thought, and everyone assumed that *au natural* was the only option. However a recent (summer 2005) *Cargo* magazine survey revealed that 71 percent of guys do some trimming in the pubic area and that 9 percent actually shave completely. That leaves only 20 percent that do no groin grooming whatsoever.

What do women want? According to the same survey, 63 percent are in favor of a little trimming and 6 percent say, "Take it off, take it all off." Twenty-two percent say leave it be. Isn't it interesting only nine percent of women say they don't care. Most of us seem to be very opinionated on this topic!

What does it all mean for you? It means you should check with your woman to ascertain her preference. I would especially do this if you like to have your woman pleasure you orally (I guess that category includes all of you), because during such encounters she will have a birds-eye view. And you don't want it looking like a nest.

If you've never trimmed or shaved your pubic hair before, don't dive in willy-nilly without knowing what you're doing. This is not—repeat not—an area where you want to slip up. That said, there are a few things you should know.

- Before starting to shave, trim any longish hair with a manicuring scissor.
- Take a warm bath or shower—or cover the area with a warm, wet washcloth— to soften the remaining pubes so they are easier to remove.
- Shave in a comfortable position that allows you to view the area well.
- Use a fresh razor to avoid ingrown hairs.
- Shave in the direction that your hair grows.

Specially developed electric razors with rotary blades are becoming widely marketed for pubic hair shaving. And other methods, including waxing and laser hair removal, are preferred by some. But simple shaving is, by far, the most mainstream choice.

Done with care, shaving your pubic hair is as safe as shaving any other body part. Plus, going bare down there is rumored to make you more sensitive to stimulation. Some consider male pubic hair shaving an art form in itself and some even maintain that it can be an exciting experience if approached properly. Hey, maybe your woman will want to do it for you. Then again, maybe not.

The Least You Need to Know

- Looking your best makes a statement about you and about your respect for your partner—it also connotes confidence and worldly success.

◆ Classic clothes and quality shoes signal a lot about the quality of the man wearing them.

◆ For hair help, find a good stylist—and always avoid the comb-over look.

◆ Men might never have learned to care for their skin the way women have, but they need to just as much.

◆ Look good down to your fingertips and toes—get the occasional manicure and pedicure and keep your nails clean and trimmed in between.

◆ Most women do have a preference when it comes to whether or not a man ought to shave his pubic hair—asks yours what she thinks, and oblige please.

Part 4

Making the Mood

Remember when you first got together with your lady? You loved to take her out on the town, and you loved to stay in and snuggle, too. If you've stopped doing either of these things, this part of the book will remind you how to start again. It will also offer a plethora of ways to enhance your home environment and to revitalize your woman with everything from well-presented food to luxurious massage. Need reinforcements? It will tell you how to find them.

Chapter 11

Out On the Town

In This Chapter

- Why date after courtship?
- The pleasures—and pitfalls—of dining out
- The lure of dance
- The appeal of chick flicks
- Planning weekend getaways and longer vacations

When you two were dating, you two were dating—literally. That may not have meant that you went out to a four-star restaurant and the theatre every night, but it also didn't mean you spent all your time together watching T.V. and eating fried chicken from a bucket.

When's the last time you took your lady out on the town—or out of town, for that matter? Okay, now when's the last time *you* made all the plans for doing so? This chapter will remind you what it's like to plan some special getaway time with your woman. You'll both be glad you did.

Date Night

There are many perfectly reasonable reasons to forget about going out together once you've settled in as a couple. Going out costs money. You're too busy with other obligations. You're both too tired after work. You have kids, pets, and—um—plants that get lonely when you're gone.

Fair enough. But for every reason you can offer to forget about dating your lady once your official courtship is over, there's a good reason to plan some special getaway time together. For example:

+ Breaking out of the routine adds zest to a relationship.

+ Getting away—for an evening, a night, a weekend, or a week—gives you a chance to talk and get to know one another again.

+ Going out gives your woman a good excuse to dress up and look fabulous.

+ Going out gives you a good excuse to dress up and look fabulous.

+ It's an opportunity to backburner the demands of work and kids and treat yourselves—you deserve it.

It's all too easy to defer to the path of least resistance and spend another day working in the yard and another night channel surfing. Planning a date or getaway away does take some planning and will tap your wallet to varying degrees. But your lady will thank you and, best of all, you will both feel renewed and reinvigorated when you return home from your foray into the world.

May I Escort You To Your Table?

Going out to eat is perhaps the most common thing couples do when they go out together. As far as a woman is concerned, that's very pleasing, because any meal she doesn't have to cook is a pretty good meal. But once couples settle in to a domestic routine, even going out for meals can become rushed and humdrum.

While it's better than nothing, a quick stop at the local diner or pizzeria is to a really good dining out date as a heat lamp is to a great day at the beach. Once in a while, it's worth it to splurge on some fine dining.

The Right Restaurant

Where to go? Imagine you are just starting to date your mate and are trying to impress her. There are three essential things you would want in a restaurant:

◆ **Flavorful, well-prepared food.** This is the most obvious requirement when you're choosing a place to dine. Choose a restaurant with a reputation for using fresh, quality ingredients and preparing food with panache. Your lady might have a preference for dishes that are more complex than either of you have time to prepare at home.

◆ **Ambience.** Setting and atmosphere are both key to enjoying a special meal out. Clanging dishes, harsh lighting, and blaring jukeboxes are out. Soft lighting and low-key background music are in. For a special date meal, you might look for banquette seating so the two of you can be side by side—but it's also fine to sit across from one another (not too far) and gaze into one another's eyes.

◆ **Good service.** A fine dining experience is almost as much about who brings the food and drink, and how the meal is presented, as it is about the meal itself. Service should be attentive, in terms of anticipating and responding to your needs, but it should also be unobtrusive. It's fine for waiters to tell you their name, but revealing their life history is another matter. (And, no, you can't go to Hooters, even if you think the service is ideal.)

What kind of cuisine to choose? Well, what's your lady's pleasure? If you're not sure, ask her what she's in the mood for. If—but only if—she's an adventurous eater, consider surprising her with an exotic cuisine that's new to her, such as Vietnamese, or Middle Eastern.

Restaurant Caveats

It's worth noting that although dining out has many pleasures, it also can include some pitfalls. You wouldn't want to make a bad impression on a date, would you? Just in case you haven't been out to an elegant restaurant in a while, here are a few do's and don'ts:

Do ...	But Don't ...
Choose a restaurant with a varied menu.	Pick one with so many choices that the menu is overwhelming.
Suggest dishes to your lady.	Order for her, unless she asks you to.
Ask the waiter for suggestions.	Feel obliged to take them.
Keep the conversation flowing.	Neglect to savor your food and your companion.
Be gracious to the wait staff.	Chat with the waiter more than with your dining partner.

continues

continued

Do ...	But Don't ...
Feel free to make special requests or send back a dish that isn't what you requested.	Be obnoxious.
Tip well.	Ostentatiously over-tip.

Above all, don't forget to make a reservation. It's very disappointing to build your lady's anticipation for a special meal and then be stuck milling about a crowded entryway or bar for hours. Besides, a reservation shows that you actually put some thought into planning the evening.

Once you do make a reservation, be punctual. Many popular restaurants will only hold a table for so long before they give it to someone else. If the restaurant you choose is extremely popular and hard to get in to, be sure to reconfirm your reservation ahead of time.

May I Have This Dance?

Once upon a time, dining and dancing used to be the quintessential "big date." I'm not about to suggest that you follow every meal you eat out with a night of waltzing, tangoing, or disco dancing. (If I did I'd scare you off from ever going out at all.)

Maybe you and you partner haven't danced together for a long time. Maybe the last occasion was your wedding. And maybe that is fine with you. But finding the opportunity to dance together once in a while—whether it's ballroom dancing, swing dancing, square dancing, or any other style—does have its advantages.

- Dance is an ideal exercise. It's a mild aerobic workout, minus any boring parts.

- Dancing requires music, and the right music can put anyone in a good frame of mind.

- Dancing increases your flexibility and stamina—so it's great preparation for other loving activities.

- Dancing slow is romantic.

- Dancing fast to soul, disco, or rock music is sexy, and gives you and your partner a chance to show off your moves.

What moves, you say? Okay, so maybe you never have had a lot of faith in your ability to look suave on the dance floor. But that's no reason to dismiss dancing as a date option. Your woman will likely be thrilled if you sign the two of you up for some lessons. Dance studios can be found just about anywhere. Even the "Y" and community colleges with adult education programs often offer opportunities to overcome the "two-left-feet" syndrome.

The nice thing about taking dance lessons is that it will give you an opportunity to regularly schedule time out of the house. You'll probably also meet some other couples with whom you'll enjoy socializing. Maybe, when the course is over, you can plan a double date.

 **Mood Makers**

Women enjoy dancing not only for its romantic aspects but because it trims and tones, and makes us feel youthful. Many people take up ballroom dance when more traditional exercise programs fall by the wayside, either because of injuries or tedium. It makes sense: the physiques of professional ballroom competitors, trainers, and dance teachers provide all the evidence of body-enhancing results.

All About Chick Flicks

Another after-dinner activity that your woman will enjoy is going to the movies. But if pleasing her is what you have in mind, you'll probably want to stay away from macho flicks that feature shootouts, stakeouts, kung fu fighting, or aggressive alien space invaders with a bent for eating earthlings. To really get her in the mood for love, consider accompanying her to a romantic movie—otherwise known as a "chick flick."

So what is a chick flick exactly? Perhaps the best way to explain the genre is to contrast it with the genre of "macho movie."

The Chick Flick	The Macho Movie
Has characters who discuss feelings.	Has characters who grunt.
Makes you laugh and cry.	Makes you yell, "Kill, kill!"
Features Renee Zellweger, Sandra Bullock, or Olympia Dukakis.	Features Clint Eastwood, Sly Stallone, Jean-Claude Van Damme.
Has child characters who triumph over adversity.	Has child characters who are kidnapped.
Includes a scene where someone sends flowers.	Includes a scene where someone sends a death threat.
Features man-woman love.	Features man-car love.
Often ends with a wedding.	Always ends with an explosion.

Chick flicks also contain various life lessons that reassure women. In such films, nice girls—even those with a few extra pounds on them—get the guy in the end (*Bridget Jones*). Guys who seem cold have warm hearts underneath (*Pretty Woman, Pride and Prejudice*). Longtime friends can become passionate lovers (*When Harry Met Sally*). Poor girls can marry up (*Sabrina*). Female friendships are strong and nurturing (*Steel Magnolias, Divine Secrets of the Ya-Ya Sisterhood*). And, finally chocolate solves most problems (*Chocolat*).

Are you cringing yet? Hey, just get yourself a bucket of popcorn and deal with it. The results will be worth it. You'll get to snuggle up with your honey, console her while she sobs, and rejoice with her when the guy gets the girl. Then, when you go home, you can get the girl. That's why chick flicks are known by another name as well: date movies.

He Says/She Says

"My husband was so adamant about not seeing chick movies that we sometimes would go to a multiplex together, split up and see different shows. I know some people like going to the movies alone but I felt silly. One night the timing was such that he missed the first part of his movie and came to mine. He ended up being such a good sport about it—I think because he liked the way I cuddled with him the whole time."
—Marla, 29

Close Getaways

Every now and then it's a great idea to get away for more than a few hours. A weekend trip, or even a single overnight can be a wonderful way to reconnect with your mate. If you don't want to spend a lot of time driving to and from your destination, get a map and draw a circle with a radius of 50 miles or so. Anywhere within this circle is somewhere you can get to within an hour. If something goes wrong on the home front, you can be back home within an hour as well.

Love Busters

Some times of the year—for example autumn foliage season or Valentine's weekend—are times when cozy inns and the destinations and dining spots around them are packed to the rafters, and hence not so cozy anymore. Consider off-season excursions if you don't want your overnight or weekend trip to feel harried.

What's to do so close to home? Lots. Almost every part of the country has some romantic bed and breakfast destinations or small cozy inns. Look for spots with peaceful environs that offer the opportunity for a nice walk in the woods, or a chance to sit in an Adirondack rocker and gaze at the stars.

If there's a particular activity your lady likes to indulge in—antiquing, attending craft fairs, going to farmers' markets, or art shows—see if you can tie your trip in with them. But do be forewarned that very popular events may be very populated with out-of-towners who've planned way ahead, so make your reservations accordingly.

Another close-to-home getaway option, which many suburban couples enjoy, is to book a weekend package in the closest big city. City hotels that are populated with business travelers during the week often offer great, relatively inexpensive deals in order to up their occupancy rate on weekends.

Once you've unpacked your overnight bags, you can treat yourself to all the cultural events that a large city has to offer. Take in a museum or two, go to the theatre, visit a club and take in some jazz. You can usually treat yourself with lots of ethnic food options as well.

Far Getaways

Got a bit more time for a getaway? Let's hope that at least once every year or two your answer will be affirmative. A week (or dare I suggest it—two?) away can literally be a second honeymoon.

If you or your mate are reluctant to be away from home for that long because "anything can happen," some careful and thorough planning should put your mind at ease. There are few corners of the world where one is really out of touch. With technology being what it is today, it's not hard to remain accessible (within reason) by cell phone and e-mail. You'll relax more if you know that anyone looking after your kids, home, cat, dogs, and so on has your full itinerary and a complete list of contact numbers.

If it makes you feel even more secure, you can pre-arrange times when you will contact these caregivers to check in with them. After you've made certain everything's under control on the home front, the world is yours for the taking. Destination choices can be found to fit almost any budget and activity preference. The only thing that's important is that you both agree on a trip that you'll enjoy.

Cruisin'

If cruising calls up images of little old ladies playing shuffleboard, it's time to update your notion of what a sea voyage is all about. Nowadays it's about anything you want it to be. Ships go just about anywhere—the Caribbean, the Mediterranean, the Adriatic, the coast of Alaska, and Central and South America. You can also pick an itinerary that goes pretty much nowhere, with lots of days on the open ocean. Or you can combine the best of both worlds, disembarking at some ports of call but taking other days to stay onboard the ship and revel in relative solitude when nearly everyone else is gone.

Onboard you can find limitless activities to entertain you and your traveling companion. A daily list of things to do onboard reads like a summer camp program for grown-ups. Take dance lessons, take a watercolor or bartending class, see a movie or show, improve your golf stroke, shop, enter a bridge tournament, soak in a hot tub, or attend a lecture on anything from herbal medicine to personal finance.

The food's great, and plentiful. But don't fall prey to the myth that you'll come home from your cruise unable to squeeze into your jeans. Virtually every ship has a state-of-the art fitness center. Most have running tracks and some have rock-climbing walls. Many cruise lines also feature light side menu choices or special spots to partake of spa cuisine.

Mood Makers

Can't leave the kids at home? A cruise vacation can be a way to take a family vacation that also allows private adult time. Most cruise lines are kid friendly—many so much so that your kids will barely give you a glance once you drop them off at the "fun factory" where they'll play video games and foosball, make movies, play Bingo, put on shows, and even enjoy all-kid meals and late-night pajama parties. Meanwhile, you and mom can soak in the sun or meet for a moonlight stroll on the promenade deck.

Active Vacations

For those really interested in staying—or getting—in shape, as well as getting away, an active vacation is a great choice. Active travel is growing exponentially in popularity. The sky's the limit on what activities you can choose. Here are some suggestions:

- ◆ **Walking tours.** Walks across nearly every scenic spot on the planet are offered for walkers of every level and preferred pace. You can traverse the Scottish moors, trek the foothills of Bhutan, or hike the back roads of the American countryside. Look for a walking tour operator that offers flexibility, daily route options for all levels, knowledgeable guides, and the support you need when you're ready for a break.

- ◆ **Bicycling Tours.** You can also bike just about anywhere and everywhere, from Nova Scotia to California's wine country to the green hills of Ireland. Tour operators offer everything from easy explorations to more challenging epic journeys. A good organization will be sure to match your fitness level to your journey—and will always have a backup van available if you want to take a day off from more difficult stretches.

♦ **Multi-Sport tours.** You can mix hiking, biking, kayaking, and water sports in many diverse locales that include the coast of Maine, the Shenandoah Valley, and the Rocky Mountains. These comprehensive multi-sport tours are great for families because everyone gets to pursue their favorite activities.

♦ **Fitness spas.** At fitness spas, guests can work out with a trainer, get a fitness evaluation, take low fat cooking classes, get a massage, and learn all kinds of wellness strategies in an environment devoted exclusively to facilitating well-being. Most fitness spas make it a point to encourage visitors to continue their newly adapted good habits at home.

♦ **Yoga retreat.** For a vacation that merges inner life and outer activity, consider a yoga vacation. Yoga retreats are offered in every style of yoga (some styles stress breathing techniques, some more strenuous postures, and some a more rapid pace). No, you don't need to head off to India or Katmandu. Yoga retreats are found all over the world—some nearer to home than you might think.

Ah, the possibilities are endless. But if the more active vacation doesn't do it for you, consider the glories of a really inactive vacation!

Island Oases

Would you and your lady like nothing better than to be beach potatoes for a week or two? There are endless island resorts from which to choose. Once there, you can partake in a little beach volleyball or windsurfing … or not. Bring a book, some sunscreen, and a willingness to slather some sunscreen on your lover.

For destinations, consider the Hawaiian Islands, The U.S. and British Virgin Islands, the Eastern Caribbean (Antigua, St. Maarten, St. Bart's, and St. Lucia, with its black sand beaches), the Western Caribbean (the Cayman islands and Jamaica, with its glorious waterfalls), and the Southern Caribbean (Aruba, Curacao, and Grenada, with its fragrant pervasive aroma of spice).

If you're watching your budget, note that many island resorts offer all-inclusive fees for room, meals, and sometimes even drinks. Check out Club Med, Sandals, and Beaches, to name a few.

Europe for Lovers

If you're willing to venture a bit farther, think about taking her on that European second honeymoon she's always longed for. Europe is home to some of the world's most romantic cities. Here's a sampling:

♦ **Dublin.** Stroll along St. Stephen's green, walk across a stone footbridge, cuddle in a cozy pub, and don't forget to read the work of Ireland's renowned poets. The remains of Saint Valentine reside in this city. Can you get more romantic than that?

♦ **Prague.** The capital of the Czech Republic and the heart of central Europe, Prague is a lover's haven with winding cobblestone roads, antique horse-drawn carriages, and a host of hidden-away intimate restaurants and hotels.

♦ **Salzburg.** This Austrian city is a favorite of lovers. It's known for its castles and baroque charm. Be sure to visit the marble hall in which Leopold Mozart and his son Wolfgang held concerts for royalty.

♦ **Barcelona.** Visit this strikingly beautiful Spanish city in April for *La Diada de Sant Jordi*. Also known as "The Day of Lovers," it's easily the most amorous day of the year—like Valentine's Day with a Latin twist. The main event is the exchange of gifts between sweethearts—men give their lovers roses, and women give their men books to celebrate the occasion.

♦ **Rome.** Stroll among the breathtaking ruins, stop by the side of a piazza to people watch and have a refreshing *limonata* (sparkling lemonade), and feast on incomparable fare wherever you choose to dine. Throw a coin in the Fountain of Trevi before you leave and you're guaranteed to return.

♦ **Paris.** Paris may be the most obvious romantic destination of all. Share a baguette, some cheese, and a bottle of wine beneath a bridge by the Seine. Steal a kiss in public without getting a sideways glance. Wrap your arms around your lover atop the *Arc de Triomphe* and Notre Dame, both of which provide stunning views of the city. A short train ride away, visit the elaborate Chateau de Versailles, the luxurious palace of the Louis XIV, the Sun King.

If you're visiting Europe, don't stick only to cities, the countryside offers wonderful romantic spots as well. While in France, take some time to explore Provence. In Italy, consider a quaint group of five fishing villages known as Cinque Terre, or Lake Como north of Milan, or the Amalfi Coast.

America's Sexy Cities

Of course, you don't have to go abroad to find cities that are ripe for romance. If you'd rather not hassle with a passport, or risk the dollar exchange rate being less than favorable, no problem. Consider taking a plane, train, or car to one of these hot spots:

- **Santa Fe.** The jewel of exotic New Mexico, Santa Fe has it all: art, music, fascinating historical tours (complete with convincing ghost stories that make you want to hug your honey). Try the spicy Southwestern cuisine, and drive just outside of town for a view of some of the most beautiful vistas you'll ever encounter.

- **San Francisco.** No wonder Tony Bennett left his heart there. Along with those "little cable cars that climb halfway to the stars," San Francisco offers beautiful parks and marinas, breathtaking bridges, and an astonishing variety of culture, cuisine, and (for your lady's pleasure) shopping. If you can, allow several days for a side trip to the wine country for some sensual sipping.

- **Miami.** No, this is not your grandmother's Miami. I'm talking Coconut Grove and South Beach, international flavors, and a Latin flair. If you can, drive South to the Florida Keys for some laid-back loving—and, what the heck, some fishing, too. Don't let your lady forget the sunscreen.

- **Las Vegas.** You don't have to be big-time gamblers, or even small-time ones, to enjoy it. Las Vegas has become synonymous with indulgence and opulence. An astonishing variety of hotels make it seem as if going to Las Vegas is actually like going to several amazing locales at once. Most of the large resorts have a menu of spa services that can reasonably be called divinely decadent. Best of all, as the ad says, "What happens in Vegas stays in Vegas."

- **Savannah.** Craving some Southern comfort? Savannah is reputed for its gracious charm, but also for its air of mystery. The downtown historic district, with its noteworthy architecture, contains some of the most romantic bed and breakfasts and small luxury hotels in the country. Possible adventures include riverboat cruises, browsing hidden antique stores (that's mostly for her) and Civil War forts (that's mostly for you). Don't miss nearby Tybee Island, Hilton Head, Saint Simon's Island, and Cumberland Island.

- **San Diego.** The weather is nearly perfect, nearly all the time. The Mexican fare is beyond satisfying. The world-famous zoo and Balboa Park make for some incredible handholding walks. Visit the Gaslight District and Old Town, and don't miss a side trip to the Hotel del Coronado—a famously romantic spot that gained its legendary status as the site where Marilyn Monroe filmed *Some Like It Hot*.

- **New York.** No list of America's sexiest cities would be complete without the daddy of them all. New York's excitement is palpable day and night; its cultural and culinary opportunities are simply unparalleled. And nothing—no, nothing—beats a twilight ride through Central Park in a horse-drawn carriage for sheer, unadulterated romance (although necking in the back of a taxi comes close).

Once again, as in Europe, don't neglect the countryside. The back roads of America contain many romantic "finds" in terms of inns, cabins, and even rustic farmhouse accommodations. The sights are awe-inspiring, the air is fresh, and getting off the beaten path means lots more privacy.

Second Honeymoons

If you're ready for the ultimate pleasing getaway, you might want to consider going all out and planning a second honeymoon. This involves arranging a trip that is especially meaningful for you both. It might involve going to a place you've both always wanted to go to, or perhaps a place you never thought about before—but it always involves heading off with the goal of celebrating and rejuvenating your connection.

Even though it may have been long ago when you first said "I do," there are some second honeymoon "do's" to keep in mind:

- This time, *do* leave the kids behind.

- Discuss making a vow renewal part of your journey—many resorts will happily help you arrange the details.

- Make it a point that each of you gets to do something you really want to on the trip—and participate in that activity as a couple.

- Don't overbook your schedule—allow time for spontaneity.

- Pack special wedding night sleepwear—for both of you.

- Surprise her with a special wedding night gift.

- Don't expect the trip to solve problems in your relationship; that's a set-up for disappointment. This is R&R.

Appendix B will give you sexy destination ideas for where you might go on your second honeymoon. But this is a case where getting there provides a large part of the fun. Take the time to plan your special trip vacation together. Consider lots of options and enjoy doing the research. Poring over maps, guidebooks, and brochures together will be a wonderful romantic prequel to what is sure to be a memorable honeymoon sequel.

Bon voyage!

The Least You Need to Know

- ◆ Continuing to date your mate after courtship is an opportunity to backburner the demands of work and kids and treat yourselves—you deserve it.

- ◆ Take some time to plan some special dining experiences—otherwise even going out for meals can become rushed and humdrum.

- ◆ Dancing together is romantic, sexy, and great exercise—if you have two left feet, sign yourself and your partner up for lessons.

- ◆ If you want to cuddle at the movies, and afterward, take your lady to a chick flick—bring a hankie for her and some popcorn for you.

- ◆ One or two nights away can be enough to reinvigorate a relationship—a week or two can literally be a second honeymoon.

Chapter 12

Sensational Surroundings

In This Chapter

- ◆ The home as comforting cocoon
- ◆ Using light and color effects
- ◆ Aroma and romance
- ◆ Mood music
- ◆ Should love trysts be scheduled?

Going out is great fun, but staying in can be a blast, too. Most women have a distinct homebody aspect to them. Home can truly be where her heart is—a respite from the pressures of the outside world, a place to unwind with someone she cares about and who cares about her. On the other hand, the home can be just as hectic as anyplace else.

This chapter will help you to turn your home into your lady's emotional and physical oasis. It's not something you'll find time for every day, but on occasion—with a little forethought—you can help turn the home you share with your partner into a sensual environment where romance can thrive.

Make the Bed Before You Unmake It

Imagine that your woman has had a long, crazy day in the workplace. Now, finally, she's heading home. She wishes she could just chill out and "cocoon" with you, her lover. But she doesn't hold out much hope that this will happen.

Sadly, her low expectations are often realized, as in this scenario: When she walks in she is barraged by her own sense of obligation and perhaps literally besieged by demands from the kids, and even from you. What time is dinner? Did you remember to pick up that notebook I need? Did you stop at the cleaners? Soon she's in the midst of domestic multitasking.

Everywhere she looks she sees another mess to tackle. There's a pile of unmatched socks on the sofa—remnants from last night's load of laundry. On the kitchen counter sits a stack of unopened mail. It's noisy, too. The TV and stereo are blaring disharmoniously. What's more, the house smells like yesterday's takeout pizza—the only thing you all had time to eat in the chaos.

Suddenly her workplace is looking pretty good by comparison. She wonders if she'll ever feel in control of her own space ever again. Maybe that is a luxury for single people only ….

Now imagine this scenario: Your partner comes home and you greet her lovingly at the door with a hug and a gentle kiss on the forehead. She looks around and sees an astonishing—but very welcome—lack of clutter and absence of disarray. The only sound she hears is that of one of her favorite mellow CDs.

There are also these things:

- Fresh, colorful flowers on the dining room table
- Two full place settings of the "good" china and silverware
- A new throw draped across the sofa
- A few interesting, new coffee table books open to some intriguing pages
- Some newly framed family photos on the mantel
- You—looking cleanly shaved and handsome in casual but neat attire

Moving into the bedroom, where she's now following your suggestion to "slip into something more comfortable," additional surprises await. The lights are dimmed. A few votive candles are flickering. There's a rose in a bud vase by her bedside. And, she can hardly believe her eyes: the bedding has been changed and a set of fresh, luxurious sheets beckons.

A man who makes the bed before he unmakes it? Who is this superhero? She examines him closely. Is it Superman? Spiderman? An X-man? A Jedi Knight? Why, no … it really is you.

And where are the kids? Safely packed away to Grandma's or a neighbor's. It's all taken care of. Her home has truly become a cocoon—and now she can turn into a butterfly.

Notice that the difference in these two scenarios doesn't depend on anything expensive or extravagant. With a little planning, it's possible to create a sensual environment that any woman would be enchanted with.

Can you create a scenario like this? Of course you can. It's like breaking down any project into its component parts: you just need to approach it logically, one step at a time.

Love and Light

Playing with lighting effects is one of the simplest ways to create a cocooned environment that is conducive to relaxation and romance. The idea is to create a canvas of light that is diametrically opposed to the lighting of everyday life. Why? Because when lighting is harsh, our mood will be the same.

The world-at-large is full of glaring lights, neon signs, and drab fluorescents. Such lights are a barrier to relaxation and intimacy. It's a softer glow that a woman associates with love. In fact, when the lights are low, studies show that we tend to stay in closer proximity to those around us.

Besides, when lighting is unsympathetic, no woman feels glamorous. Diffuse, dimmer lighting makes people look their best. When a woman wants to objectively examine her face for little imperfections, she looks in a brightly lit make-up mirror. But when she catches a glimpse of herself in a mirrored wall at a softly lit, elegant restaurant, it's as though all those tiny wrinkles, blemishes, dark spots, and under-eye puffs are magically minimized.

Wait! Don't get carried away and attempt to rewire the entire house. You don't need to swap out all the light fixtures to achieve ambience with lighting. With a few deft tricks, you can alter home lighting to achieve a desired effect of calm and a flattering aura.

◆ Install dimmers. Almost any light—including overhead chandeliers and track lighting—can be hooked to a rheostat, which instantly regulates light intensity with the turn of a dial. You can find rheostats at the hardware store.

♦ Replace the white light bulbs in your lamps with pink bulbs. Her skin will look smooth and rosy. And, hey, so will yours.

♦ Use candles as a simple, inexpensive way to alter your lighting. Just a few can fill any room with an ethereal glow. They're inexpensive and versatile, so feel free to experiment with different shapes, sizes, and scents.

♦ If you have a fireplace, use it to create a dramatic centerpiece of light that will draw your lady in like a proverbial moth to a flame. While it's a nice masculine touch to go out and chop your own firewood, that is also time consuming. As a shortcut, for those nights when you're not feeling like Paul Bunyan, lay in a supply of DuraFlame logs so you can start a fire quickly. Or consider converting a wood-burning fireplace to gas, which allows for instant mellowness with the turn of a knob.

Love Busters

Women love scented candles, but not at the dinner table. Their aroma can interfere with the taste of the food, since the senses of smell and taste are inextricably intertwined.

Aside from feeling better and looking better in more ambient lighting, your lady will feel less inhibited whenever the lights are low. If tonight's the night you're thinking of trying something new in bed—a new toy or position or technique—use lighting to help alleviate any initial shyness and self-consciousness—for you as well as your partner.

Color Her Pleased

Another way to embellish the sensuality of your home cocoon is to experiment with color. Whether we are consciously aware of it or not, we are constantly reacting to color signals in our environment. Advertisers and product marketers understand this principle well. That's why they manipulate our reactions to color to sell everything from frozen foods to fabric softeners to luxury automobiles.

But it wasn't marketing experts who invented the notion of influencing behavior through color. Mother Nature uses color as a big part of the intricate process of attraction and mating. The plumage of an exotic bird, the brilliance of a flower awaiting pollination—these are but a few examples. Take a hike in springtime and you'll witness nature's template in action. Follow Mother Nature's lead and any clever fellow can use color to induce feelings of intrigue and excitement, or contentment and calm in his lover.

No need to go overboard here either. I am not suggesting that you start repainting rooms or sending your furniture out to be re-upholstered. Add color in small doses, using it as accents. Use pillows, blankets, quilts, small area rugs, and paintings or wall hangings and—perhaps easiest and most lady-pleasing of all—fresh flowers. Employing colorful objects is a simple way to bring on the mood you want to create.

Red Is for Passion

Of all colors in the visible spectrum, red causes the greatest bodily response. Red also incites strong emotions. Being in red surroundings can raise the heart rate and pulse. This "warm" color can literally make a lady feel hot. Historically, red is the color most strongly associated with passion. That's why Valentine's hearts are always red. When you send red roses to your woman, it's a signal that your feelings are strong and heartfelt.

Deep, subtle shades of red, such as crimson and scarlet, are especially associated with sexual temptation and eroticism. ("Scarlett" O'Hara, a classic strong female heroine, wasn't called that for nothing.) If you're tempted to buy your lady red lingerie, stick with these hues as opposed to the bright in-your-face red you'd find on a Ferrari. Too much of an orange-red shade can be exhausting and overwhelming.

Pink's Not Just for Barbie

Pink is the pastel that results from adding white to red. From girlhood on, females seem to be attracted to pink. It's perceived as soft, delicate, pretty, and feminine. As you may know if you have a daughter, this preference for pink can be somewhat exploited by toy and clothing manufacturers. Perhaps you're a little pinked out as a result.

Don't be so quick to dismiss pink. You can add some to your environment without having your home morph into Barbie's dream house. It's worth it, because grown women still consider pink a warm and romantic hue.

Looking for some pink flowers? Your choices are almost limitless. Try pink mums, geraniums, carnations, pink primula, and a wonderful blossom called "painted lady" (also known as coneflower). In winter, try some pink poinsettias.

A little pink will give you a little lift as well. It's a color associated with health and wellness—feeling "in the pink."

Blue Is for Soothing

Blue is a soothing and reassuring color. Use it when you want your lady to feel calm and relaxed. Use cobalt blue to stir erotic thoughts, but temper blue with white for an association with heavenly delights.

Ask your florist about some brilliant blue choices, such as Virginia bluebells, smooth ruella, and a beautifully named choice called "Venus's looking glass." There are many blue wildflowers as well—like wild blue phlox, bergamot, and blueflag—but when they're out of season, consider silk flowers in blue hues.

Beware of overdoing blue, however. Although it calms in smaller doses, blue can bring us down if we're exposed to large expanses of it. (That's why we sing "the blues.")

Purple Is for Luxury

Remember your color wheel? Purple combines the class and elegance of blue with the power of red. That's why purple is considered grand and luxurious. It's always been associated with royalty.

In America, purple used to be associated with older women, but that is true no longer. Of late, purple has become increasingly popular with women of all ages. You can use lavender shades in particular to signify sensuality and youthfulness.

Purple blooms appear to be a favorite of Mother Nature. They include pansies, petunias, lilacs, violets, pussy willows, purple daisies, and purple freesias.

 Mood Makers

Women tend to adore that most intriguing and temperamental of purple flowers: the orchid. Orchids have fascinated and mesmerized people since early times. They have been the symbol of love, luxury, and beauty for centuries. Greeks looked at them as a symbol of virility. Orchids can be expensive, but you can keep them ever-present by getting your lady a coffee table book featuring the many varieties of orchids. Along with striking oversized color photos, these books offer detailed advice on the art and cultivation of the flower in a domestic environment.

Yellow Is for Freshness

If you have a room that doesn't get a great deal of light, you can bring the sunshine in with lemon yellow or coral touches. Yellow is the most reflective and bright of all the primary colors, and in psychological terms it signals something new and unanticipated. Yellow has many wonderful associations in addition to sunshine. It is the color of fresh lemons and creamy butter. Yellow is perceived as cheerful and friendly. When it veers toward gold, it is perceived as glowing.

Yellow blossoms include sunflowers, day lilies, Dahlberg daisies, daffodils, moonbeams, and—of course—yellow roses and yellow tulips.

Green Is for Renewal

Green has so many shades and tones that it can evoke a spectrum of different responses. Mixed with a hint of yellow it connotes the renewal of spring. Soft sages and moss greens are restful. So is aqua, which is blue-green tinted with white. Jewel-tone greens, like emerald and malachite, are seen as luxurious and make one's environment seem rich and well appointed. You can easily add varied shades of green to your surroundings in the form of house plants and small trees.

Earth Tones Say "Natural"

Browns and beiges are comforting, natural tones. They say, "All is well in our world." Brown is for hearth and home. Put some fresh, crusty bread in a hand-woven basket to delight your earthy woman. Look for some household items in shades of bamboo and sand.

Easy as Black and White

White connotes innocence and purity. Its presence in the boudoir can make a woman feel likes it's her "first time" all over again. White flowers for the bedside include lilies, phlox, goatsbeard, lamium, tree lilacs, rune anemones, and Japanese honeysuckle. Do you have any idea what kinds she carried in her wedding bouquet? If you reprise that theme you will be a huge hit!

Black is a highly provocative color, perhaps because it is also a color that implies a hint of danger. We women like to wear black for our men because of these associations, and also because we believe it tends to make us look thinner. Think how svelte your woman might look in a luxurious set of black satin sheets.

Love Makes Scents, Scents Make Love

Scent, in the form of biologically produced *pheromones*, plays a role in sexual attraction and behavior. But all scents are really a kind of chemical communication. They send out signals and we respond on a visceral level, even if we are not thinking about the aroma or consciously noticing it.

In matters of romance, it is not incorrect to say that women are led by the nose. Throughout history a link between perfumed scents and desire has been a constant. When Circe set out to seduce Ulysses, she used a powerful aromatic potion. When the Queen of Sheba moved to Jerusalem, she tried to win King Solomon's heart with fragrant spices.

It sounds like women were behind most of the aromatic plotting, with men in their thrall. But, in fact, research shows that women are the more aromatically susceptible gender (possibly because of their role as child-bearers) and regard smell as an even more significant signal than do their male counterparts.

Tongue Teasers

Pheromones are natural scents that, although undetectable to the conscious mind, serve as powerful forces of sexual attraction. Pheromones are produced by glands nears a person's armpits, nipples, and groin. Although research is inconclusive, they're probably detected by something called the VNO (vomeronasal organ), a small cavity in the nose.

One scent your woman doubtless likes is your unique smell. Each person has a one-of-a-kind odor that is tied to his or her immune system. It is produced by the segment of our DNA called the major historo-compatibility complex (MHC). Because we require an immune system that offers the widest array of protection against disease, we tend to seek out mates whose MHC differs greatly from our own. In a classic experiment, a Swiss researcher at The University of Bern asked women to sniff and select a variety of men's pre-worn cotton T-shirts. The women consistently favored the shirts of men whose MHC differed from their own as well as the ones whose scents reminded them of previous or current lovers—thereby offering proof that MHC had influenced their romantic predilections.

But although you are probably already pleasing your woman on an olfactory level, you can certainly do more. No, don't leave smelly T-shirts around the house! But do take care not to over-douse yourself in cologne that covers your natural scent. A little dab will do.

Instead, enhance her aromatic pleasures by introducing other subtly pleasing scents into your environment. Flowers, scented oil burners, candles, room sprays, and incense are some of the simplest ways to do this.

But what scents, other than yours, appeal to your women's sensual side? Individuals may have very particular favorites, but of the many scents available the following have wide appeal:

◆ **Vanilla.** The scent of vanilla is said to produce an increase in sexual arousal almost instantaneously. There's doubtless some in the kitchen cupboard that holds your spices.

◆ **Sandalwood.** An extremely calming and earthy scent, sandalwood can alleviate stress that might interfere with romance.

◆ **Lavender.** Lavender is a sexy scent with a bit of a bite to it.

- ◆ **Anise.** Anise has a sweet licoricelike odor. It's been used for centuries to stimulate feelings of love and well-being.

- ◆ **Rosemary.** Rosemary is known as the herb of love and remembrance. Plant her some in the garden or in a window box.

- ◆ **Sage.** This herb is said to balance female hormones and increase libido.

- ◆ **Thyme.** Burning thyme as an essential oil is said to offer relief to women with menstrual or pre-menstrual symptoms.

- ◆ **Myrrh.** Myrrh is a dried sap of the *Commiphora myrrha* tree. Prized since ancient times, it is said to have healing and rejuvenating properties.

- ◆ **Musk.** Musk is believed to closely resemble the smell of testosterone, which is itself a pheromone.

Again, don't overdo scents. Any aroma can become overbearing in mass quantities. (You know how you feel when you encounter a female that is literally drenched in perfume.) Go easy on the room sprays, in particular, and burn incense sparingly. If you're using something in a concentrated essential oil form—as is done in aromatherapy—water it down.

Love Busters

If you're using incense, don't leave a trail on her tabletops. "Ash catchers" are available for burning incense sticks cleanly and safely. Many are made of carved wood and serve as interesting conversation pieces.

Sounding Her Out

Now we turn to appealing to your woman's auditory sense, her sense of sound. That can mean getting a set of wind-chimes to soothe her, or placing a white noise machine beside the bed to block out the annoying drone of the world at large. But it can, of course, also mean pleasing her with music. Choosing the appropriate romantic music can easily get a woman in the mood for love.

Each of us is aware of how powerfully music can alter our emotions. Music can make us laugh; it can make us cry. It can make us feel hot and sexy and uninhibited. And once we're in the midst of lovemaking, music can give us a second wind. It can heighten our senses, make us more imaginative, and—in some cases—increase our sexual stamina.

Of course which music you choose is of paramount importance. Needless to say, it's a personal choice, but nevertheless some general rules apply.

- Choose mellow, not manic music. Fast, frenetic music, like rap and disco, has its place—but even if your lady is a fan, it's probably not the right choice when you're planning a relaxing feast for the senses.

- Keep lyrics loving and uplifting. Country can be conducive to romance, but forego whiny or vengeful "you left me, you dog" sentiments.

- Have a variety of music on hand. If we listen to the same thing over and over, we tend to block it out. It just becomes droning background noise.

- Avoid anything so unusual or experimental that it may be jarring. Tribal trance music, Gregorian chants, and atonal jazz may be intellectually interesting, but not tonight.

- Avoid vocalists who like to "belt" out a tune. Vocal acrobatics may be awe-inspiring, but they can also be distracting.

- Make sure there's enough rhythm to provide a little bit of bounce—but avoid tunes that call up images of "Dudley Moore in under shorts" routines.

Perhaps the biggest musical *faux pas* of all when it comes to romance is going with the cliché. Barry White, Michael Bolton, Marvin Gaye singing "Let's Get it On." No, no, and no way. Though these talented artists have produced great love songs, women have heard them too often. Their very familiarity has rendered them ridiculously obvious. Go for more creative choices. Entice your lover with songs she will respond to on a more personal level.

Still not sure what to try? Many music stores allow you to preview CDs in the store, and you can also listen to tunes on the Internet. A few artists you might want to sample:

- Harry Connick, Jr.
- John Coltrane
- Michael Bublé
- Frank Sinatra
- Billie Holiday
- Stevie Wonder
- Eric Clapton
- Tony Bennett
- John Mayall
- Michael McDonald
- Natalie Cole
- Sadé
- k.d. lang

Mix it up with Latin selections, a touch of tango, and some classical pieces. Check out CDs that are pre-arranged collections of songs for loving. Or create a personalized play list on an iPod that you then connect to play through stereo speakers.

Finally, keep the volume at a moderate level. Blaring is hard on the ears and unkind to the neighbors. It also distracts one's attention from the pleasure of the aural experience.

He Says/She Says

"When my husband and I were dating in college we often made music tapes for each other. That was years ago. Recently he burned me a CD of romantic songs he knew I'd love. It was perfect, but the truth is I was thrilled before I'd even played it. It brought back memories of those great times when we would take time out of our day just to do a little something extra for one another."
—Gina, 33

Should You Schedule Your Tryst?

Should you surprise your woman with a romantic at-home evening? Sure, if you can pull it off. Spontaneous love trysts are fantastic. But let's look at some of the things that can interfere with them:

1. Fatigue. Both physical and mental exhaustion can sap her sex drive.

2. Over-commitment. Too many obligations might compete for your attention.

3. Guilt. She might have the nagging sense there is something else she should be doing.

4. Unsynchronized schedules. You're getting a second wind when she's falling asleep, or vice versa.

5. Lack of privacy. Kids, cats, dogs, all think your bedroom is open for business 24/7.

6. Interruptions. If it's not the kids, it's the phone, the fax, the pager, the doorbell.

7. Specific worry. A particular problem or concern is preoccupying her.

8. Free floating anxiety. She may just have had "one of those days" and find it hard to segue to a radically different kind of night.

9. Procrastination. Oh, what the heck, you can put it off until tomorrow, or the next night, or the next.

If you're hoping to surprise her, be careful not to sandbag her. Scope out her schedule ahead of time. You'll both be sorely disappointed if she walks in to find a carefully crafted sensual scenario on a night when she has made a commitment to be at a town council meeting or the PTA. If she's brought a pile of work home, she may be tempted to put it aside, but feel torn about letting her boss or co-workers down.

At minimum, try to give your partner a little bit of a "heads up" by sending her a steamy e-mail or leaving her an intriguing phone message during the course of the day. Now she'll have the fun of anticipation—and you run less risk that she'll come home too drained to respond as you'd hoped.

On the other hand, a bit of formal planning may be just what you need. There is nothing unnatural about it. After all, lovers throughout history carefully plotted when and where they would join up for special, sacred time together. With so many potential distracters, it's a good idea to schedule a night of cocooning on your calendar in advance at least every once in a while. Then she can have the additional fun of focusing on your "appointment" ahead of time. Her passion and excitement can only build.

The Least You Need to Know

- ◆ With a little forethought you can, at least on occasion, turn your home into a cocoon that keeps the hectic world at bay.

- ◆ Lighting choices can create a sensual atmosphere and relaxed mood.

- ◆ Knowing your woman's response to various colors can help you create a pleasing environment for her.

- ◆ Scent is a powerful mood maker, as well as an agent of seduction—but go easy, or it can be overpowering.

- ◆ The right music can soothe—or stir—your woman.

- ◆ Special sexy nights at home might not occur spontaneously as often as you both would like—so schedule some now and then.

Chapter **13**

Refresh and Restore Her

In This Chapter

- ◆ Cooking for your lady
- ◆ Sexy foods with a reputation
- ◆ Finding household helpers
- ◆ Helping your lady to delegate
- ◆ Relaxing her with massage

If you want to revive your woman's desire, first you must revive your woman. Sometimes you might want to pamper her yourself. Another option is to enlist others to lighten her load. Still another is to get her to lie down—for the sole purpose of massaging her weary—though lovely—limbs.

This chapter will tell you how to refresh your lady, so that her pleasure in you will be refreshed as well.

Food for Love

Taking your lady out to dine will always win her favor. But have you ever considered preparing food for her yourself? Not many things say "I love you" as well as that.

Please don't say you don't know how to cook. If you can read, you can cook. That's why there are recipes—step-by-step guides to making anything from a burger to a bouillabaisse. You can find recipes anywhere—online, in cookbooks, in magazines (*Real Simple* magazine is an excellent choice) and on food packaging. Or just call your mother and ask her for some suggestions. Come on, you know she'd like to hear from you anyway.

If you've never so much as boiled water before, don't sweat it. It really doesn't matter what you prepare, and your dishes certainly needn't be anything complicated. Even if you overcook or undercook your fare, or forget to put the chicken in the chicken fricassee, your woman is apt to think of your offering as ambrosia of the gods. Why? One: because you made it. Two: because she didn't have to.

I realize, of course, that many men are expert cooks. There are probably more male chefs than female chefs in the restaurant business. So if you feel the urge to get fancy, or are a veteran cook, by all means go for any elaborate fare that suits your lady's palette. She won't say no to your duck a l'orange and chocolate soufflé. However, if you're a true novice, start simple. Try some of these ultra-basic preparations.

- Pasta. Boil water. Take pasta out of package. Cook for length of time noted on package—too long and you've got limp noodles. Toss with olive oil or tomato sauce. (Paul Newman can help with the latter—his jarred sauces will make any red-blooded woman swoon.)

- Roast chicken. Buy a Perdue Oven Stuffer roaster. Turn the oven on to the suggested temperature on the package. Roast. A little thermometer pops up when it's done. Carve and serve with green beans (microwave some frozen ones) and rice (rice is prepared somewhat similarly to pasta).

- Homemade pizza. Yes, you can order a pizza, but it's a nice alternative to buy a pre-made pizza shell at the grocery store. Sprinkle the shell with shredded mozzarella and add all her favorite toppings—for example, olives, broccoli florets, or sun-dried tomatoes.

- An entrée salad. Start with a bag of pre-washed mixed greens and adorn with her favorite veggies. Festoon with croutons, and if she likes nuts add some slivered almonds. Now turn it into a meal by topping it with sliced chicken or canned or fresh tuna.

◆ Fresh fish. Marinate a filet of your lady's favorite fish in equal parts white wine, lemon juice, and olive oil. Sprinkle with a touch of dried rosemary. Bake at 350 degrees for 15 minutes.

◆ BLTs. Even a nicely made sandwich will be much appreciated. Grill some Canadian bacon or turkey bacon (both have less fat and calories than traditional bacon strips). Now add the "T" (that's tomatoes) and the "L" (that's love—and, oh yes, lettuce, too). And don't forget to add the mayo.

Once you've whipped up your kitchen creations, no matter how humble, show them some respect. Don't just toss food on a plate. Arrange it attractively (for example pre-cut your pizza and sandwiches into wedges). Garnish them with colorful tidbits like baby carrots or yellow grape tomatoes. Serve condiments in small bowls, not in their original jars.

If you'd rather wave a credit card than a spatula once in awhile, that's no problem. It's perfectly acceptable to stop by your local gourmet food market or the take-out section of an upscale supermarket for a variety of delicacies. Go in with an open mind—and an open wallet—and try to imagine what might capture your woman's fancy. Always shop with freshness in mind. Don't try to save on soggy day-old fare.

Mood Makers

If you like to grill outdoors in the summer, you can be a year-round cooking champ with a George Foreman grill. It's fast because it cooks both sides at once. And it's specially designed to siphon grease into a separate tray. The latter feature really appeals to women watching their figures.

Food for Sex

While you're in your culinary mode, you might be interested to know there are some foods that come with a folkloric reputation as romance boosters. Although Western science may disagree that they impact the libido directly, anecdotal evidence on their behalf has persisted for centuries across many cultures.

As it turns out, these foods are also quite healthy to eat, and experts agree that what's good for overall health is good for one's sex life as well. Being in better physical condition can certainly lead to better sexual performance. So there's no harm in adding some of these delectable edibles to the dishes you lovingly serve your lady. Experiment if you dare!

◆ **Aromatic spices.** Cardamom, cloves, and saffron are sensual fare on many levels. They are said to produce desire, perhaps because they are so pleasing to smell, see, and taste that those exposed to them feel predisposed to enjoying even more sensual tingles.

♦ **Onions.** The oldest of the supposed edible aphrodisiacs, the use of onions as love aids dates far back. During the era of the Pharaohs, Egyptian priests weren't allowed to eat onions as it was thought this would tempt them to break their vow of celibacy. French newlyweds still feast on onion soup during their honeymoon to restore their energy and rekindle desire after a strenuous wedding night.

♦ **Garlic.** Greeks, Romans, Chinese, Japanese, and others around the world have used garlic as a sexual stimulant. We do know it stimulates the taste buds, making the rest of a meal even more appetizing. Of course garlic does leave its signature on the breath. If you and your woman are both garlic fans, eat it together—but never go solo.

♦ **Peaches.** They are cool, delectable, and pleasing to the palate. For centuries the Chinese have claimed that peaches also spur the sex drive. There's no hard evidence, but think how erotic it could be to hand-feed your lady a nice slice of ripe, juicy peach.

♦ **Bananas.** These phallic fruits also have an aphrodisiac reputation. In fact, their shape may have been what started the rumor. Nevertheless, bananas are high in potassium and very good for you. Peel slowly and invitingly.

♦ **Cucumbers.** The cool smell of cucumbers is said to be especially appealing to women. Like bananas, they also have a phallic shape—and if you're beginning to see a theme here, you're not alone. But even if shape is most of what's behind the cuke's cachet, there's no harm done. Multiple servings of veggies a day are a boon to one's overall diet.

♦ **Pine nuts.** Since Roman times, these tiny tree seeds have been thought of as sexual helpers. No proof exists, but they certainly are the key ingredients in a great pesto. For a lusty pasta topping, toss some into a food processor with olive oil, basil, and parmesan cheese.

♦ **Truffles.** Napoleon and the Marquis de Sade consumed these rare mushroom-like delicacies for their amatory powers, though probably it's their very rarity that led to their desirability. Truffles are notoriously hard to find in the wild, and truffle hunters in Italy and France use pigs and dogs to sniff them out. But you only need to hunt around a gourmet shop. One caveat: These morsels are also very expensive. Black truffles can sell for up to $500 a pound. So watch that household budget!

♦ **Caviar.** Caviar was prized by expert lovers including Casanova, Dostoevsky, and Rasputin. As a general rule, caviar is costly, but there are some very affordable varieties. It's very romantic to spread a little on a cracker and slide it between your lover's parted lips.

♦ **Oysters.** Love Goddess Aphrodite was born from the sea, and as such, many types of seafood have reputations as aphrodisiacs. Oysters earned their amorous stripes long ago because they contributed zinc to nutritionally deficient diets. This improved overall health and therefore led to a more robust sex drive. The genitalia-like appearance of oysters didn't hurt either.

Tongue Teasers

Placebo is Latin for "I shall please." A placebo can be any treatment or substance believed by its administrator to be without effect. Yet those who receive the substance may experience intense effects, which they attribute to it. In controlled scientific experiments, placebos are often sugar pills or starch pills.

Will your woman melt in your arms if you treat her with items from the foregoing list? Don't rule it out. The mind is incredibly powerful. If I were to give you a sip of sugar water and tell you it was a very rare and powerful love potion, it might well put you in the mood for loving. When we believe that some substance induces a particular effect, we may experience that effect profoundly even if that substance is completely inert. This is known as the *placebo* effect.

At the very least, concocting aphrodisiac treats for your lover will earn you an "E" for excellent effort. What woman wouldn't want to be surprised with a tray of caviar and oysters followed by a spice-steeped entrée followed by an array of fresh fruits? She'll feel pampered and adored—and that's the point.

Hired Help

There may be times when you would like to shop for, cook for, and serve your lady but honestly can't spare the time. There may be times when you'd like to help her clean the house but are just too overwhelmed with other work and family commitments. Well, welcome to her world! Now you know what your partner is up against much of the time.

What to do? Enlist the help of trained professionals. Break out that checkbook and do your bit to help the service economy.

Virtually every kind of household help is available. There are people who clean houses, people who organize closets, people who cater virtually any kind of food.

There are even services that run all manner of assorted errands and that will stand in line for you at places like the Department of Motor Vehicles.

Where to find this kind of valuable domestic assistance? Check your local Yellow Pages, search online, and—best of all—look through the ads in your local newspapers (especially the giveaway "penny saver" kind). If you can't find exactly the kind of help you seek, ask your neighbors for their recommendations, or try to enlist some trustworthy local teens. High school and college students are full of energy and always seem to be in need of some ready cash.

Helping Her Let Go

Some women do have a problem when it comes to letting go of any responsibility that they consider theirs. A caring partner—that's you—can help even the most "Type A" woman to delegate. This involves alleviating any guilt she may feel at letting others do what she considers to be her jobs.

He Says/She Says

"For a long time I thought I would feel like a failure if I let anyone else clean my house. My mother never would have dreamed of such an indulgence. But with everything else I had on my plate, I have to say that cleaning the floors and the bathrooms just wasn't giving me any personal satisfaction. My husband did pitch in, but he also traveled a lot so his help was inconsistent. One year, on Mother's Day, he and the kids presented me with a year's prepaid cleaning service. These folks came every two weeks and did all the heavy duty stuff. I could still deal with daily straightening in between, which I like because I am a bit of a neat freak. Now they renew their gift every year—and I would never want to go back to the way things were before."
—Angela, 38

There are a number of helpful ways in which you can reassure her that it's okay to stop shouldering the entire burden. Remind her of the following:

◆ It's all right to use money to buy time. In fact, this is one of money's best uses. Time to restore oneself and enjoy life's pleasures is of inestimable value.

◆ No one can continue giving to others when they're running on empty. Yes, your woman may pride herself in doing things for you and for the entire family. She may love the feeling of being useful. But she won't be much use to anyone— least of all herself—if she is approaching burn out.

◆ Not everything can be her number-one priority. Sure, there are some things she may not want to let go of. This is a good time for her to prioritize. What are the things that someone else can do reasonably well and that do not require so much of a "personal touch" as others? Those are the first things to delegate.

Be aware that this kind of discussion can get a little touchy. Be sure your woman knows that you do, in fact, consider her indispensable. Helping her to delegate is not the first sign that you are trying to replace her. Make sure she knows that you value her for what she does, but that you value her even more for who she is.

Say It with Massage

Once you've catered to your woman's appetite and relieved her of some of her household duties, you can really give her a treat to help refresh her. What's more, now she'll have the time to enjoy it. The treat I'm referring to is that of a sensual massage.

At the end of a long day, many women say they can imagine nothing so pleasurable as letting their cares melt away as their body is lavished with thoughtful attention—the aim of which is solely to relax and reinvigorate them.

Types of Massage

Many kinds of professional massage are available. You can certainly give your lady a gift certificate to indulge in a single massage or a series of them at a local health club or day spa. Investigate the many options available, for there are almost as many kinds of massage as there are pleasure points in the human body. Here are just a few:

♦ Sports massage is used to keep the body flexible, help the muscles recover from overexertion or injury, and help prevent athletic injury.

♦ Deep tissue massage is a general term for different styles of massage—including Feldenkrais, Rolfing, and Trager—that focus on the body's deeper muscles and connective tissues.

♦ Reiki aligns body energies by placing the hands above various parts of the body in a particular sequence.

♦ Shiatsu incorporates acupressure and other techniques to manipulate the body's *chi* and remove energy blocks by stimulating pressure points.

Tongue Teasers

Chi is a name for the life force, the vital energy that runs throughout the human body along paths known as meridians. Those who believe in the concept of chi say that an imbalance in this energy can lead to fatigue, listlessness, and even disease. Since about 1400 B.C. in China, massage has been one of the methods used to balance chi.

- Thai massage combines yoga, stretching, twisting, acupressure, and deep massage.

- Stone massage (also known as thermotherapy) combines heat, cold, and pressure, in the form of smooth hot and cold stones that are applied to and removed from various body parts in a certain order.

A professional massage is still considered by most to be a costly luxury, and as such is a relatively rare event. But massage doesn't have to be a rarity for your woman, and a stranger needn't administer it. There's a type of massage that is a little different from any of the preceding categories—and you can do it. That type is known as sensual massage.

Your Sensual Massage

The term "sensual massage" may sound like a euphemism for sexual stimulation. However, right off the bat, let me assure you that is not what we're talking about here. Naturally, any sensual experience can bring on an erotic mood, and may be a natural segue to lovemaking. But, first and foremost, the reason to offer a sensual massage to your partner is to offer her delicious tactile sensations—no strings attached. Although sensual massage usually takes place between sexual partners, it makes no demands on the person being massaged except that she relax and enjoy. It takes the emphasis off any kind of performance.

A good way to approach a sensual massage is to simply offer a nice back rub and see how that goes. If you're a beginner at giving massages, you're doubtless wondering exactly what it is you should be doing after the initial back rubbing. A good plan is to start massaging with slow gliding stokes along the entire back of your woman's body. Alternate from featherweight pressure to a somewhat heavier touch, then back again. Next, you can expand into some other techniques. Some of these are commonly used by professional masseurs and masseuses; others strike a more intimate note:

- Give little finger kisses by touching your partner as if you were playing an up-tempo tune on the piano.

- Press areas that feel knotted and tight with the heels of your hands.

- Cup your hands with palms facing downward, and softly thump up and down her body.

- Glide the palm of one hand over her entire body, barely grazing the skin.

- Try rapid, rubbing strokes that warm the skin with friction.

- Knead your lady by gently grasping an area—such as a calf, thigh, or upper arm—and working your hands as if you were kneading dough.

- Trace the outline of her lips with the tip of your index finger.

- Caress her jaw line by gently rubbing your fingers from the tip of her chin to the tops of her ears.

- Press your thumbs into the neck tendons that stretch from the bottom of her ear to the top of her shoulders. (This feels especially wonderful to anyone who hunches over a computer for much of the day.)

- Place your hands on her scalp, spread your fingers wide, and swirl them around with light pressure.

- Give her happy hands and feet by using the balls of your thumbs in circling motions on these extremities.

- Stroke the muscle that begins at the outer edge of her armpit and runs down the side of her body.

- Provide soft pressure with your palm at the base of her spine.

- Spread your palm just above her genital area; then pull your fingers inward, grazing this very sensitive skin ever so gently.

- Stroke the insides of her thighs with your palms.

The most important element of sensual massage is to be continuously responsive to your partner. Ask her what feels good. Be aware of how her body is communicating likes and dislikes to you. If your woman is pulling away or tensing up, alter what you're doing. If she's moaning with pleasure, do what you're doing some more.

As time goes on, you'll learn what strokes, rhythms, intensities, and special tricks turn your lady to putty in your manly hands. Just remember to keep an open mind, vary your touch according to her mood, and break the routine by trying a few new moves now and then.

Finishing Touches

To add another dimension to your sensual massage, use a lotion or oil. Massage oils and lotions render the body silky and slippery, making it easier for the massage-giver to stroke and for the recipient to luxuriate. Most of them also smell wonderful.

Be advised, however, that some women may be very particular about what kinds of lotions are applied to their bodies. Be sure to tell her what you're planning on using and don't just spring it on her as a surprise. If she says, "What's in that stuff?" don't take offense. Just read her the ingredients.

Once you've gotten your lady's agreement, rub a little bit of whatever you'll be using on the back of her hand to get her accustomed to the texture and scent. Once your lady gets comfortable with the oil or lotion, rub the substance into her back, arms, legs, buttocks, chest, neck, and shoulders.

When choosing an oil or lotion, be sure it's one specifically formulated for massage. These will leave less of a sticky residue than, say, hand lotions. Also, lighter is better. A lighter substance will be easier to work with. In addition, a subtle scent will be more pleasant than a heavy, overwhelming aroma. With scent, you can have too much of a good thing.

Love Busters

Never pour massage oil or lotion directly on your woman's body—it gives an unwelcome chill. Hold and rub it in your hands first to warm it. Use the palm-warming technique each time you apply more.

Another thing to keep in mind about massage oils is that many of them create stains that are difficult to remove. So either use sheets your woman is willing to part with (and good luck with that!) or buy a special sheet to put on your bed, floor, or whatever surface your massage will take place on.

The Least You Need to Know

- Few things say "I love you and care about you" more than preparing delicious and well-presented food for someone.

- Some foods enjoy a reputation for inspiring desire—and since they tend to be tasty and healthful foods there's no harm in incorporating them into your culinary offerings.

- When you can't help your lady out with chores, call in reinforcements—professional helpers offer assistance with almost any household task.

- Help your lady delegate without the guilt—let her know her time and well-being are what matter to you most.

- When it comes to massage, try doing it yourself—offer a sensual (not sexual) massage to melt her cares and her tension knots away.

Part 5

Love to Love Her

This part of the book offers instruction in the subtle, age-old art of seduction. It also ensures that your landing will be as smooth as your initial approach. Even the most skillful lover can learn a few new tricks, so this section details the ins and outs of foreplay, oral sex, and positions for intercourse that will enhance her gratification. It also includes advanced material for the adventurous who'd like to surprise their partners with something new and unexpected and expand their lovemaking repertoire with toys, erotica, and some esoteric techniques. Finally, it offers a chapter on giving your woman pleasure by letting her enhance your pleasure, too.

Chapter **14**

A Monogamous Casanova

In This Chapter

- ◆ Secrets of the world's most famous lover
- ◆ Seductive flirtations
- ◆ A guide to female anatomy
- ◆ Her favorite fantasies
- ◆ Fantasy roles and rules

Few things render a man more justifiably proud than completely satisfying his woman sexually. Needless to say, being on the receiving end of her man's devoted efforts in this area is extremely pleasing to any woman.

Although you may not realize it, you have within you the power to evolve into the kind of lover you've always wanted to be. This chapter will give you the necessary basic training by providing lessons in everything from the art of flirting to primers in female anatomy and female fantasies. But, remember, like most worthy endeavors, good loving begins with nothing more than the right attitude. You can learn a lot about that from a man who lived and loved long ago: Casanova.

Casanova's Secrets

Giovanni Jacopo Casanova (1725–1798) was a notorious Italian adventurer. His 12-volume memoir included long, provocative discourses on his passionate and prolific love affairs.

Casanova was one of history's most charming and irresistible seducers. All agreed, too, that his follow-through was as good as his serve. Women who enjoyed trysts with Casanova marveled at his unfailing ability to determine exactly what they craved and to give it to them.

What were Casanova's secrets? First, he worked at his craft. His quest was to fashion himself as the ideal lover for any partner. As he himself put it: "The cultivation of the pleasures of the senses was ever my principal aim in life. Knowing that I was personally calculated to please the fair sex, I always strove to make myself agreeable to it."

Second, Casanova truly adored women. Unlike the infamous seducer Don Juan, who lived to subjugate women, Casanova was genuinely interested only in pleasing them. He couldn't get enough of them.

So far, so good. Like Casanova, you too can make it a goal to elevate your loving to an art form. You too can cultivate and convey an attitude of adoration toward the object of your affections. But there is one caveat: Casanova did not limit his amorous attentions to one woman. He shared the love, so to speak. While that might work for an eighteenth century adventurer, it won't cut it for you. What your woman craves is a monogamous Casanova—a man who will make it his business to lavish his loving upon her and only her.

It can be done. And it all starts by mastering one of Casanova's key strategies—the flirt.

The Art of the Flirt

Casanova was a master at building anticipation. When he found a woman who tempted him, he crafted his every move, every glance, every word, to convey to her a promise of things to come. He was, in plain English, a big flirt.

Flirting is a basic and universal human impulse. Most of us flirt more or less instinctively when we spy a future prospect for a relationship, or when we're just beginning to court. Sadly, though, once we are in a committed relationship we often let the art of flirting flounder. It's a symptom of the sort of complacency that can take a toll on a relationship.

Flirting restores a bit of the initial mystery to a long-term relationship. It also stokes the libido of both the flirter (you) and the flirtee (your woman). Forgot how? It's well worth taking a brief refresher course.

- **Be subtle.** The key to seductive Casanova-style flirting is to do it in an understated manner. You can bet that Casanova wouldn't have made any headway by crass or blatant overtures. "Hey. Baby, I'm your handyman—wanna see my tools?" would hardly have earned him the favors of a beautiful woman (although he might have had a nice black eye to show for his efforts). To flirt is to hint, not to hit over the head.

- **Involve your eyes.** When it comes to sending powerful messages of love, longing, and seductiveness, the eyes have it. Let your eyes take in your woman's body. Then cast them, in turn, on her eyes, her lips, and her eyes. Hold her gaze. This says, "I wish I were touching you right now."

- **Lean in.** Everyone has a zone of intimate space around them. In our culture this zone is about two feet in circumference. Successful seduction involves the brief, subtle breaching of that invisible barrier. Lean in toward your woman. Allow your arm or leg to briefly brush against her, but make sure this touch is just a light grazing. Then move away again.

- **Mirror her posture.** When two people are attracted to one another, they adopt what researchers call postural echoes. Mirror-image postural echoes—where one person's left side reflects the other person's right side—are the strongest indication of rapport between any couple. As you consciously arrange your body and limbs to mirror your woman's (e.g. by leaning forward with your left arm on the table as she is leaning forward with her right arm on the table) you will create a congruent connection.

- **Listen.** Let your body talk say, "I'm listening to you. I think what you have to say is fascinating and important." To show you're listening, tilt an ear toward her and nod. Be sure not to just look like you're paying attention. Casanova would truly listen. Women would tell him what they dreamed of and he would be able to bring their dreams to life.

- **Talk in low, intimate tones.** Make it seem like you're sharing secrets. Be playful and flattering and funny. Stay away from mundane topics. Now is not the time to talk about who's going to balance the checking account or take the cat to the vet.

Your woman will be so delighted to be flirted with in this manner that it probably won't be long before she starts to give you signals that she wants to take things to the next level of intimacy. But, hey, not so fast. Keep building that anticipatory tingle until she can barely stand being without you a moment longer.

Female Anatomy: A Road Map

Once a woman invited Casanova to pleasure her with his lovemaking, she was in for a pleasant revelation. Here was a man who not only talked a good game, but played one as well. Where some men, even some men in long-term relationships, think of a woman's body as *terra incognita* (an unknown land), Casanova knew his way around the terrain.

When you're driving, I'm sure you pride yourself not just on knowing where you're going, but on knowing 10 different ways to get there. When you're loving, take the same approach.

Her Not-So-Obvious Pleasure Zones

The main thing Casanova knew about a woman's anatomy was to treat her entire body as a sexual organ. Every square inch of a female is an erogenous zone. Never limit yourself to concentrating only on a woman's breasts and genitals. Instead, try your hand—and tongue—on lots of hot spots.

- **Her hair.** It's an incredible sensual experience for a woman to have her man run his fingers through her hair. Don't stop there. Kiss her locks; smell her hair and tell her how wonderful the scent is.

Love Busters

Blow into one of your lady's ears and it may send her into rapture; blow into the other and it may leave her cold. Who knows why, but most seem to have a strong individual preference for left or right. Find out through trial and error, but then make a note for your mental map of her body.

- **Her neck.** The neck is actually one of the most erotically sensitive spots on the female body. But, no, don't give her a hickie. You're not in high school anymore. Cover her neck in tender kisses to get her all fired up. Where do you think the word necking came from?

- **Her ears.** Bundles of nerve endings in and around the ears render them super-susceptible to touch. Use the pads of your index finger and thumb to massage her outer lobes with slow, firm movements. Use your mouth to gently nibble and blow. Wet willies, meaning a tongue in the ear, are not female favorites, generally speaking, but you can always ask.

◆ **Her toes.** Not every woman likes to have her toes played with, but those who do really, really like it. Having her toes nibbled, kissed, or gently sucked can literally send chills up a woman's spine.

◆ **The small of her back.** This zone responds well to manual massage and to soft, grazing licks. Go for it, and loosen her lumbar.

Beyond these not-so-obvious spots, there are of course some other spots that have often held the spotlight. Do you know exactly what's what—not to mention what kinds of stimulation suits each spot? Casanova made it his business to know, and so should you.

The Clitoris

Above a woman's vagina is a smaller opening called the urethra, where urine comes out. Above the urethra is the hood of a small pink knob known as the clitoris. The clitoris can generate some intensely pleasurable sensations. In fact, it seems to have been made for pleasure alone, because the clitoris is the only sex organ with no known reproductive function. Many women say that oral or manual stimulation of the clitoris is the easiest way for them to achieve orgasm.

The word clitoris comes from a Greek word meaning "little hill." It's been recently discovered, however, that the clitoris is much bigger than previously thought. Its network extends in two arms about nine centimeters back into the body and high into the groin.

Mood Makers _____

The hood of the clitoris may be camouflaged by pubic hair. A good way for you to find the clitoris is by touch. During sexual arousal, the hood becomes puffier and puffier but the clitoris remains inside it. If you place your finger on the hood and press down you'll discover a shaft of rigid tissue.

Don't become confused. The clitoris seems to shrink out of sight in the instants just before a woman climaxes. This is a sign of turn-on, not turn-off. It occurs because the hood of the clitoris is becoming engorged with blood.

Women are very particular about how their clitoris is stimulated. And what a woman wants my vary depending on how aroused she is. Your partner might savor a gentle, teasing caress. Or she might like firmer pressure. She might enjoy the same kind of stroke over and over, or she might find that repetitiveness makes her clitoris numb. If you want to experiment with touching her clitoris, trace the alphabet on it with your finger or tongue. You'll most likely find a winning touch before you can say "A, B, C."

Trying to stimulate the clitoris too early in lovemaking can be uncomfortable for some women, for others direct pressure after they're aroused may be painful. So you need to experiment and note your partner's responses.

The Mons Pubis

Also known as the mons veneris (mountain of Venus), this is the mound of pubic hair covered in fatty tissue that covers the pubic bone. Pressure applied to this area by the palm of the hand, or by an erect penis pressing up against it, can be very pleasurable.

The Labia Minor

These smooth inner lips of a woman's genitals are super hot spots. Ninety-eight percent of women in the famous Kinsey studies of sexuality reported being able to feel a touch on the inner or outer side of these lips.

The Labia Majora

These are the fleshy outer lips of the vagina. They are considered far less sensitive than the labia minor, although they engorge with blood during arousal. The outer lips are formed from the same embryonic tissue as the male scrota.

The Vaginal Vestibule

Mother Nature has generously supplied the funnel shaped area just above the inner lips of the vagina, as well as the first inch and a half of its interior, with a wealth of nerve endings. By comparison, the deep inner walls of the vagina have far fewer nerve endings to stimulate.

You know the phrase, "Size doesn't matter"? Well, the fact that the entrance to the vagina is so sensitive is one of the reasons that a man's penis size is not of paramount importance to a woman's enjoyment of intercourse.

The G-Spot

The G-spot was named for Dr. Ernst Grafenburg, a German gynecologist who discovered this erogenous zone on the inner upper wall of the vagina. Some women don't believe they have a G-spot. But this is just a term for an anatomical area, and many women do find it pleasurable when stimulated. The most recent theories about it are that it is, in fact, part of the clitoral network—the spot where the elongated arms of the clitoris crisscross. Because it doesn't contain as many nerve endings as the clitoral head, the G-spot tends to respond to a more consistent and deep massage-type stroke than the clitoral hill.

If your partner wants to have you help locate her G-spot, have her lie down on her back and insert one or two fingers into the vagina with your palm facing the ceiling. If you bend your fingers slightly and feel along the vaginal walls you will find a roundish, sensitive area somewhere between the bladder and the pelvis. (Often before a G-spot orgasm occurs a woman will experience a feeling of pressure in her bladder.) If you keep rubbing this spot, she may like it. But if she doesn't find the sensation enjoyable, don't fret. Just move on to a known hot spot.

Love Busters _____

There is no "better" or "more mature" type of orgasm. G-spot and clitoral orgasms are equally wonderful. Never feel—or make your woman feel—that not achieving any particular kind of orgasm is a sign of inadequacy. Wherever orgasm originates, and by whatever methods, it creates a powerfully pleasurable wave of sensation. When it comes to giving your lady an orgasm, the end always justifies the means.

The Perineum

The perineum is the area between the vagina and the anus. It's made of tissue similar to that of the vaginal lips and therefore contains numerous nerve endings. Although this area is very stimulating for a lot of women, it often goes unexplored.

This area is extremely sensitive and fragile, so stick to a feathery touch at first. If your lover is aroused by this for some time, you can apply a bit more pressure. To ease the path, use a little lubricant (more on lubricants in Chapter 19).

The Breasts and Nipples

The breasts are, in fact, rich in nerve endings and ripe with pleasurable possibilities. All breasts respond sooner or later to sensual touch. Start teasingly—for example by touching a breast softly. Then lift your hand away for a moment before continuing. When her nipples become hard that's a sign of arousal. It indicates that your partner could well be ready for more intense stimulation.

What a woman enjoys with regard to her breasts can change depending on the time of month due to hormonal changes. Always look for feedback when giving pleasure.

The Buttocks

Many women enjoy having their buttocks attended to—some with more gusto than most men might imagine. Because the rear end isn't sensitive in the way a nipple or a clitoris is, more pressure can be applied. Your woman might enjoy having you knead and squeeze her buttocks. It's true that many women are self-conscious about their behinds, but having her man spend time in this zone may give her a whole new appreciation of her backside.

Whatever zone you are spending time on, linger there for a while. Lovemaking is not the Tour de France. It's never about covering a lot of ground in the shortest period of time.

Love Busters _____

According to *Time* magazine, 14 percent of cell phone users said in a worldwide survey that they had interrupted sex to take a call. Don't you be one of those people. Make your woman secure in the fact that your attention is on her and only her. Besides, think how silly you'd feel if the call was a wrong number, or your mother.

Her Favorite Fantasies

Do women have sexual fantasies like men do? Yes, yes, and yes. Virtually every study on sexuality shows that the overwhelming majority of women have sexual fantasies at various times and in various situations.

Sexuality and imagination go together so naturally that you can't have one without the other. Most women want to keep at least some aspects of their sexual reveries private. But what if some of their fantasies could move into the realm of reality? Another thing Casanova did well was to play into women's fantasies. In his empathic and non-judgmental company, women felt free to imagine—and sometimes to play at bringing their imaginings to life.

When you are in a committed relationship that has gone on for a while, you might think of your sex life with your woman as having boundaries—lines you've been afraid to cross. But self-imposed boundaries can be pushed back if you and your woman mutually decide it's okay.

Have you ever stopped to wonder what, exactly, women like to imagine when it comes to sex? According to a compendium of surveys, the following rank high on the average female's list of steamy sexual scenarios:

1. Sex with a stranger. There's something about a "mystery man" that's incredibly intriguing. Many women fantasize about a night of no-strings-attached passion with a man whom they know little about (first names only, please) and whom they'll never see again.

2. Sex with more than one. Some women like to think about being part of a three-some (or as the French say, a *menage-a-trois*). Others think about orgy-style samplings in an even larger group. The idea of all that naked flesh, including her own, is part of the turn-on.

3. Sex as performance. Being an actress in an erotic movie is a true favorite of many. The idea of having an audience can really make her feel desirable.

4. Being a dominatrix. Some women like to think about ordering a man to please her, making him beg for what he wants, and maybe even tying him up and spanking him. It's a fantasy that has a certain appeal even to some very mild-mannered ladies—maybe because those dominatrix outfits are so hot and stiletto heels make a lady's legs look great.

5. Obeying her master. On the flip side of the dominatrix coin, we have the sexual subjugate. Many women are turned on by the thought of being commanded and surrendering to a man's sexual demands. Still others relish the idea of disobeying, which is really quite naughty.

6. Girl on girl. Lots of women wonder what it would be like to share their body with another member of the fairer sex. And most who do say they'd want their man to watch. Really!

7. Being a prostitute. No matter how prestigious her career, a woman may wonder what it's like to be paid for providing sexual services. Sometimes they're street-walkers; sometimes they're high-priced call girls—like the kind in the Mayflower Madam's stable.

8. Making love in an exotic location. A moonlit beach, an African veldt, a private Lear jet: these are but some of the locations women sometimes visit in their sexual reveries.

 Mood Makers

Does knowing about female fantasies turn you on? That's only natural. To learn more, try browsing through romance novels. You can order them online if you're too shy to do this in a bookstore.

9. Making love with a celebrity. Now don't be upset. You think about the very same, don't you? Except your fantasies probably don't revolve around Brad Pitt.

10. Like a man. They might say they just want to try it once, but many women want to try being the penetrator (e.g. using a strap-on dildo) instead of the partner who is penetrated.

11. Like a virgin. She's pure and naive; he's the irresistible charmer who "takes advantage." This is a common scenario in many bodice-ripper romance novels, and therefore, maybe one of the most widespread fantasies of all.

Where do these fantasies come from? The genesis of sexual fantasies is complex. They may evolve out of deep-seated psychological preoccupations, some of which go all the way back to childhood. Or their source can simply be a provocative scene in a book or movie.

Fantasy Roles and Rules

Does a woman having a sexual fantasy mean that she actually wants to do the thing about which she is fantasizing? In many cases, the answer is no. You can't assume that because someone has a thought about being paid for sex or engaging in group or same-gender sex that this in any way fits in with a woman's image of herself in the real world.

On the other hand, some women might want to toy with the idea of acting out on some of their sexual fantasies in a safe, accepting environment (i.e. with you, their committed partner). All they've been waiting for is the right moment.

Why not take the time, when you are both relaxed and the mood is rife with sensuality, to ask if your partner would like to tell you about any of her fantasies? If she's agreeable to this first step, you can ask if she'd like to act one out. Fantasy can transport the two of you anywhere, anytime. Once there, you can make love "in character." Although you're not strangers, or client and call girl, or master and slave, you can role-play if you both have a solid amount of mutual trust.

There are certain things you can do beforehand to make the fantasy-to-reality transition both a sexually satisfying and emotionally safe experience.

◆ Discuss the details of the fantasy and see if the scenario is something in which each of you can actually picture yourselves engaging.

◆ Talk about positive consequences that might result from trying out the fantasy (would it be fun; would it turn you both on?).

◆ Talk about any potentially negative consequences that might result (such as embarrassment or jealousy).

◆ Sketch out a kind of storybook script for the fantasy (what is the plot; who are the characters?).

◆ Consider watching an adult film together that incorporates this type of fantasy (more about erotica in Chapter 19).

◆ Dabble in the fantasy before trying it out in a full-fledged way by improvising a few lines from your script the next time you make love.

◆ Agree ahead of time that either one of you can stop the fantasy play at any time, and agree on a word or signal that means "return to reality."

Naturally, if you act out a fantasy and don't care for it, you don't have to do it again. But that doesn't mean you can't try another. Like many couples, you and your woman may find that fantasy adds a thrilling new dimension to loving and expands the range of your sexual bond.

He Says/She Says

"When my husband asked me—after 10 years of marriage—if I'd ever want to act out a fantasy of mine with him I couldn't believe my ears. First I was embarrassed. How did he know I had fantasies? Then I started giggling, to hide my embarrassment. But, a week or two later, I found myself able to whisper my fantasy in his ear. Then he looked a little embarrassed, but eventually we went for it, and it has been great."
—Candace, 40

The Least You Need to Know

◆ Casanova, the notorious lover, lived to please all women—you can adapt his secrets of adoration and attentiveness while living to please only your woman.

◆ Flirtation, done with the proper subtlety, restores a bit of the initial mystery to a long-term relationship and fires up the libido.

◆ Learning about female anatomy means not just knowing where you're going, but also several different ways to get there.

◆ Nearly everyone has sexual fantasies, and your woman is likely no exception—ask whether she wants to act out any of her fantasies.

◆ It's never sexy to keep a fantasy scenario going past the point where one partner feels uncomfortable.

Appetizers

In This Chapter

- ◆ What foreplay is—and isn't
- ◆ Foreplay outside the bedroom
- ◆ Foreplay bedroom techniques
- ◆ From foreplay to more play

You've all heard of foreplay, right? You know it's something women enjoy and something you're supposed to do. Being the concerned lover and sensitive guy that you are, you are probably pleasing your woman with some enticing foreplay already. But are you doing it as well as you could? Well, that's what this chapter is all about.

Executed with skill and sensitivity, foreplay can cause your woman to experience depths of sexual ecstasy she may not have even realized existed. Delivered with spirit, self-confidence, and panache, the appetizers served up as love's first course will enhance lovemaking and intimacy for you both.

What Is Foreplay?

Foreplay literally means "the play that comes first." It can involve a broad range of the activities that a man and his woman indulge in together as they create readiness for ultimate sexual satisfaction. I know you're with me so far. But where a lot of men go wrong is in thinking of it as a kind of wind-up before the pitch—something obligatory and functional, but hardly on a par with the main event.

For women, foreplay is more than a physical build-up. It is an inextricable part of her continuum of sexual pleasure. Think of it this way: When you take your lady to an elegant restaurant that offers a delicious variety of foods, you would hardly encourage her to rush through the first dish that was put before her so she could move on to the next. On the contrary, you would want her to savor every bite. In fact, many of the very best restaurants tantalize diners' palates with not just one appetizer, but a parade of vividly flavored treats. Each hors d'oeuvre sets up for what's coming next. That's a good analogy for a woman's ideal concept of foreplay. One delight should lead seamlessly into another—with small moments of respite in between—building to a crescendo of intensity.

What Is Foreplay For?

Ask most men the purpose of foreplay and they will say it is to arouse a woman's body. But a man devoted to pleasuring his woman ought to know foreplay stimulates both a woman's body and her mind.

Certainly, the effect of foreplay on female physiology is profound. During love-making's first course, dozens of chemicals, including a powerful hormone called oxytocin, flood a woman's bloodstream. The chemicals make all of her more sensitive to touch. Other physical consequences of foreplay include ...

- An increased flow of blood to the pelvic area.

- The production of fluids that act as natural lubricants.

- An increased heart rate.

- An increase in respiration.

- A rise in blood pressure.

- A flushing of the skin.

- A swelling of the breasts and hardening of the nipples.

- The emergence of the clitoral head from beneath its hood.

On a psychological level, foreplay fulfills a complementary function. It makes a woman feel appreciated, even adored. When a man showers his woman with loving kisses and caresses, she instinctively feels that he is caring for her and catering to her. His movements, the sounds of pleasure and satisfaction he makes, and the words he whispers all contribute to her overall sense that he considers her attractive and desirable. She relishes the fact that he is so completely focused on her that he has nothing else on his mind but to experience her and love her.

Finally, foreplay serves another very crucial role in relationships: it offers a means of learning what turns a lover on most. Foreplay gives a guy the perfect opportunity to spend time understanding what his partner likes and what she really needs to be stimulated fully.

He Says/She Says

"The way my husband gives me his full attention during our foreplay is one of my greatest pleasures. I know for sure that every other thought except being with me has flown right out of his head. He's not thinking about work or football or tinkering with his car or anything else. I'm the center of his universe. That alone is a real rush."
—Terri, 33

Stay alert and observant. Notice what you do that makes her moan and sigh with delight. Notice which techniques and rhythms simmer her down and which ones bring her back near the boiling point. (Use both in alternation to really drive her wild with desire.)

Don't be shy about asking out loud either. This is a good time to solicit feedback from your woman, and you may find she feels less inhibited about indicating her preferences now than at any other time. It can be very exciting for a woman when her man asks her if she likes what he's doing and if she wants more, or if she wants him to try this … or that … or maybe even the other. Both of you will benefit from learning and communicating during foreplay.

Mood Makers

Try looking into your woman's eyes and saying, "Tell me how you want me to love you tonight." That will set her reeling with delight—especially if you've never said that sort of thing before.

Foreplay Outside the Bedroom

We usually think of foreplay as something we do in bed. But it is certainly not necessary to wait until bedtime to begin stirring up a sense of anticipation in your woman. There are lots of ways throughout the day to say that you are having thoughts about her that are both naughty and nice. A lightly lascivious phone call from work is a good way to add some spice to her day. So is a Post-it love note left on her dresser or makeup mirror. If you get up and leave the house before she does, try leaving one flower perched on her pillow—or place a fresh, flakey croissant on the kitchen counter so she can savor something rich and satisfying with her morning coffee or tea. If she leaves before you or you both leave together, try dropping a chocolate kiss into her purse or leaving it beside her coffee mug the night before. Later, over dinner, make all-important eye contact. Then hold her gaze a moment longer than you ordinarily might and give her a playful wink.

Foreplay can even be conducted in public. If you're out together, let her know you're happy to be seen with her and that you'll be even happier to get her alone later on.

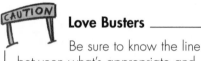

Love Busters

Be sure to know the line between what's appropriate and inappropriate in terms of public displays of affection. No woman wants to be "manhandled" in public. As much as you might long to touch her breasts or pat her behind, control yourself! There will be plenty of time later.

Put your arm around her or hold her hand as you walk along together. Flash her a smile from across a crowded room. If you're dining out and have a table that affords you the opportunity to be inconspicuous, try initiating a little game of footsie. The fact that you can take things no further in the moment is very exciting in itself. Delaying gratification can create an amazing pull and establish an aura of sexual energy around the two of you that is palpable. Besides, gratification delayed is often the sweetest gratification of all. What we cannot have immediately we value all the more.

Thoughtfulness Is Foreplay, Too

Remember, too, that no matter how attracted your wife or girlfriend is to you, and no matter how much she would appreciate your loving ministries in theory, she won't be able to respond to you in practice if she is simply too overburdened and exhausted. So, believe it or not, sometimes a little extra help with the kids and the housework can be the hottest form of foreplay.

Imagine this scenario: You've just finished dinner, which your partner took the time to prepare. Now, there are dirty dishes to be tackled, and leftovers to wrap and put in the fridge. As usual, your partner takes charge of this as well. Tonight she's in a bit of a hurry though, because both of your kids need help with their homework and one of them is in rather desperate need of a bath after a muddy slide into home plate at the afternoon's Little League game.

Oh, and the dog needs a walk—but that's usually your job. So, you get Fido's leash and say, "See ya." Your plan is to get some fresh air with your pooch, take out the trash—because, hey, you do your share—and then watch T.V. or catch up on your car magazines, kiss the kids goodnight, and hope that your wife (who looks especially enticing as she's bending over to pick up a juice box that your littlest child has just hurled across the room) is in the mood for a little intimate encounter. In fact, you can't wait to try this new foreplay technique you just read about that is reputed to drive women crazy.

Now imagine this scenario: You've just finished the dinner that your partner cooked for you and your family. You say, "Thank you for that wonderful dinner, honey. I know how hard it is to get dinner ready for this crowd with everything else you do. How about I bring home takeout tomorrow?"

Next, you talk with your partner about what needs to get accomplished at home that evening. You notice she looks a little tired but you don't mention that. Instead you say, "Sweetie, I think you deserve a night off. I'm going to walk this puppy and then come back and clean up around here. Don't lift a finger, I mean it. You relax for a bit. I'll take care of the kids' baths and homework if you promise me that you will go and relax in a bath yourself. I don't want you doing anything else tonight except taking a little time out to pamper yourself."

Okay, now in which of these scenarios do you think you are more likely to get the chance to try out your new foreplay maneuver?

If you said the first one, do not proceed with the rest of this chapter until you go back and reread the earlier ones on being a considerate, helpful guy.

If you said the second one, you understand that part of getting your woman ready for love is to show love in the daily things you do for her. Congratulations! You may now proceed to the bedroom.

Foreplay in the Bedroom

Bedroom appetizers come in many wonderful flavors. Lovemaking foreplay can encompass kissing, stripping, teasing talk, stroking and caressing, finger play, oral play—and just about anything else you both enjoy.

But before we move to all that, let's address one question that I know is on your mind. How long should foreplay last? This question has both a technical answer and a practical one.

The technical answer, according to the research of both Dr. Alfred Kinsey and Masters & Johnson is that over 92 percent of women achieve an orgasm during a sexual encounter when their partners spend 21 minutes or more on foreplay.

Twenty-one minutes may seem like a long time, but if you think about it, you routinely devote that amount of time, and more, to things far less important than bringing your woman to a state of bliss that will inspire both her gratitude and her desire to reciprocate. Twenty-one minutes is …

- Less than the length of one sitcom with the commercials taken out.

- Less than the time in one football quarter with the timeouts added in.

- Less time than it takes to warm up the charcoal on your outdoor grill.

Besides, the practical answer to the question of how long foreplay should last is as long as it takes your woman to get fully turned on. That could be 15 or 20 minutes; it could be half an hour or more. No matter—as long as you are both enjoying yourselves with a wide and wonderful array of appetizers.

Kissing and More Kissing

While there's certainly no rule on how to begin bedroom foreplay, a kiss can be a great way to start. Surely you've kissed your woman lots of times before. But there's kissing and then there's kisssssssing. A kiss can be an art form in itself, a tour de force displaying supreme skill and inspiration.

Try preceding a long, slow kiss by cupping your lady's face in your hands and gazing into her eyes for two or three seconds. This signals your adoration and appreciation of her—and also lets her know that you are going to take this one wonderful step at a time.

Mood Makers

If you're both in the mood for some "caveman" kissing variations, you can play with the idea that your woman is completely in your power. One way to do this is to move your hands to the back of her hair and hold onto it firmly from the roots (no pulling please) while you kiss her. Another caveman variation is to back your woman against a wall while you kiss her hungrily.

Now, use your tongue to gently part her lips. Let the tongue roll, lick, flick, and encircle. Don't be afraid to explore. But never try to thrust your tongue so far into your woman's throat that it feels like you're about to perform a tonsillectomy.

Women thoroughly enjoy kissing and being kissed. In fact, a common complaint is that their partners don't kiss them for long enough. So … take … your … time. Kissing is never boring, especially if you add new dimensions to your kisses by varying their rhythm and pace. Transition from intense, passionate kisses back to lighter, teasing ones. Try kissing around her lips for a little while; then return to her mouth. Your woman will be surprised and intrigued as you take things from a boil to a simmer and then back again.

Don't neglect to kiss her neck—which, as you learned in Chapter 14, is one of the hottest hot spots on the female body.

> **CAUTION**
> **Love Busters**
>
> Brush before you kiss. Floss, too, and use a mouthwash. Bad breath can take all the fun out of kissing. To enhance spontaneity, carry a pack of mouthwash strips in your back pocket. You can peel and pop a strip at a moment's notice.

Caress Her, Undress Her

Kissing and caressing go together naturally. Run your hands up and down your partner's back; move your hands in circular motions at the base of her spine. Knead her back from the bottom to the top and back down again. Stroke her neck, ears, arms, and wrists. Then work your hands up her sides and down toward her outer thighs.

But wait! I know what you're thinking. Down boy. It's not time yet to move on to touching her breasts—and it is certainly not time yet to move on to her genitals. Prolong your buildup by avoiding contact with these areas for a while longer.

> **CAUTION**
> **Love Busters**
>
> Don't rush. Avoid making any contact with her genitals for the first 10 to 15 minutes of foreplay. This will delay gratification and stoke the fires.

At this point, if you are standing, your teasing stroking of her outer thighs makes for a nice segue into a really exciting maneuver. Try lifting her up and wrapping her legs around your waist as you prepare to carry her toward your bed. Lay her down—then break off contact for a moment as you look her over adoringly.

Now you can begin to remove her clothing, piece by piece. As you do so, kiss and lick each successive body part that you expose—her shoulders, the insides of her elbows, her

> **He Says/She Says**
>
> "I get so excited when my boyfriend gives lots of attention to my breasts during foreplay. It's more than just a physical sensation of arousal. It's knowing how much he is enjoying himself that turns me on."
> —Beth, 29

tummy. And, now, yes it's time to kiss and caress her breasts. When you do, another rush of the hormone oxytocin will be released into her bloodstream.

Making the Breast of It

One thing that's important to know is that all breasts, large and small, contain the same number of nerve endings, but women vary greatly when it comes to breast sensitivity. Over-stimulating a woman's breasts before she is ready can be numbing or painful for her—particularly during some parts of her menstrual cycle. Try taking a "less is more" approach. Start out by kissing, sucking, or fondling the breasts softly; then pull away for a moment before continuing. This gives her that all-important thrill of anticipation.

Don't focus solely on the twin "bulls-eyes" of her nipples. In fact, stick to indirect stimulation until you notice that her nipples have become hard. This indicates that they are aroused. Even if your partner pushes your mouth or hands directly to her nipples, don't give in right away. Just continue moving slowly toward them. Take your time and tease her. Now, if you like, you can try wetting your fingers and rolling her nipple around a bit before bringing your mouth to it. Be alert to the response you're getting as your touch becomes more vigorous. When in doubt ask, "Is this okay. Is this too much?"

How Your Clothes Go

If you've been doing a yeoman's job up until now, you may find that your lover has already taken the initiative in removing some of your clothing. She may have removed or unbuttoned your shirt and unbuckled your belt. So now may seem like the logical time for your pants to come off. However, if you keep them on for a while you can get her juices—and yours—flowing even more with some "dry sex."

> **CAUTION**
>
> **Love Busters**
>
> Few visual triggers are more likely to undermine the mood of foreplay than a man wearing nothing but his socks. Avoid the budget porn movie look and pull those argyles off before your trousers and underwear go.

Place your body over hers. Now begin mimicking the movements you'd make if you were actually penetrating her. She'll feel your hardness and imagine what may be in store. Now your pants can come off. But, please, not until you've removed your socks.

The Fire Down Below

A clear sign that it's time to involve your partner's genitals in foreplay is that she is instinctively spreading her legs. Once you're at this point, you have many delightful options to choose from. One is to use your fingers to stimulate her.

Most women masturbate by rubbing a finger or two over their clitoris in a back-and-forth or circular motion. You can do this, too, and it is most helpful to ask how she likes it done. If she's not too shy, it's even better to have her show you how she likes it done.

Before you do something so direct, however, try experimenting with some of these various teasers:

♦ With one finger, tickle her vaginal opening as lightly as possible.

♦ Give her a labial massage by exploring the inner and outer lips of her vagina—tracing, pulling, and rubbing gently.

♦ Place your palm on her mons pubis (the mound where her pubic hair is), then move your hand in a small circular motion, then raise your fingers slightly and tap her vaginal lips lightly about 10 times (after a few moments rest, repeat this again).

♦ Give her a light, gentle caress that barely touches the inner thighs and pubic hair until her pelvis begins to arch upward—then insert your thumb in her vagina, as you rest your fingertips on top of her pubic bone.

♦ Lay your free hand over the lower part of your lover's abdomen and experiment by applying different kinds of pressure with the top hand while fingers from your other hand are inside her vagina.

♦ Use a fingertip to tickle her clitoris very, very lightly.

Another wonderful option at this point is providing your woman with some incredible oral sex. Once again, don't go right for the "target" of her clitoris. Instead, use your tongue to lick her neck, her abdomen, her inner thighs, and her outer labia. And that's just the beginning. There is, in fact, so much to say and to learn about this highly pleasurable topic that the entire next chapter of this book, Chapter 16, is devoted to it.

Love Busters

Some women enjoy deep, vigorous thrusting of the fingers into their vagina; some tense up under this kind of stimulation. This is another one of those situations where it is best to both observe and to ask about her preferences directly.

Foreplay and More Play

All the romantic and playful sexual activity you and your partner engage in will serve to make both of you more aroused and more responsive. If you put enough time and imagination into foreplay your woman will be saturated with desire.

If you are planning to segue from foreplay into intercourse, how will you know when your woman is ready? The easy answer may seem to be "when she's wet"—meaning when her vaginal area is well *lubricated*. But how wet is wet enough?

A woman's vagina generally begins to lubricate soon after sexual arousal, which can result from physical stimulation, like what takes place during foreplay, or from merely thinking about sex. Beads of liquid form on the vaginal wall and the vulvovaginal glands secrete a few drops of thicker liquid. Both processes combine to facilitate intercourse by allowing greater ease of movement as the sex organs make contact and move to create friction.

But it's important to understand that a woman may be highly aroused and still not very well lubricated. This may have to do with many factors, including her estrogen level (this is impacted by her menstrual cycle, as well as whether or not she is menopausal), her diet, and even the amount of stress she might be under. Do not take offense if your woman is not as wet as you think she should be. But do know that intercourse without proper lubrication can be very uncomfortable. Refer to Chapter 19 for some tips on using lubrication enhancers.

Tongue Teasers

Lubrication, commonly known as "getting wet" refers to a natural sexual readiness process that occurs within 10 to 30 seconds of a woman becoming sexually aroused. The vascular engorgement of the tissues that lie beneath the vaginal wall begin the process.

Of course, another excellent way to find out whether or not your partner is ready for intercourse is to inquire. Try using the moment for some inventive spicy talk. Ask, "Are you ready for me, baby?"

Another thing you may be wondering is whether or not you should proceed with intercourse if your partner has already had an orgasm during foreplay. Some women prefer to climax before intercourse, others prefer to reach their orgasm during intercourse. And some like to do both! That's all good. The key is in simply knowing what your woman's personal preference is.

Finally, although foreplay is most often thought of as a prelude to sexual intercourse, that doesn't always have to be the case. You may want to pleasure your woman with your fingers or tongue until she climaxes … and perhaps climaxes yet again. She will be only too happy to return the favor—although on occasion you might even consider letting her know that this time is all about taking care of her.

Whatever you and your partner choose to do, try thinking of foreplay less as a linear, goal-directed activity and more as a process that creates a series of pleasure waves—ebbing and flowing, cresting and falling. Conceptualizing foreplay as a pleasure unto itself will enhance lovemaking and open up endless new possibilities for you both.

The Least You Need to Know

- ◆ Foreplay is more than getting ready for an experience—it is an experience in itself.

- ◆ The purposes of foreplay are to arouse both body and mind and to enable partners to learn about what excites one another.

- ◆ Foreplay can—and should—begin outside the bedroom, often with a gesture that shows love and appreciation.

- ◆ At every stage of foreplay—kissing, caressing, undressing, and the rest—pull back briefly now and again to build desire and anticipation.

- ◆ When in doubt about whether a particular technique is too vigorous or too gentle, observe your partner's reactions—and don't be afraid to ask.

- ◆ Foreplay can be a segue to intercourse or to other means of sexual gratification—in any case it helps to imagine it less as a goal-oriented activity and more as an opportunity to imagine, to explore, and to create desire by expressing it.

Chapter 16

Tongue Loving

In This Chapter

- What women love about oral sex
- Getting past inhibitions—yours and hers
- Best positions and techniques for performing oral sex
- Advanced oral tricks to please her
- Signs of female orgasm

If this book had only a single chapter on pleasing a woman sexually, this would be the one. The majority of women cannot get enough of a man who performs oral sex frequently, skillfully, and enthusiastically.

It's not surprising, though, that many men don't feel confident with their level of expertise in this area. Unless you've had the good fortune of knowing a woman who was willing and able to instruct you in this art, you might approach oral sex by just burrowing in, sticking out your tongue, and hoping for the best. Very often, men say that oral sex is something they'd like to get better at. It's a sure bet that your partner will be grateful if you avail yourself of this opportunity for self-improvement.

Why She Really, Really Likes Oral Sex

Just what is it about oral sex that pleases women so much? For one thing, there's the sheer physical gratification. But woman, as you well know by this point, do not live by the physical alone. It is but one of the many different ways that oral sex—otherwise known as *cunnilingus*—provides pleasure to her. There are others as well.

Tongue Teasers

The act of performing oral sex on a woman is technically called **cunnilingus**. This is derived from the Latin *cunnus* meaning "vulva," and *lingere*, "to lick." In slang, performing cunnilingus is also known as "going down" and "eating out."

- Oral sex offers concentrated stimulation where she feels it most.

- Orgasm resulting from cunnilingus can happen quickly and intensely.

- The tongue is so soft and flexible it can offer sensations that no other body part can.

- When a man performs cunnilingus, it signals that he is focused on gratifying his partner.

- It makes her feel totally accepted, even adored, because it indicates that her man loves her taste and her scent.

- A woman finds it incredibly sexy to see the top of a man's head lodged between the "V" of her thighs.

- It makes her very wet, and is thus great preparation for intercourse.

- It gets her man very excited, and thus very hard.

- There's no risk of pregnancy.

- It's a great way to have sex during pregnancy, even in the later months.

- She can just lie back and enjoy herself.

Oral sex makes the vast majority of women happy for so many reasons that every man determined to please his woman ought to have oral sex techniques in his sexual repertoire.

Overcoming Inhibitions

Despite the many pleasures and benefits of oral sex, it should be noted that some women feel shy or otherwise reluctant to have their lover get so very, very up close and personal. Even if part of her really wants to try cunnilingus, another part may pull back. She may feel very vulnerable in such a situation. She may feel insecure about how her vulva looks, tastes, and smells. If this is a part of her body with which she herself feels somewhat unfamiliar, she may also feel confused about exactly what it is you'll be doing, and even concerned about whether or not you will hurt her. In some cases, women resist oral sex simply because they feel it is taboo.

According to the *Redbook Report* on female sexuality, 62 percent of women find oral sex highly enjoyable and another 28 percent find it somewhat enjoyable. Only 6 percent say they don't care for it. Talk to your lover to find out which category she falls into. If she's in the latter 6 percent she may well change her attitude once she knows yours is positive—although, as with all sexual matters, there's no need to force an issue with so many pleasant alternatives available.

To assuage any fears she may have, you will need to reassure your partner that going down on her is something you want very much to do, and that you are eager to experience her in this fashion. You'll also want to manifest confidence in your abilities (which you will well be able to do by the time you complete this chapter.)

Of course, it will be hard to convince your woman to overcome her own inhibitions if you have not come to terms with your own. So let's have a look at what some common male objections are, and at strategies for getting over those particular reservations.

"I'm Sensitive to Odor."

Some guys feel squeamish about the smell of a woman's genitals. But with routine hygiene, your woman will simply smell natural—a bit salty and musky. Many men find the up-close scent of a woman a super turn-on once they experience it. However, if you're really concerned about being overwhelmed, suggest a joint shower as a prelude to sex.

Mood Makers

There are many scented lubricants made specifically with oral sex in mind. You and your woman can experiment. Now, oral sex can taste like eating a strawberry sundae.

"I Don't Care for Pubic Hair."

You will probably be less concerned about pubic hair once you try oral sex and realize that it won't interfere with your pleasure or hers. It is true you may end up with a strand or two between your teeth. Just chalk it up to an occupational hazard. An ordinary toothbrush will remove it.

On the other hand, if a preponderance of public hair is really an aesthetic problem for you, you can discuss your lover's opinion of trying either a *Brazilian wax* or a *Hollywood wax*. Both are very much in fashion and if she's never tried either, she may find she feels surprisingly sexy after this type of grooming.

Tongue Teasers

A **Brazilian wax** removes all pubic hair except for a vertical strip in front. A **Hollywood wax** leaves things all bare down there.

These services, along with standard bikini waxes that trim excess hair on the upper thighs and groin, are available at many day spas. It can be awkward—or worse—to attempt to wax this sensitive area at home, and the results are not as effective as they are when waxing is done by a pro. One thing to note: if your partner gets into the waxing habit, she'll have to keep it up every couple of weeks to avoid stubble.

"I Don't Want To Hurt Her."

As when your lover performs oral sex on you, the trick to not inflicting discomfort is simply not to involve the teeth. Also, rest assured that if you were doing anything to cause pain, your woman would tell you. No woman will grin and bear it when it comes to this sensitive area of the body. If there's a problem, just correct it. No need to make a big deal out of it.

"Oral Sex Is Hard Work."

Oh, be a sport, won't you? Of course oral sex takes some effort, but it is well worth it. If you are really feeling exhausted, come up for air now and again, using your hands to stimulate her while you take a breather.

"I'll Never Get Good At It."

The first secret to getting good at oral sex is the same secret to becoming skilled at anything: practice, practice, practice. The second is to be responsive to your partner's desires. Read on to learn about basic and advanced techniques, but bear in mind that when it comes to oral sex, your partner can be your best guide. Encourage her to let you know what feels best.

To begin, all you really need is an open mind and a "can-do" attitude. As Woody Allen rightly said, "Eighty percent of success in anything is showing up."

Positioning for Oral Sex

The main idea behind positioning for oral sex is that both partners should be comfortable and that the man should have ample access to the woman's entire pelvic area. What seems to be most efficacious is the woman on her back pose, although there are a few others you may wish to use for occasional changes of pace.

Woman on Her Back

This is the position a woman will be most likely to instinctively assume in preparation for cunnilingus. In this position she'll lie supine with her legs less than a foot apart and bent at the knee. Her back will be flat and her pelvis will be slightly tilted upward.

You should position yourself so that your torso is vertical with regard to her genitals— your bodies should be in a straight line relative to one another. This means you'll need room to stretch out, so your partner's head will need to be near the head of the bed.

You should be able to slide your hands beneath your partner's backside. If she would like, and if it would make access easier for you, slide a pillow under her buttocks. (This also will help prevent neck strain on your part.)

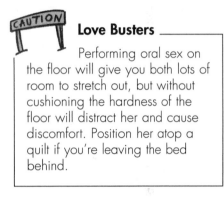

Love Busters

Performing oral sex on the floor will give you both lots of room to stretch out, but without cushioning the hardness of the floor will distract her and cause discomfort. Position her atop a quilt if you're leaving the bed behind.

Bury your nose lightly in her mons pubis and lightly press the area between your nose and upper lip against the front of her pubic bone. The idea is to allow your tongue to have a wide range of motion across the length of her genitalia.

Her Legs Aloft

As variations on the woman on her back theme, you can lift one or both your lover's legs over your shoulders. Some women find this position extremely stimulating and some men feel it give them easier access.

Simultaneous Mutual Oral Sex

Commonly known as sixty-nine position, simultaneous mutual oral sex is something couples tend to either really enjoy or eschew. Its advantage is instant reciprocity and the opportunity to reach a climax together. But many feel that it is too distracting to be the simultaneous giver and receiver of pleasure. The only way to know whether this pleases you and your partner is to give it a try.

There are a couple of options for the sixty-nine technique. Many consider side by side, head to toe, the most comfortable approach and the easiest to sustain. You can also be on your hands and knees over your partner, but this can be fatiguing and hard to sustain. Either way, some women find it harder to reach an orgasm when oral sex occurs during sixty-nine, because the man's tongue makes contact with her genitals from a less than optimal angle.

Woman Sitting Atop

In this position, the woman kneels so that she can lower her vulva over her lover's face (in the vernacular, she "sits on his face"). Some couples like the excitement that this "dominant female" approach allows, and it does make for better access than sixty-nine. One drawback: it can be tiring for a woman to kneel for a long period of time.

Oral Sex While Standing

I know that you, as a man, might relish receiving oral sex from a standing position. It's exciting to see your lover kneeling before you, devoting herself to your pleasure while on her knees. Some women feel the same when the shoe is on the other foot, so to speak. However, in this stance, cunnilingus will probably work best as a kind of warm-up for other activities. It's difficult to get the angle right for a woman to achieve a climax.

The Basics

Every woman has individual preferences when it comes to having oral sex performed on her. Nevertheless, it can't hurt in any endeavor to have a basic game plan to follow. Then, as things move along, it's fun to experiment with different plays. You can always take a basic technique and then refine it and improvise upon it.

- ◆ **Kiss around.** Start by planting appreciative, adoring kisses around her vulva, but not directly on it. Kiss her outer and inner thighs and lower abdomen. Get her enthused about what's coming next.

- ◆ **Think ice cream.** Approach your partner's labia as you would a sugar cone filled with your favorite flavor. Long, gentle, languorous licks—given with a flat tongue—are how you want to proceed. Don't imagine it's a hot summer day and you need to keep your ice cream from melting. Instead, savor the flavor. Lick her inner vaginal lips from bottom to top numerous times, brushing the head of her clitoris as you go past it. Pause for a moment in between licks to let the sensation resonate for both of you. If you gently press a hand on her mons pubis and oppress slightly upward as you lick, you will increase the surface area that you have available to lick.

Mood Makers

How long should cunnilingus take? How long have you got? Approach this activity as if you had all the time in the world. If your partner feels she should hurry up and have an orgasm, she will tense up instead.

◆ **Get a rhythm, then change it.** Repeat your long, slow licks for a few minutes. Now vary your licking a bit with some quick flicks and semi-circles. Try licking across the clitoral head horizontally and diagonally. Use some secondary licks—not aimed at the head—as teasers to get her even more aroused.

◆ **Try a little suction.** Pucker your lips around the clitoris and gently—I said gently—suck. See how your partner responds to this stimulus. If it is too intense, back off and resume licking.

◆ **Involve your hands.** Hands can be great helpers in performing oral sex. You can use them to part the lips of the vagina, and to gently squeeze her buttocks. You can also insert a finger or thumb into her vagina while you are stimulating her clitoris—but do be aware that while some women adore this move, others find it distracting. Test the waters.

◆ **Let her do some work, too.** Part her labia with your thumbs and push your tongue into her vulva, and then be still. She will instinctively grind herself into you.

◆ **Hold her in place.** From your vantage point, you will have a bird's eye view of your lover as she approaches orgasm. When her inner labia darken and her clitoris retreats under its hood once again, she is about to come. Use your hands and your mouth to hold your lover in position. Bring her legs as close together as possible, which will make it easier for her muscles to contract. If she—or you—veer off course even a little bit her orgasm may elude her.

◆ **Apply focused rhythm and pressure to the head.** To bring on her orgasm, reestablish a rhythm of quick, catlike licks across the head of the clitoris. Use more pressure now than you did in your initial licking.

◆ **Keep at it while she climaxes.** While your partner is in the throes of orgasm, continue to apply pressure. This will prolong her contractions and keep her orgasm from fizzling abruptly. Don't stop until you sense her body relaxing. It's likely she may, at that point, signal you to stop by placing a hand on your head or gently pushing you away. Don't take offense. She just needs to recover!

As you work your way through all of the foregoing steps, take a moment here and there to check in with your partner. If your head is properly positioned you should be able to look up, make eye contact, and observe how your woman is doing. The sounds and movements she makes will provide additional clues. You can always stop for a moment and ask her if she likes one particular kind of stroke or another, but in the clinch her body language and moans will probably be all you need to direct you.

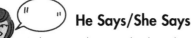 **He Says/She Says**

"I love it when my husband goes down on me, because he doesn't make it seem like a chore. I've heard women complain that this can be something men seem to want to 'check off their list' so they can rush on to intercourse."

—Deborah, 32

Once your mission is accomplished, let your face linger for a while near her genitals. Plant more gentle kisses on the insides of her thighs, indicating how much you have appreciated the opportunity to gratify your lover in this way.

But resist directly continuing to stimulate the clitoris after she has climaxed. This feels too intense for most women. Some find it irritating, even painful. If you're moving on to intercourse after cunnilingus, be aware that your partner may well need a minute to catch her breath before commencing a new activity. Segue by stroking and kissing her all over.

Variations on the Theme

Ready to add more variety to your oral sex adventures? There are many ways to diversify your partner's range of sensations. Try a few of the following tricks to arouse her:

- **The Hummer.** Sound vibrations can add to her pleasure. Try softly humming with your lips against her vaginal lips. If you're feeling whimsical, try humming a whole tune, like Jingle Bells or Happy Birthday To You. (One caveat: don't blow air directly into the vagina, which, though rare, could cause an air embolism.)

- **The Outback.** Run your tongue lengthwise up and down her perineum—the space between the base of her vaginal entrance and her anus. This area is thick with spongy erectile tissue and contains many nerves that are extremely sensitive to touch.

- **The Ice Man.** For a frosty treat on a hot night, try going down on your lover with an ice cube in your mouth. She'll undoubtedly flinch at first, but then relax into the sensation. Some people like to use this technique after the woman has had one orgasm and is feeling flushed. They say it is likely to give her another climax before long.

- **Hot Stuff.** Take a sip of a warm beverage before your first vaginal kiss. Warm seltzer water adds a bit of fizzy fun.

- **Under the hood.** Although part of the clitoral head will naturally pop out from beneath its hood during oral sex, many women say they prefer it if their partner uses his finger to expose even more of the head. Devotees of this method say it offers a much more intense orgasm.

> **CAUTION**
>
> **Love Busters**
>
> Some women complain of whisker burn if their lover has a beard or mustache. If this is a problem, apply conditioner to your facial hair, ideally at least an hour or so before your intimate encounter.

- **Reach up and touch someone.** Let your hands roam up while you're going down. Use them to squeeze your lover's breasts and caress her nipples.

- **Taps and tugs.** Gently tickle or tap her inner labia as your tongue focuses in and around her clitoris. Try a gentle tug on the inner labia and see how she responds.

- **G whiz.** As your tongue works its magic, use your finger to stimulate your partner's G spot. Insert a finger into the vagina and then crook it upward as if you were beckoning her toward you. It will press against the sensitive spongy tissue of the vaginal ceiling, which swells up when aroused. Depending on your partner's preference, this can also be done with two fingers—your index and your middle digits.

Fancy tricks can be fun, but don't worry if they're not your style or if your lover doesn't take to them. Most women don't need a brass band when it comes to cunnilingus. An eager partner who has mastered the basics will thrill them every time.

Did She Come?

Did your woman have her orgasm? For some men it's easy to tell. Their women are the type who thrash about and cry out. In fact, some women come so loudly their lovers feel like they're being cheered for scoring a tie-breaking championship touchdown. If this level of gusto describes your partner, then asking the question, "Did you come?" is somewhat beside the point. If you have to ask, she didn't.

But not all women are so effusive, and therefore not all men are certain about whether or not their partner has climaxed. The principal way to know if a woman has had an orgasm is that there will be spasmodic, involuntary contractions in her pelvic area—and sometimes complementary ones in other parts of her body. On average, these contractions will last 10 to 20 seconds. Don't confuse her milder pre-orgasmic throbbing with full-blown contractions. While extremely enjoyable, and still part of the process, these preliminary pleasures are not the whole enchilada.

Other signs that your woman is experiencing a climax can include:

- Rapid breathing
- Increased body temperature
- Racing, pounding heart
- Bearing down in the pelvic area
- Tightening of the stomach muscles
- Swelling breasts
- Erect nipples
- Flushed face
- Flushed ears
- Perspiration
- A stiffening body
- Widened nostrils
- Increased vaginal secretions

If you are making oral contact with a woman when she orgasms you may well notice a change in the way she tastes. Her juices will be thicker and sweeter. You may also find that your woman grabs at your hair and ears as she comes. Don't be distracted! She just needs something to hold onto.

Mood Makers

Some women prefer cunnilingus as a prelude to intercourse and do not wish to climax during it. They want to save that for later. If that's your woman's preference, know when to stop. Don't feel bad that you didn't make her come this way, so long as she is satisfied overall.

Now we come to a question that puzzles a great many men. Could your lover actually be faking her orgasm? According to sex researcher Shere Hite, more than half of all women have faked orgasm with a male partner. Makes you wonder, doesn't it?

One thing this statistic signifies is that men are not being very observant. If you pay attention with your eyes, ears, and body, you will find ample evidence of orgasm. Another thing it signifies is that lots of women are so interested in pleasing their man that they will fake a climax in order to make him feel good.

In the long run, however, this won't make anyone happy. If you think your partner is faking an orgasm, it's a sign that you may need to communicate better about your sex life. Don't accuse her of faking—that will probably just make her feel embarrassed and defensive. But do inquire as to how you can make her experience more complete.

The Least You Need to Know

◆ Women appreciate oral sex because of the unique sensual and emotional pleasures it provides.

◆ Even if your woman has never experienced oral sex, she may be very receptive to your suggestion.

◆ Oral sex offers so many pleasures to women that it's worth reconsidering any inhibitions you may have.

◆ Like any sexual technique, oral sex takes effort and practice, but practice makes perfect.

◆ Fancy tricks offer a nice change of pace, but most women will be thrilled by an enthusiastic partner who's mastered the basics—as Woody Allen says, "most of success comes from showing up."

◆ Women's orgasms are accompanied by definite physiological responses that show she is making it, not faking it.

Chapter 17

Playing With Positions

In This Chapter

♦ Beyond the old stand-by positions

♦ Man on top and woman on top positions

♦ Side-by-side positioning

♦ Sitting, standing, and kneeling positions

♦ Anal play

Most people have a favorite position for sleeping. You probably also have one for reading in bed and for watching T.V. These are habits you're not likely to break. But when it comes to positions for passion, consider that some habits are made to be broken. Experimenting with some new positions can please your woman by adding new sizzle to your sex life and by incorporating ways to up her pleasure quotient during intercourse. This chapter will tell you how.

Beyond the Tried and True

If you've ever looked at any book on the topic of lovemaking you've probably come across positions for intercourse that appeared so exotic and impractical that you imagined you, your partner, or both of you ending up in traction due to a severely thrown out back. The ideas might have turned you on, but you might have felt somewhat daunted when it came to giving these new things a go. Besides, why mess with something that seemed to be going pretty well anyhow?

Fair enough. There's nothing wrong with you or your love life just because you and your partner may not have tried 50 different positions for sex, let alone twisted yourselves into spine-defying knots while hanging from a chandelier. You're certainly not alone if you've settled into one or two favorite positions. Many couples do this. Then, they either alternate these positions during different lovemaking sessions or segue from one to the other during a single session.

There's no reason to think your partner finds this devotion to the tried and true displeasing. But wouldn't it be nice to mix things up now and again? After all, as pleasant as it is to sit down to a staple favorite dish for dinner, it's also nice to be served an unexpected delicacy.

Besides, while many men feel that sexual intercourse is equally enjoyable in any position, women often find that certain positions are more likely than others to bring them to a climax. Spicing up your bedroom repertoire can rekindle a level of enthusiasm you and your lover might have forgotten was possible.

Mood Makers

There's scientific proof that new positions up one's arousal level. In a research experiment, a group of male and female college students were shown the same sexually explicit video once a day for four days. Most of them showed diminished excitement by the third day. By the fourth day, some of them were bored. On the fifth day, the researchers showed a new video with the same actors but a new sexual position. Viewer arousal rocketed to nearly the same level as the first day. Novelty—that is, anything to which we're not habituated—intrigues us.

Now, don't get apprehensive about throwing your back out. I'm not suggesting that every guy take it upon himself to become a sexual contortionist. If really exotic positions are of interest to you, you can certainly explore some texts like the Kama Sutra—the ancient Hindu lover's manual that is best known for its detailed cataloguing of sexual positions—some of which look as if they might require several trips to the chiropractor after the loving is over.

In all seriousness, the Kama Sutra is a wonderful resource that offers a lot of information about physical love and pleasure. It's inspirational to view the incredible diversity of sexual positions. But if you want to start a little more gradually, there are plenty of positions possible for people with virtually every level of agility, strength, and stamina.

Before we move on to some positioning advice, I'll share a secret with you. While virtually hundreds of positions have been drawn, photographed, and written about, they are all variations on a few basic themes: man on top, woman on top, man entering woman from behind, side-by-side sex, standing sex, and sex in a sitting or kneeling position.

Man on a Mission

The most common position for lovemaking is known as the *missionary position*—in which a woman and man lie facing each other, with the woman on the bottom and the man on the top. In a survey in which 1,500 women responded to an online poll conducted by *Glamour* magazine, more women (30 percent) chose the missionary position as their position of preference for lovemaking than chose any other style.

Are they just being "traditional"? That could be part of it. But the missionary position has a lot to offer. This position allows for easy entry and deep penetration. Many women consider it the most romantic position because it allows lovers to gaze at one another's faces and easily lends itself to kissing and hugging before, during, and after intercourse. The position also allows for a good deal of clitoral stimulation. Partners can grind their groin areas together so that his pubic bone stimulates the clitoris, or either partner can reach down and stroke the clitoris with a finger.

Tongue Teasers

The **missionary position** got its name from Christian missionaries in the South Pacific and Africa. The missionaries maintained that based on their interpretation of the Book of Genesis, in which man is said to be the superior gender, this was the heavenly-ordained way to make love.

Although some people consider this position uninventive, many exciting add-ons are possible. There are many things you can actively do to increase your woman's pleasure, and your own, while doing it missionary style. These include:

- **The leg lift.** Have your lady lift and bend her legs a little so that her feet rest on your buttocks. This allows your pubic bone to gently rub against her clitoris. It's just a tiny movement away from the basic position, but can really have an appreciable effect.

- ◆ **Over the shoulder.** Place your lover's legs over both your shoulders. This allows you to attain the deepest possible penetration. But take care: with this position, it's possible to get in too deep, which can cause your woman pain. Take cues from your partner and move slowly.

- ◆ **Legs closed.** If a woman keeps her legs together, it forces you to enter her from a sharper angle toward the clitoris. Also, the vagina tightens more around your penis, so added stimulation and sensations will result.

If your woman feels up for something a bit more athletic, another missionary-based technique is to have her wrap her arms and legs around your body and pull up toward you so that her body is no longer touching the mattress or any surface below. This "pull-up" moment may not last long—in part it depends on your strength and her size—but it's a fun sensation, like floating in space while having sex.

Feel free to think of your own variations. Who knows? Maybe you'll come up with a winner that will surprise you both.

Put Your Woman Above You

Twenty-eight percent of women polled by *Glamour* magazine said that the woman-on-top position was their favorite. One likely reason is because when a woman straddles the man and either lies or sits astride him, she does the thrusting. Yes, it's more work for her but, unlike sorting your socks, it's work she truly enjoys.

The woman-on-top position allows the woman to be a more active participant in controlling her own sensations. She can control the depth and speed at which penetration occurs. By slightly shifting her center of gravity she can also alter the angle of penetration.

One caveat though. Some women feel self-conscious in a woman-on-top position. This is usually true if they are insecure about the look of their body. So remember what you learned in Chapter 4, and make her feel beautiful at every opportunity if you want to give her incentive to enjoy this positioning option.

Some women also resist this "superior" position because they assume their man will resent them taking more control of intercourse and being the "dominant" one. But I'll bet you find this an extremely exciting proposition. If you've never tried being on the bottom, let her know you're ready, willing, and able.

As with the missionary position, there are a number of things you can do to increase pleasure in the woman-on-top mode:

- Caress, lick, or suck your lover's breasts, which are within convenient reach of your hands and mouth.

- Stimulate her clitoris manually.

- Encourage her to stimulate herself manually while you watch.

He Says/She Says

"My fiancé told me he loves it when I'm on top because he can see how beautiful my body is. That was a super turn-on for me." —Kelly, 30

As with all of the position categories, woman-on-top allows for super-spicy "advanced" variations. Try having your woman squat over you for even deeper penetration (good for her quadriceps, too). Try having her face backward to alter the angle of penetration.

Coming From Behind

In this position the woman supports herself on her hands and knees while the man enters her vagina from behind. For variation, the woman might support herself on her elbows, or perhaps lie flat.

Many women feel that this style of sex makes for some of their most erotically charged lovemaking. Some say they adore the feeling of being "taken" this way. An added feature of this style of lovemaking is that penetration can be very deep.

It's true that the rear entry position doesn't accommodate eye contact. The easy solution for this: try doing it in front of a mirror.

Among the other things you can do to enhance this position:

- Stimulate your partner with your hands as you penetrate her.

- Fondle her breasts from below.

- Start the usual way, then have your woman push her rear back so she is sitting on her heels.

The man-from-behind position is commonly known as doing it doggie style. That's because rear entry is how dogs mate—as do most mammals. Some women don't like this terminology because of its animalistic connotations. But that's exactly what others love about the term. The idea of being an animal during sex can be quite stimulating.

Side-by-Side

Many couples may not have experienced the joys of side-by-side sex. They have a lot to look forward to. Side-by-side positioning can make for gentle, slow, relaxing sex, because in this position the man can typically thrust for a long time before reaching an orgasm.

If you and your woman enjoy snuggling in the romantic "spooning" position while you doze off, you don't have far to go before turning this into a lovely lovemaking session. Afterward, you can drift off in one another's embrace. In side-by-side sex, both partners lie on their sides with their legs apart. If they like, one partner's leg can rest over the other. If the woman lifts her knees up a bit, she may find it allows for easier penetration.

To embellish side-by-side sex …

- Have your lover draw her knees all the way up into the fetal position for greater tightness.

- Caress her breasts as you thrust.

- Stroke her clitoris while you are inside her.

- Lay side-by-side facing toward one another and have your lady wrap her legs around yours.

He Says/She Says

"I love making sideways love in the morning. It's a wonderful transition from a dreamy state to wakefulness. The memory makes me feel loved all day long."
—Abbie, 34

The scissors position is a popular variation on side-by-side sex. The woman lies on her side and raises one leg. The man enters her from the front, as he would in missionary style. Both of you can move around freely without tiring, and you can have full access for fondling her breasts and rear.

A Standing Date

Why should a woman stand up when she can take a load off her feet? The answer, say ladies who like to do it in a vertical position, is that having sex standing up seems risky, urgent, and therefore very erotic. A "gotta have you now" dynamic underscores fast, spontaneous sex.

Because it's a position that can be achieved without the removal of much clothing, standing is also considered the ideal way to have a quickie. And while women certainly like lots of foreplay and prolonged lovemaking sessions as a rule, a hot and heavy quickie is a nice occasional exception to that rule.

One caution: standing sex requires some degree of balance and flexibility. Usually one partner is shorter than the other, so you have to find a way to align yourselves for intercourse. What often works best is for the woman to wrap her legs around your waist. To avoid back strain on your part, it helps to have your partner supported by a wall behind her.

You can jazz up a standing position with these techniques:

- Keep as much clothing as possible on and suggest your woman do the same.

- Have your partner wear really high heels so that she can align her genitals with yours.

- Try merging a standing position with rear entry—she stands on tiptoes and you bend your knees to achieve a good angle.

- Concoct a joint fantasy about doing it in an elevator, or sneaking off to a coat closet at a party or restaurant.

Standing is one of those positions that you most likely won't use a majority of the time. That's why it's so much fun. It's like allowing yourself and your woman to indulge in tasty fast food once in a while.

Sitting or Kneeling

Sitting and kneeling positions also allow for a break in the routine. These positions can enhance a woman's tightness and provide a sharper angle for entry.

Here's a kneeling favorite. Get your woman to lie on the bed while you kneel and sit on your ankles, between her thighs. Take hold of her thighs and slide her toward you. Her bottom and lower back should be elevated while her ankles or lower legs rest on your shoulders. In this position you can apply clitoral pressure with your hands or your woman can massage her clitoris with her fingers. You can also massage her stomach, hips, and thighs. Keep in mind that this position is not designed for rapid lovemaking, but rather a slow and intimate session.

As for sitting, try having your woman straddle you, facing toward you or away, while she is seated in your lap. Initiate a session in a nice, comfortable easy chair. You can also do it sitting upon your bed, face to face. What women especially enjoy about this position is the deep intimacy that comes with being eye level with their partner. Even though your movements are somewhat restricted, you get a lot of full-body contact.

A nice thing about sitting or kneeling positions is that they are easy to transition into from other positions. For example, if you are in the woman-on-top position, you can just pull her legs forward and you can sit up. In the man-on-top position, you can do likewise.

Pleasing Pillows

In missionary, doggie, spooning, and many other positions, you can increase your lady's comfort and make the experience more penetrative by using pillows as love-making aids. For example, in doggie style, you can place one or more pillows beneath her abdomen or groin. In the kneeling position, where you pull her thighs toward you, you can place a pillow under her lower back.

While you can use the pillows that are normally in your bed, it's fun—and somewhat more sensible in terms of laundering issues—to use pillows specifically made to enhance sexual pleasure. One kind is the angling pillow, sometimes known as the "liberator." It comes in four sloped triangle-shaped components that can be used separately or together (feel free to mix and match). This kind of pillow is made from microfiber, which eliminates slipping and sliding. The nylon shell is water-resistant and lubricants and massage oil can be easily cleaned off.

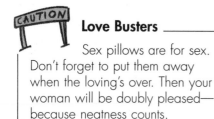

Love Busters

Sex pillows are for sex. Don't forget to put them away when the loving's over. Then your woman will be doubly pleased—because neatness counts.

Another kind of sex pillow, called the "sweetheart" is shaped like a fluffy red heart. It's soft and velvety and very girl-friendly. Its stuffing even has scents of rose and lavender.

When introducing anything new in the sex department, it's a good idea to broach the subject first before springing on your lady. She may not react as positively as you'd hoped if she walks into her bedroom and sees her bedspread or sheets adorned with foreign objects. It might be fun to shop for sex pillows together, and it's easy to do so online. Try www.justpillows.com, or specialty shops that sell sexual toys (more on this in Chapter 19).

About Her Back Door

Now we come to what some women, admittedly, think of as a sore subject. Although many heterosexual couples enjoy anal sex, some people—especially some women—are put-off by the idea.

Nevertheless, you might be surprised how many have tried this style of lovemaking. According to the Kinsey Institute, 43 percent of married women have done so. Of those, about 40 percent say they found the experience a positive one.

A woman's anus contains many nerve endings that, when stimulated, can generate many pleasurable sensations. Even so, some women just aren't interested in trying. They feel they get quite enough pleasure via other sexual means, thank you. They may associate anal sex with an unbreakable taboo, or they may fear what is likely to be some initial discomfort.

Like many men, you might be intrigued by the concept, even if you have never said so aloud. Men who have tried anal penetration contend that the anus provides a very tight fit. A pleasurable amount of pressure is applied to the penis by the anal muscles. Many also admit to enjoying the psychological rush that comes from entering "the forbidden land." Even so, if your woman is firmly against considering the idea of anal sex, you must respect her right to say no. This activity, like any other, must be completely consensual.

Talk about it first. Ask your partner if she has had any previous experience with anal sex. She might tell you about specific medical problems she has—such as hemorrhoids that cause her to be reluctant. Please be sensitive to any concerns on her part. Don't try to pressure her into trying something she does not want to do. If she is turned off by the idea and only agreeable because she thinks it will please you, reassure her that there are plenty of other things you can do that will make you happy, and move on.

If, on the other hand, your partner expresses interest in finding out what erotic benefits anal sex has to offer, the proper way to begin is with extreme gentleness and ease. Also, keep in mind that anal sex is not just anal intercourse but that it also encompasses stimulation of the anus by a finger and oral stimulation. These pleasures can be an end unto themselves or a wonderful way to test the waters and find out if your lover wants to explore going further.

The easiest and gentlest way to begin to stimulate the anus is by softly rubbing your partner there during intercourse or—perhaps better yet—during oral sex. Massage the area slowly—with a clean, nail-trimmed, and well-lubricated finger—and see how your lover responds. If she yells, "Stop that!" or pulls your hand away, you will know you're barking up the wrong tree, so to speak. If she moans or sighs with pleasure or otherwise indicates she wants more, then you can insert your finger a little further. Keep listening for cues and reading her body language to see if she continues to be comfortable and agreeable every step of the way. Also, be aware that even a small change in angle, depth, or pressure can make a big difference in what she is experiencing. So go very, very slowly.

If gentle thrusting of a finger or two fingers feels good, your partner might be ready to try intercourse. If so, put on a condom—a safe sex must—and insert the head of your penis slowly. If this is the first time, be aware that insertion of the head may be all her sphincter muscle will allow. If she is very relaxed, however, you may be able to penetrate a bit deeper and begin thrusting rhythmically. Never force any movement. When it's time to withdraw, do this slowly as well, because quick withdrawal can also cause discomfort.

Mood Makers

While the vagina can supply some of its own lubrication, the rectum does not. Any anal play requires a lubricant, and lots of it. Apply it to the anus as well as to your finger, or to your penis if you are attempting intercourse. Some lubricants are specifically formulated for this purpose and they are usually of the thicker, heavier variety.

Know, too, that it is unhygienic to insert a finger or penis that has penetrated the rectum into the vagina. If you are planning to move on to vaginal stimulation or vaginal intercourse, stop and wash your hands or genitals beforehand.

If it turns out this style of lovemaking is agreeable to you both, you will likely find that it avails more and more pleasure as time goes on. As both partners become more relaxed, penetration can become easier and deeper. If it's not for you, so be it. There are so many wonderful ways to make love, you needn't feel that any one of them is the be-all and end-all. Remember, no form of lovemaking will ultimately be pleasurable unless both parties are wholeheartedly enjoying it.

The Least You Need to Know

♦ Varying sexual positions will increase your woman's arousal level.

♦ You don't need to be an acrobat or yoga master to try new lovemaking positions—simple variations are possible without requiring a visit to the chiropractor.

♦ All sexual positions, no matter how esoteric, fall into one of six simple categories: man-on-top, woman-on-top, man-from-behind, side-by-side, standing, and sitting/kneeling.

♦ Pillows for sex add comfort and add intensity to female orgasms by allowing for deeper penetration.

♦ Anal sex may be unappealing to some women, but many heterosexual couples enjoy it—if you want to broach the subject, do so gently.

Chapter **18**

Ultra-Orgasms

In This Chapter

- Fundamental principles of Tantric sexuality
- Getting started with Tantric techniques
- Start and stop techniques
- Enhancing and extending orgasms
- The role of attitude in sex

A creative and enlightening way to continue to explore the pleasures of lovemaking with your partner is to learn a bit about what is known as the Tantra. Rooted in eastern spiritual philosophy, Tantra incorporates practices aimed at making lovers feel more connected to one another, and also connected to a higher level of consciousness through sexuality.

Tantra also offers what are reputed to be transcendent and rapturous bodily sensations. Your willingness to experience Tantra, even in moderation, has the potential to please your woman on the physical, spiritual, and emotional plane. This chapter will get you started.

The Tantra Mantra

Now, hold on. If you're thinking about skipping this chapter, because it just doesn't seem like your cup of tea, let me address a couple of apprehensions you might have. First, you may think that Tantric sex practices are only for those whose idea of a good time is sitting in esoteric yoga positions trying to levitate. Not so. It is true that *Tantra* contains a myriad sexual positions and techniques that require a good degree of flexibility and fortitude, but many are achievable by "amateurs." There's no reason to feel incompetent if you only wish to dabble.

Tongue Teasers

Tantra is derived from a Sanskrit word meaning "woven together." The origins of sacred Tantric practice and doctrine can be traced back at least to the Indus Valley civilization that was contemporary with the Sumerian and the beginnings of the Egyptian Old Kingdom.

Stop focusing on the things that your body can't do. No true Tantric practitioner would be unhappy with his body and its form and limitations. That's because Tantric sex calls for lovers to experience their bodies as manifestations of the divine. Yes, even those love handles and aching lumbars should be honored and treated with respect.

Now we come to another apprehension. If words like "divine" and "spirit" are throwing you off, rest assured that your particular spiritual or religions beliefs will not be compromised by incorporating a Tantric perspective. In short, Tantric philosophy espouses:

◆ **Approaching your partner with reverence.** Tantra helps lovers deepen their respect for, and even awe of, one another. It celebrates the undeniable ways in which male (yang) and female (yin) complete one another. Many of its positions allow for eye contact and full-body closeness meant to stimulate the heart in addition to the hormones.

◆ **Staying focused on the moment.** A key underlying principle of Tantra is that the journey takes precedence over the destination. Lovers who adapt Tantric love-making techniques may devote hours to a sexual interlude, while delaying climax as long as possible. No more of your mind wandering off to your job performance review or your chores or your checkbook smack in the midst of sex.

◆ **Becoming more self-aware.** Tantra teaches lovers to become more in touch with their bodies, and to be in greater control of them. For example, it teaches simultaneous deep breathing and meditation techniques that enable you to enjoy sex more by becoming more relaxed. It also offers means of developing certain muscles that are used in lovemaking. Finally, it offers methods of delaying orgasm so that sexual encounters may be extended.

So to sum up what could be called the Tantra mantra: this approach to sexuality teaches reverence, focus, and self-awareness. These are beneficial traits in any context, and available to all through this intriguing route.

Perhaps your woman has heard of Tantric sex and been curious about it. Even if she has not, she would almost certainly be interested in exploring with you ways to get closer and to prolong your sexual encounters—providing, of course, that you have read the earlier parts of this book and have taken care to help her out so that she is not too exhausted for prolonged sexual activity.

> **CAUTION**
>
> **Love Busters**
>
> If you are going to introduce the idea of Tantra, be sure you take it seriously. Eliminate distractions, and devote some time to your efforts. While you're at it, make sure your woman doesn't have two loads of laundry running. If she does, help her fold and sort before you begin. Tantra is the opposite of the "wham-bam, thank you ma'am" approach to sex. It requires an uninterrupted window of opportunity.

Starting Down the Path

Getting started with Tantric techniques means being prepared to nurture intimacy. All that's required is the desire to discover more about yourself and your partner. Start slowly by trying a few basic preliminary techniques.

Synchronized Breathing

An integral part of Tantric sex is harmonized breathing between partners. These breaths should be long, slow, and conscious. You can practice such breathing on your own by:

♦ Inhaling through the nose slowly, noticing the cool sensation in your nostrils

♦ Letting the breath flow all the way down into your diaphragm and abdomen, filling these spaces with energy

♦ Holding the inhalation for several seconds

♦ Exhaling through the mouth so that the exhalation lasts a few seconds longer than the inhalation

Practicing this type of breathing in step with a partner affirms your unity as a couple—the blending of yin and yang. A lovely, peaceful way to experience breathing together is to lie in the spoons position with the man cradling the woman. This allows you not only to hear but also to feel each other's inhalations and exhalations. Practice slowing and elongating the breaths until you are inhaling and exhaling as one. This mirrored breathing technique is at once relaxing and erotic.

A variation on this is for one of you to breathe out at the same tempo as the other breathes in. Experiment with both techniques to find what works best for the two of you.

Soul Gazing

Eye contact is fundamental in Tantric sex. The idea is to look not so much at one another as in to one another. Through intense gazing, it is said that lovers can directly experience one another's souls.

Start by dimming the lights—but don't turn them all the way off. Disrobe and sit across from one another in comfortable cross-legged positions. It's fine to arrange pillows so that you can both sit as comfortably as possible.

Now, don't stare, but do gaze deeply into your partner's eyes as she gazes into yours. If you like, you can affirm in words how much you love each other and how important you are to one another, but silence is perfectly acceptable, too, because it will be a very profound sort kind of silence that—in its own way—communicates a great deal.

After a few minutes of gazing at one another without touching, join hands. Now begin breathing in sync, just as you practiced in the spoons position. Now you are making contact with your eyes, your hands, and your breath. Begin to notice the palpable energy that is flowing between you. It might actually feel like a tingle, a bit of an electric current.

Mood Makers

Even if you take nothing else away from Tantra, upping the level of eye contact you and your partner have before and during lovemaking will deepen your relationship and enhance your physical pleasure. Think of eye contact as an erotic meditation.

How long should you remain in this state? As long as you both find it pleasurable. Do not be in a rush to move on, because the longer you stay in this state, the more enjoyable any ensuing lovemaking activities will be.

I know it seems hard to imagine when you are beginning, but ultimately you may want to soul-gaze for 20 or 30 minutes or more. But starting with even five minutes will give you a new perspective on your partner and the bond you share.

Some Tantric Positions

If you and your partner are ready to move on to sexual intercourse, there are myriad positions suggested by Tantra. In fact, there are so many that if you are intrigued you might well want to pick up a book completely devoted to the subject—like *The Complete Idiot's Guide to Tantric Sex* by Dr. Judy Kuriansky (Alpha, 2001)—for more ideas.

Some of these positions are easier to achieve than others. You should try what you're comfortable with and not worry about those that seem difficult for you to attempt. What's most important is to note what all the positions have in common: the goal of heightening not only physical pleasure but also emotional and spiritual connection. In any position, the couple should try to remain cognizant of energy exchange between yin and yang.

The Lotus

In this quintessential Tantric position, the man and the woman sit facing one another, with the man's penis inside the woman's vagina. She wraps her legs around his behind, and he either does the same or leaves his legs outstretched. This position offers full body contact and facilitates eye contact.

The Goddess

In this man-on-top position, the woman draws up both her knees until they nuzzle the curves of her breasts. She places her feet in her lover's armpits. This is a favorite of petite women—also those with some flexibility. It can take a bit of practice to act like a Goddess.

The Cup

The couple lies side-by-side, face-to-face. Although his penis is inside her vagina, the man does not thrust. Instead the couple creates friction by both moving their thighs back and forth and up and down. After some time, the man can begin thrusting gently.

The Foot Yoke

Seated erect, the woman folds one leg to her body and stretches the other out in front of her. The man mirrors her position. As they move closer, each keeping one leg outstretched, she slides so that she nestles atop him. He then enters her.

The Serpent

The woman can lie down on top of the man, or the man can lie down on top of the woman. Neither partner spreads their legs. The penis is inside the vagina, while the two bodies, from head to toe, are flat on top of each other in full contact.

The Suspended Position

The woman sits in her partner's hands, which are cupped around her buttocks. Her arms are around his neck, and her thighs grip his waist. As the man remains still, she thrusts, pushing her feet back and forth against a wall.

> **Mood Makers**
>
> To help get into position more easily and precisely, you might consider purchasing a Tantric chair, available for order over the Internet. The chair's design creates a platform enabling both lovers to be entirely supported during intimacy. With the chair, many new angles and positions are possible. Embarrassed? Don't be. Because the chair is also designed to fit unobtrusively into one's home décor, you won't need to explain its purpose to your in-laws or other guests. It simply looks like a comfortable designer chair.

Starting and Stopping

In any sexual position used for the Tantric method, the idea is to go slowly. The build-up to orgasm is considered extremely important, and the longer it lasts the more intense orgasm will be.

In Tantra, it's not uncommon for various forms of foreplay to go on for a couple of hours. Yes, I said a couple of hours. What do you mean, "Get a life?" Hey, it's still not as long as a NASCAR race or a basketball playoff with double overtime.

One Tantric technique said to especially intensify orgasm involves a kind of cresting and falling foreplay known as "riding the wave." First, the man inserts his penis in the woman's vagina and rests it there. He then withdraws it and uses it to massage his lover's clitoris and vaginal opening before sliding it back in. The cycle is repeated multiple times, with both parties repeatedly feeling they are a hair's breadth away from climax. When climax does occur, it's an especially ecstatic experience.

The Full-Body Orgasm

As a result of breath control, eye contact, extended foreplay, and start and stop techniques, it is possible for a woman to have something known as an full-body orgasm (FBO) during lovemaking. FBO may sound like an acronym for a labor union or a government spy organization, but it's actually much more exciting. In a typical female orgasm, sensation emanates from, and remains centered in, the clitoral or vaginal area. In a full body orgasm, sensation is experienced in every part of the body. Quivers and tingles may begin anywhere—for example, the toes, the backs of the knees, the thighs, the abdomen—and then radiate and reverberate all over. In addition to contractions during the climax, a woman in the throes of an FBO frequently experiences a surge of heat and a sense that an electrical current is passing through her body.

Full-body orgasms during Tantric sex are also noted for their spiritual component. They are a means of achieving unity not only with one's lover but also with the entirety of creation. This may sound a little lofty, but in actuality orgasm is one of those all too rare experiences in life that allow us to enter an altered state of being and transcend everyday mundanities. It is not surprising that many Eastern mystics have equated this "loss of sense of self" with spiritual bliss.

During any orgasm, one has the sense of stepping, however briefly, outside the barriers of linear time. Those sublime seconds seem, in their own way, to last an eternity. With Tantric sex, orgasms allow one to linger even longer in such a gloriously suspended state.

He Says/She Says

"Orgasms are different for me now that we have slowed down and extended our lovemaking. First, I feel my pelvis and abdomen get all tingly and hot. As my partner keeps touching me in that perfect place my whole body wells with sensation. Soon I'm vibrating from head to toe. At that point, he could literally touch me anywhere and it would prolong the ecstasy. After it's over, I feel completely fulfilled from our lovemaking."
—Grace, 35

By relaxing and bringing more awareness to sexuality, it is possible to experience oneself as a conduit for universal energy. Some might say this is because our chakras—bodily energy centers—become unblocked. Others provide a less metaphysical explanation and say this sensation is a result of one's own psychological preparation to "let go" and be open to enhanced experience. However we explain the logistics of spiritual sensations during orgasm, the result is one that will enhance any relationship—because it enhances feelings of love, gratitude, and awe.

Some research has been conducted on the benefits of enhanced and extended orgasms. Benefits are reputed to be numerous. They include:

- A reduction in sympathetic (adrenalinelike) nervous function.

- An increase in parasympathetic function (associated with relaxation and well-being).

- A release of beneficial hormones and balancing of their levels.

- A sense of mental clarity and increased ability to solve problems intuitively and in new ways.

- A sense of peace.

Those who experience extended orgasms also report a strengthened self-esteem. They say they feel more powerful and effective in all areas of life. And, yes, they also have a lot of fun.

Secrets of Sexual Self-Control

According to Tantric beliefs, men can also bring another dimension to their orgasm. What would you say if I told you that you might be able to have multiple orgasms without ejaculating? Men who become adept at practicing Tantra achieve *dry orgasms.*

 Tongue Teasers

The term **dry orgasms,** referring to male orgasms in which semen is not ejaculated may sound like an oxymoron—but it is not. Physiologically, it is possible for a man to have an orgasm without ejaculating. On the other hand, it is also possible for a man to ejaculate without much physical pleasure at all. Orgasm and ejaculation are functions that are activated by separate parts of the nervous system. Although they often do occur simultaneously, each of these functions can be experienced independent of one another.

The theory, as explained by Tantra experts, is that when a man ejaculates he expends energy and is thus "spent." The idea is that if he saves his semen he can have more energy for orgasmic sensation and more peaks in his sexual experience. He can also continue with lovemaking for a much longer stretch of time.

The techniques that assist one in developing these skills can be learned and mastered with specific breathing and movement exercises and meditations. These steps enable a man to be aroused and relaxed at the same time. The techniques are not difficult per se, but they do take time and concentrated effort to master. If this is a course of action that intrigues you, you can learn more about them in specialized books such as Taoist master Mantak Chia's *The Multi-Orgasmic Man* (Harper San Francisco, 1997) and *The Multi-Orgasmic Couple* (Harper San Francisco 2002).

Even if the idea of separating orgasm from ejaculation does not appeal to you, men can still have full-body orgasms. As in women, these orgasms will create sensations well beyond those in the genital area.

"Riding the wave," as described earlier in this chapter, is very conducive to bringing on an FBO. In addition it helps to keep your eyes open and take in all the visual stimulants associated with making love to your woman. Keep your focus strong as well. Be aware of all the pleasurable sensations that lead up to orgasm, and breathe consciously and rhythmically as your climax begins.

Above all, relax. Don't be so concerned about when you're going to come. As with many things in life, detaching anxiety from orgasm makes it all the easier and more enjoyable to experience.

> **Love Busters**
>
> There are two caveats to be aware of with regard to dry orgasms. First, speak with your physician if this is something you want to pursue, because some people have voiced concern about whether this practice might lead to prostate or bladder problems. Second, nonejaculatory sex is not birth control. A woman can still get pregnant from pre-ejaculatory fluid on the tip of a man's penis.

Permission Granted

When it comes to Tantric sex or any kind of sex, the most potent sex organ in the human body is the brain. On one level, the brain must process stimuli and instruct the body as to how to react. On another level, though, it must interpret any stimuli with regard to any attitudes you hold.

Depending on what opinions a person holds about sex and sexuality, one brain may register an experience as erotic; another may register the same experience as neutral, or even offensive. The brain can even undermine sexual experience by diverting attention away from pleasurable bodily sensations by introducing irrelevant even unnerving thoughts. If you're not committed to enjoying your sexual experience and do not feel comfortable giving yourself and your partner this gift, you may spend the majority of time during a sexual interlude planning your estimated quarterly taxes.

If you want to enjoy sex—Tantric or otherwise—more, and help your partner to do the same, it's a good idea to take stock of your attitude toward sexuality. It probably has been shaped by many things, including your cultural and religious upbringing, the media to which you've been exposed, and the influence of your parents, teachers, and peers. But are the things you learned as a child and adolescent relevant to your contemporary reality? They may or may not be. If there is a "nagging voice" in your background telling you that various aspects of sex are wrong or "dirty" they are surely inhibiting your ability to experience a full range of pleasures in your committed relationship. The same, of course, holds true for your partner.

Talking about how your sexual attitudes were shaped, and addressing those of them that may be outmoded can be a weight off both your shoulders. There's no reason why you and your lover should play by anyone else's rules. You need to grant yourselves permission to be in charge of and take responsibility for your own sexuality.

It's for the two of you to determine what is and isn't acceptable when it comes to your sexual bond. It really isn't anyone else's business. This is not to say "anything goes" and that no discriminating values apply. But you and your partner can determine your values together and vow to jettison any lingering "shoulds" and "shouldn'ts" that no longer seem to make sense.

When you make a conscious attempt to look at and re-evaluate your sexual influences, the result can be extremely liberating. The process can also bring the two of you much closer together.

CAUTION   Love Busters _____

> If you're hearing negative voices in your head when you have sex, you're not crazy. These are echoes from your past, voicing values that you've absorbed without scrutinizing them. To enjoy yourself more, learn to dispute any negative self-talk. If a voice says, "Stop," you can counter it by affirming in your mind that you and your partner are enjoying what you're doing, that there is nothing to be ashamed of, and that you are going to continue to pleasure your partner in this way.

Further Your Tanric Knowledge

Many informative websites offer extensive knowledge and links to resources regarding Tantric sex. One of my favorites is tantra.com. Here you can learn about techniques, access articles, and even enter discussion forums.

There are also a wide variety of books on Tantra. In addition to the ones mentioned earlier in this chapter, some very popular ones include:

◆ *The Art of Tantric Sex* by Nitya laCroix (DK Adult, 1997). The book's focus is on channeling energy during lovemaking.

◆ *Tantric Love: A Nine Step Guide to Transforming Lovers into Soul Mates* by Ma Ananda Sarita and Swami Anand Geho (Fireside, 2001). This amply illustrated book offers exercises to join the souls of man and woman.

◆ *Tantric Secrets For Men: What Every Woman Will Want Her Man to Know About Enhancing Sexual Ecstasy* by Kerry Riley and Diane Riley (Destiny Books, 2002). For pragmatists, this work contains straight, down-to-earth talk about Tantric sex minus a lot of the Eastern mysticism.

There are also numerous videos and DVDs about Tantric sex. One favorite, part of the *Better Sex* video series, is "The Tantric Guide to Better Sex" (Sinclair Institute, 2005). Finally, you and your lady can take workshops in Tantric love at a number of spas and retreats, such as the Omega Institute in Rhinebeck, New York (see Appendix B for details).

The Least You Need to Know

◆ Tantra stresses reverence for one's partner, staying focused in the moment, and self-awareness and self-control.

◆ Synchronized breathing and eye contact are simple and effective ways to get started with Tantric practices.

◆ A common goal of Tantric sex positions is to heighten not only physical pleasure but also emotional connection.

◆ As a result of breath control, eye contact, extended foreplay, and start and stop techniques, women and men may have full-body orgasms.

◆ Enhanced and extended orgasms have numerous physical and mental benefits, and induce a sense of spiritual connectedness.

◆ In sex, as in most things, attitude is key—give yourself permission to deepen your sexual experience.

"V" Is for Variety

In This Chapter

- The allure of love accessories
- Love toys to please her
- Lubrication aids
- Erotica for her
- The art of the striptease

S. J. Perelman once quipped, "Love is not the dying moan of a violin—it's the triumphant twang of a bedspring." There is nothing like variety to make those springs twang. This chapter will tell you how to incorporate woman-pleasing toys and erotica into your life in order to liven things up and add a delicious new element of fun and adventure to your love life.

Love Accessories

Women love to accessorize. Accumulating accoutrements for any activity makes that activity itself more fun. Notice that if your lady starts taking yoga classes, she will soon buy herself yoga outfits, yoga books, and a yoga mat. If she takes up gardening it will be garden tools, garden gloves, and a garden hat. Why should sex be any different? There are lots of ways to accessorize lovemaking with what are commonly known as sex toys. Besides offering the fun of shopping itself, accessories can enhance physical and mental stimulation.

If you're thinking, "Sex toys! Oh, my partner will never go for that!"—think again. Sex toys have become more and more mainstream in recent years. They're regularly reviewed in magazines. They're sold on websites and at a growing number of specialty boutique-type shops, some owned and operated by women. A number of books have been devoted exclusively to the topic. Maybe, without telling you her secret, your partner has even sneaked off with a few of her girlfriends and attended one of those popular shop-at-home sex toy parties. Here you thought she was off buying Tupperware!

On the other hand, maybe your lover is like many women who, although curious, have never touched a sex toy. Maybe she isn't even sure what sex toys are. Perhaps you're the same way. Maybe you've never had time to explore these kinds of accessories because you've been too busy searching for the perfect golf clubs or the ultimate set of Allen wrenches.

So here's a primer: sex toys are any objects that can be used to make sex more enjoyable. They are different from sensual aids—satin sheets, scented candles, and mirrors—in that sex toys are directly involved in sexual activities. Sex toys can include vibrators, dildos, penis rings, restraints, and—for the really adventurous (not to mention the physically fit)—sex swings and slings.

The following sections will elaborate on sex toy options, but before you head off on a shopping spree, here are a few things to keep in mind if you are hoping to introduce sex toys into a relationship for the first time, or to incorporate new toys that you have never used before:

- Test the waters. Ask your partner what she might like to try. Ask if she's intrigued with the idea of what you want to try.

- Respect her urge for privacy. Acquiring sex toys needn't involve visiting a sex toy emporium (though there are lots of upscale ones that cater to discriminating clientele). It can all be done online from the privacy of your home.

- Be prepared to start slowly. Even online "window shopping" can be a turn-on.

Your woman may protest that you and she need no props in order to make passionate love, that your bodies alone are more than enough. No doubt they are, but novelty usually infuses lovemaking with a jolt of new energy. Once you've introduced the topic, let the idea sit with your woman for a while. Don't force the issue. Now that you've piqued her curiosity—and stoked her urge to shop—she may well be the one to raise the subject again.

Good Vibrations

Vibrators are among the most common sex toys. You can purchase a garden-variety vibrator just about anywhere you can purchase household appliances. That's convenient, because you can pick up a new toaster or vacuum cleaner at the same time. Even if you get a basic model that doesn't appear in any way sexual—the kind where the vibrator's packaging says it's designed for massage and relaxation—any vibrator can do very pleasant things when applied to the genitals.

Vibrators meant to be specifically sexual, however, are much more aesthetically pleasing. They come in more shapes, sizes, and colors than you can imagine. They range from traditional eight-inch phallus-dimensioned contraptions to sleek, finger-fitted devices.

Vibrators can be loud or soft in sound, strong or gentle in touch, fast-paced or deliciously slow. In fact, there are so many ways to vibrate that some women have been known to joke that these types of toys can render men superfluous. Don't worry. I said it was a joke.

Many women do use vibrators to please themselves while their men are otherwise engaged or on the road. But you can certainly get in on the vibrator action when you're around. You can use a vibrator as part of foreplay, to get your woman in the mood. You can also integrate it into your lovemaking by watching your partner use it or by helping her use it. In addition to being used on the vulva, vibrators can be placed between a man and woman during intercourse, producing bonus sensations for both lovers.

 **Mood Makers** _____

Rabbit-type vibrators, made famous on *Sex and the City*, are billed as "doing everything but the dishes." The velvety-textured shaft twirls for G-spot stimulation, the rabbit ears flutter along the clitoris, and "pearls" roll and tumble at the vaginal opening. Some rabbits come with cords; others are cordless. The cordless style is easiest to manipulate, but whatever you do, don't forget the batteries.

Pleasing With Plastic

Dildos are penis-shaped plastic, latex, or silicon items intended to be inserted into the vagina or the rectum. Unlike vibrators, they don't move unless you move them. That means one has quite a bit more control over the amount of stimulation and speed of thrusting.

Dildos come in many styles. Some are crafted so that they very much resemble actual penises. Why bother with a plastic penis if the "in the flesh" model is available? Because dildos are very rigid and stay that way indefinitely. Now, don't take offense. Every guy can use a stand-in sometimes and many couples like to use dildos to prolong their sexual encounters.

A dildo can be used by a man on a woman, or the woman can use it on herself as her partner watches. A dildo may be especially useful when used in addition to oral or manual stimulation of the vulva.

All Tied Up

Some women like to reinforce their fantasy scenarios by using a variety of restraints for bondage. Some women feel freer to express themselves when restrained, while others enjoy being "forced" to relax and just receive pleasure. Whatever the motivation, restraints can add an element of perceived risk and danger to a sexual encounter, which many people find enthralling.

I know what you're thinking: Why spend a lot of money on restraints? Can't I just use some of my old ties—maybe the wide paisley ones my woman forbids me to wear? Well, yes. But your woman will get into the spirit of the thing more if you spring for something a bit more specialized and more elegant than yard sale fodder.

A wide variety of restraints are available in every material from silk and velvet scarves and ropes to leather cuffs and buckling bonds (which allow you to clamp your lover's wrists or ankles together in a single, swift motion). Of course, there are always metal handcuffs—and would you believe you can get some of these adorned with rhinestones? (What girl doesn't like a little extra bling?)

Blindfolds are also related to the bondage dynamic. For some women, not being able to see what their partner is doing can add significantly to arousal. Homemade blindfolds tend to slip off or feel uncomfortable, so do look into those that are specifically crafted for your activities. If you really want to try a basic version first, try a sleep mask—the kind you might use to catch a nap on an airplane. You might have a collection of them if you're a frequent flyer, or you can buy one in any drugstore.

With This Ring

For you, there are a wide variety of rings—leather, metal, or stretchable jelly—designed to be worn at the base of an erect penis, where they encourage blood flow to remain in the male organ. Penis rings provide adornment—in case you also enjoy a little bling—and some men find the rings can slightly add to the size and firmness of an erection. The type of penile rings that have a knob or other extension can stimulate a woman's clitoris or labia during intercourse.

Love Busters

Never use a ring that is too tight or that causes discomfort. It can cut off blood flow to the penis and be very dangerous. Never leave a ring on the penis for more than half an hour. Jelly rings are great because they're stretchable and can be easily removed as needed.

For Swingers

Ever think about running away and joining the circus? Now you can stay home and still feel like something of a trapeze artist. Sex swings and slings are specially designed for holding a man or woman in a semi reclining position with the legs apart. The swing hangs from an eyebolt or a special stand, and allows for all manner of positions that would be difficult or impossible to achieve without its support.

These items are expensive and many consider them "over the top." It's not where I would start experimenting with sex toys. That would be like heading out for the advanced trails the first time out skiing. If you and your woman are sex toy novices, stick with the bunny slope. But, hey, if you're up for a window-shopping trip, they're at least fun to look at. Let your imagination run wild.

A Tube of Lube

Lubricants are not sex toys, strictly speaking. But they are certainly sex aids that many couples find indispensable. We used to think of sexual lubricants as a classic tube of KY, but there are many more varieties now. A delightful range of flavored lubricants that includes cherry, strawberry, vanilla, piña colada, mint, banana, peach, bubblegum, chocolate raspberry, caramel cream, and—of course—passion fruit. There are even lubes that warm instantly when you put them in the palm of your hand and rub.

Speaking of which, women are really warming up to the idea of experimenting with different types of lubricants, and that in turn is opening them up to being more inventive in the bedroom in general. So think of expanding your lube repertoire as dipping your toe in the waters of pleasurable possibilities.

Lubes are the slippery secret behind sensational sex. You and your partner may not think you "need" a lubricant if she doesn't have a problem with vaginal dryness. The truth, however, is that lubricants benefit everyone. They enhance friction and ease penetration. Because they eliminate soreness, they also help to promote longer sexual encounters.

He Says/She Says

"At her bridal shower, one of my wife's bridesmaids gave my wife a basket of lubricants. I know she blushed and laughed like crazy. Those tubes sat in a dresser drawer for years before we pulled one out on a whim. Now we're definitely sorry we didn't dip into that basket sooner! We've already bought many refills."
—Clark, 30

If you've never tried a lubricant, you're not alone. Sex surveys show that some lovers resist them, saying they're "unnatural" or "messy." But those who use lubricants swear by them. Even if your lover self-lubricates very well, slippery aids have a lot to offer.

Don't feel for a moment that by using a lube you are doing anything to undermine Mother Nature. Yes, it's wonderful that Mother Nature thought up self-lubrication. But added lubricants are just as natural as any other lovemaking enhancer: seductive lingerie, mood music, dim lighting, or a steamy video.

Some tips on enjoying lubricants:

◆ Choose a lube that doesn't remind your woman of her gynecologist's office. Many women have a negative association with the kind of lubricant jelly applied to speculums in gynecological exams. (If you don't know what a speculum is, let's just say it's a necessary nuisance needed for internal exams—and no woman considers them a pleasure.) Stay away from anything that smells medicinal.

◆ Put lube where it counts. The best place to use a lube is on anything that will be inserted or penetrated, as well as any part of the body that will be stroked or rubbed repeatedly.

◆ Incorporate lube application into your foreplay. Some lovers view lubes as an interruption. Yes, it takes a moment to squeeze some lubricant onto your hand and then apply it, but you and your partner can do this to one another, or you can watch with anticipation as she applies lube to herself.

◆ Try a tasting session. Lubes can work very well for oral sex, but before you try it find out which flavors and textures suit your palate.

◆ Read the entire label. An oil lube will break down the latex in condoms; water-based lube won't. An ingredient called Nonoxynol-9 can be irritating to women with sensitive skin—and men, too. That ingredient also tastes unpleasant and numbs the mouth, so lubes containing it are poor choices for oral sex.

◆ Don't go overboard. If you apply too much lube you will know it, because your sensations will diminish. This is easy enough to remedy, though, especially with a water-based lube. Just wipe some off with a towel or some tissues. (That said, you can never have too much lubricant when you are having anal sex—as discussed in Chapter 17.)

In addition to lubes, and for a novel change of pace, try erotic body dusts—a light powder that you can sprinkle on and rub into your lover's skin. Body dusts are infused with sensual scents like wild berry or honey. While they don't generate slippery friction, they'll leave your lover's body extremely smooth for a unique feel during lovemaking. For added fun, most body dusts come with a feather tickler to use when applying the dust. Now it's your turn to play "French maid." Mmmmmmm.

Erotica for Ladies

One way to garner ideas and inspiration for your woman's fantasies, and to stoke her appetite for loving, is to partake of some adult entertainment together. This may be something you've never even considered. In fact, you might be thinking: "Hey, wait, porn is a guy thing."

Pornography—in the sense of explicit material that primarily conveys visual images of sex—arouses guys because guys are visual creatures who get excited by what they see. But women can get excited by imagery, too. In fact, some scientific evidence suggests that we, as a gender, might be surprised to see how stimulated we might become if we were to expose ourselves to graphic entertainment.

Tongue Teasers
The word **pornography** comes from the Greek word *porneia*, which literally means "writings of and about prostitutes."

In a Northwestern University study, more than 90 gay and straight men, women, and male-to-female transsexuals were shown erotic film scenes with a probe attached to their genitals to indicate when they were aroused. The men and the transsexual subjects were aroused only by scenes that featured members of their preferred-partner gender. Women, however, were aroused by all of the material—whether it featured lesbian scenes, gay male scenes, or mixed-gender scenes. Possibly this is because women—by and large, have had relatively little exposure to pornography, and what's new and unanticipated is arousing.

Whatever the reason, we're clearly not immune to the impact of explicit material. Nevertheless, generally speaking, we prefer a storyline involving a relationship of some sort in order to feel fully engaged with sexually stimulating material. That's why we appreciate erotic scenes within the context of romance novels or within feature films that have a plot involving romance and passion.

No, I'm not talking about romantic chick flicks—though as you learned in Chapter 11, your woman will feel very romantically inclined toward you if you sit with her through one of those without snoring, guffawing, or tossing popcorn. I'm talking about mainstream R-rated movies. Many mainstream films, available at any video store, are apt to get us in the mood. These include:

- *Bull Durham*, with Susan Sarandon, Tim Robbins, and Kevin Costner
- *The Thomas Crown Affair*, with Pierce Brosnan and Renee Russo
- *The Postman Always Rings Twice*, starring Jack Nicholson and Jessica Lange
- *Body Heat*, starring William Hurt and Kathleen Turner
- *No Way Out*, with Kevin Costner and Sean Young
- *Risky Business*, starring Tom Cruise and Rebecca DeMornay

These movies contain scenes that are steamy, while not overt. It certainly doesn't hurt that they have some wonderful eye candy for us, too. (Don't sulk. We still think you're cute. And you get to look at the female stars while we look at the hunks.)

If you've never seen these movies, you won't be sorry for having done so. They're all entertaining, as well as, hot. Even if you have seen them, think what fun you can have watching them with your lover—each of you knowing what the other one is thinking about.

If you want to experiment with more explicit adult films, a female-friendly way to start is the Shane's World series of erotic movies. These films are produced and directed by women. The filmmakers bring a half dozen real people and adult video stars together at various locations for a few days. Because non-scripted human connections are being made, the sex scenes can be far more appealing to us relationship-oriented types. It's like X-rated reality T.V.—*The Bachelor* on steroids.

Love Busters

Pushing the boundaries of your partner's taste isn't sexy; it's exactly the opposite. Reactions to explicit material are subjective. Never insist that your partner watch any material she finds distasteful or degrading.

If you'd like to sample a whole potpourri of films and see what might strike her fancy, modern technology provides a way. Many cable T.V. systems allow subscribers to download movies of all kinds directly and view them at their convenience. Fees are tacked onto your monthly bill. Understandably, this might be much more appealing to your lady than renting erotica at the local video store where she usually checks out Disney movies for the kids.

An Audio Alternative

If erotic films are not your woman's thing—or if you'd like to try expanding into other media—try an interesting alternative that has come on the scene: audio erotica. There is now a variety of adult audio CDs in which women tell erotic stories. The theory behind this new medium is that listeners will have an enjoyable, interactive experience because they will instinctively visualize the intimate situations to which they're listening.

An added bonus: erotic CDs are ultra-portable. You and your lady can listen to women sharing their sexy stories and enticing fantasies as easily as you can listen to music. You can even use your computer to transfer the material to your iPods. It could be just the thing for your listening pleasure when you're apart but thinking about one another.

The Book Nook

If your lady has a literary bent, she might be intrigued with the erotic Sleeping Beauty trilogy. Its three books—*The Claiming of Sleeping Beauty, Beauty's Punishment*, and *Beauty's Release*—written by A.N. Roquelaure, a pseudonym of famed *Interview with a Vampire* author Anne Rice. The author set out to pen this very graphic fairy-tale-with-a-twist in order to prove that women can write erotic as well as men. They can.

Additionally, Lonnie Barbach has compiled a number of erotic story collections, including *Pleasures: Women Write Erotica* and *Erotic Edge: 22 Erotic Stories for Couples*. These make wonderful read-aloud choices. Believe me, your woman will think it sexy and sweet that you want to read her a bedtime story. Finally, you might also try browsing through magazines, such as *Penthouse* letters, together.

Striptease Her

Now I'll tell you another secret about women. Among the many, many erotic possibilities, there is one that nearly every woman I've ever talked with has thought about. Many have even tried it to some degree—much to their men's delight. That activity is the good old-fashioned striptease.

Whether you believe it or not, your lady may be dying to do a little bumping and grinding, and maybe even a little pole dancing (broom handles or bedposts are nice stand-ins) for you.

A striptease is a great way to let you know how sexy she thinks she is—and without a doubt you will agree.

How to get her to live out her fantasy if she's shy? Try doing a Full Monty or Chippendale's-type routine yourself. Come on, you know you want to. And while a little spontaneous stripping is always welcome, it's nice to put a little effort into it and make it a really special event. Here's how:

1. Prepare what you wear underneath. This is the one time you can break the underwear rules outlined in Chapter 10. Go for it, good-looking, and put on that tiger print banana sling if you dare.

2. Select your music. You'll want something with a good beat to inspire Elvis-style hip swiveling. But don't choose music with a tempo that's too fast. It's best to take your time.

3. Remember the "tease" part. This activity is more about the teasing than the stripping. Tantalize your audience of one by moving suggestively.

4. Maintain eye contact. It sends your woman the message that you're doing this for her, and only her.

5. Fling. As you take off an article of clothing, toss it in your lover's direction. (Remember fling, don't wing. Hitting your woman in the eye with a belt buckle ruins the mood.)

6. Stretch out your ending. Once you've removed everything but your skivvies, slow down and tease even more. Allow your lover to really enjoy herself as you give her a glimpse of your equipment, then cover up again.

7. Obey the no-touching rule until you're done. But when you are done—touch!

He Says/She Says

"I couldn't believe it when my husband put on Sister Sledge's "We Are Family" and started strutting around the bedroom taking his clothes off. At first I thought I'd die laughing. But it was obvious he was really into doing a routine and I became entranced. I couldn't believe he'd thought this up. I started yelling, "Take it off. Take it all off!" And he did!"
—Mary, 37

If you're shy about stripping for your woman, practice in front of a mirror. Think of it as a dress rehearsal—or, rather, an undress rehearsal. Tip: you may want to close the blinds if the neighbors are home.

The Least You Need to Know

- Sex toys can add extra excitement to your lovemaking because they add the spark of the new and offer ways to enhance pleasurable sensations.

- If you and your partner have never tried sex toys, you can start to dabble slowly—try going window-shopping on the Internet for inspiration.

- A woman doesn't need to have a "dryness problem" to use or appreciate a lubricant; lubes can enhance the pleasure of any sexual encounter.

- Adult films, audio CDs, and even books can offer new ideas and inspiration—your woman will most enjoy erotic material that has a good storyline and that details relationships, as well as, sex.

- Stripteasing for your woman is a surefire pleaser because it creates a feeling of anticipation—and may prompt your woman to let lose her own strip teasing fantasy.

Chapter 20

Letting Her Please You

In This Chapter

- ◆ Why any woman can be a better lover
- ◆ Helping her initiate sex without feeling silly
- ◆ Guiding her to your erogenous zones
- ◆ Helping her overcome oral sex inhibitions

Would you be pleased if your woman was more skilled in bed, and more sensitive to your sexual needs? What if she were even more enthusiastic and more adventurous when it came to lovemaking? These are rhetorical questions, of course. *What guy wouldn't be pleased*?

Well, this may come as a surprise to you, but your woman would very much enjoy giving you more pleasure. Few things make a woman feel more sexy and desirable than really satisfying her man. You may not realize it, but you have it in your power to help your partner evolve into the kind of lover she's always longed to be. This chapter will tell you how.

The Good Girl/Bad Girl Paradox

Do you ever have the feeling that just beneath the surface there is a part of your partner that would like to be less inhibited? Do you suspect that there's a part of her that might be a little wild, maybe even a little naughty? You're probably right. If you'd like to know why it's hard for many women to explore their sexuality as fully as they might, you can gain some insight by imagining, just for a bit, what it's like to grow up female in a society that gives a girl a lot of mixed messages where sexuality is concerned.

Perhaps you've heard the term "double standard" used with regard to how young men and women are socially prepared to become sexually active beings. This refers to the fact that while males are implicitly given the message that it's good to become an experienced lover, women are often explicitly instructed that their "goodness" revolves around holding on to their chastity for as long as possible. Even when they do begin to have a sex life, many boundaries are put around what is and isn't acceptable behavior.

Examining the language that surrounds sexuality offers some very interesting evidence for this double standard. A man who is good in bed and forthright about enjoying sex—and lots of it—might be called a "stud." That's a word with a generally positive association. But what is a woman with similar characteristics called? If you just flinched, you have gotten the point. Some of the words that are used to describe a woman with a high sex drive and a high level of sexual expertise are, in fact, not so nice. From a very young age, most girls are led to believe that while a man might happily dally with a woman who is, shall we say, free-spirited and open-minded in this area, they will only settle down with a virtuous female.

You might argue that the rules have relaxed a bit in recent decades, but actually as bold female sexuality has become more celebrated in the media—Paris Hilton can sell hamburgers like no one else—lots of ordinary women have only become more confused. Even Paris, in her private persona, was ostracized when a tape of her personal love life was circulated.

What's a woman to do? How does she know if her man really wants a playful vixen or a demure maiden? Telling her that a guy wants a partner who's "a lady in the living room and a hooker in the bedroom" (not to mention a Martha Stewart in the kitchen) doesn't really help to ease her confusion. Is she supposed to change her *modus operandi* every time she walks through a different doorway? Does her man really want a woman with multiple personality disorder?

The end result of all her perplexity is that a woman might hold herself back sexually, even in a committed relationship. There are lines she may be reluctant to cross. But all of this can change for your woman if you, in the most loving way possible, encourage her to cross them for you.

Let Her Be Your Temptress

With your encouragement, your woman might be able to give herself—and you—the gift of moving more deeply toward experiencing the heights of sexual pleasure. With the right attitude on your part, she will know she is free, within the context of your monogamous relationship, to be not a "bad girl" but a true temptress—expressing her mature sex drive in ways that may have never occurred to her before. What she might like, first and foremost, is your implicit and explicit permission to "go for it."

Tempting your woman to unlock her inner temptress doesn't require a heavy-handed approach. You'll only achieve an outcome opposite of that which you desire if she feels that your encouragement to do more means she's not doing enough as it is. Let her know how attractive you find her (remember the tips in Chapter 4), and indicate how much you enjoy your lovemaking. That's a crucial first step in inspiring her. Now …

♦ Let her know that you'd like to discover if the two of you could give each other even more pleasure in more ways. After all, the only sex either of you is ever going to have is with one another, right?

♦ Inquire about her fantasies, and about whether there is anything she's ever thought of doing with you that she's been too shy to try?

♦ When she's doing something you enjoy, give her positive feedback such as, "Yes, yes, take your time, lover."

♦ If she's missing the mark, gently guide her hands or tongue, or other appropriate body parts, and then reinforce her with more positive words that encourage her to linger.

♦ Watch or read some erotica together, and ask, "Could you ever see yourself doing something like that—I could!"

♦ See if you can coax her into doing a striptease—lots of women are secretly dying to try.

♦ Inspire her to explore by doing unto her the kinds of things you would like done unto you—women are natural givers; they enjoy reciprocating favors.

At the end of a lovemaking session where you sense your lover has pushed her boundaries, even more positive reinforcement is in order. Tell her how thrilled you were. Praise her efforts, even if you sense she could use a little more practice. Never give her the sense that her performance is being graded, or you'll give her performance anxiety.

Help Her Initiate Sex

One of the gripes many men have about sex in their relationship is that their women never, or rarely, initiate sex. They have an excellent point. Most women simply don't do this often enough, if at all. If this is the case with you and your partner, don't misunderstand why she's so reluctant. Certainly don't take it as a sign of rejection or lack of interest.

Sometimes men joke that women don't initiate sex because they don't have to. But often the reality is that women don't initiate sex because they feel embarrassed and self-conscious doing so. These feelings also tend to be the result of social conditioning.

Our society taught us that girls needed to wait for boys to ask them to dance, to invite them out on a date, to ask them to go steady, or to propose marriage. Naturally, it was up to the man to indicate when he wanted to make love. We were led to believe that if we were sexually forward, we would be considered aggressive and unappealing. It might scare a guy away!

I bet you think that sounds ridiculous, but social conditioning dies hard. If you would like your woman to be the one to get the ball rolling in the bedroom, give her some ideas about how she might go about it. For instance …

- ◆ Collaborate with her to develop a special "sign" that indicates her interest, like leaving a rose on your dresser or putting on a special CD.

- ◆ Suggest she put a Post-it note on your pillow reading, "How about it, handsome?"

- ◆ Give her some homemade coupons redeemable for a night of hot loving, and have her redeem them when she's in the mood.

- ◆ Ask her to experiment with the very direct approach—by plopping herself in your lap and giving you a long, deep smooch.

Initiating lovemaking can encompass a wide range of styles, from the subtle to the brazenly outrageous. As with all matters in the romance department, take your woman's unique essence into account. Help her find an approach that suits her personality and style.

> **CAUTION Love Busters** _____
>
> When your woman finally takes the plunge and initiates sex for the first time, don't put her off. Be receptive, even if her overture is at a time you wouldn't have anticipated. Unless you're really incapacitated—perhaps in traction—oblige her by being extremely attentive and enthusiastic. If you reject her too many times in these situations, she might stop trying. Instead, explain to her what times might be better for you.

Introduce Her to Your Hot Spots

As part of sex and foreplay, you naturally want your woman to touch you where it feels good—really, really good. But does she know where all of your erogenous zones are? For that matter, do you? Perhaps you've been so preoccupied with giving her the tingly pleasure of the perfect touch that you've never taken time to explore the multitude of ways in which she can stimulate you.

The Outer Zones

Yes, I know you know how she can stimulate you directly. But what about all those peripheral areas that are ripe for some rubbing, grazing, licking, or stroking? You might think that your woman should instinctively know which of your spots are hot and which of your spots are not. But how can she be if even *you* are somewhat unenlightened?

If you really want to let your woman please you, the two of you can embark on an exploratory journey, unlocking the hidden potential of all your hot spots as you go.

What feels good to you is, of course, a highly subjective matter. But here is a menu of ideas from which you might want to pick and choose. Have your lover …

- Trace the outline of your lips with the tip of her index finger.
- Gently move her fingers from the bottom of your ears to the tip of your chin.
- Massage your earlobes.
- Gently rub her hands through your hair in circular motions while lightly scratching your scalp.

- Press her thumbs into the neck tendons that stretch from the bottom of your ears to the top of your shoulders.

- Make gentle circling motions on the nerve ending-rich areolas that surround your nipples, and lick your nipples themselves (yes, you might be as sensitive there as she is).

- Stroke the muscle that begins at the outer edge of your armpit and runs down the side of your body.

- Give a light, feathery touch to the tiny hairs above your tailbone.

- Apply soft pressure with her palm at the base of your spine.

- Spread her palm just above your groin; then pull her fingers inward, grazing this very sensitive skin ever so lightly with her fingernails.

He Says/She Says

"To make our lovemaking more enjoyable, I encouraged my wife to 'let her hair down'—literally. I asked her to unpin her long hair, which she usually wore clipped back during sex, and let it fall across me as she bent over me. What an erotic feeling."
—Edward, 41

Remember to keep reinforcing your lover when she touches an area that, shall we say, rings a bell. If something doesn't feel especially good, gently move her along with a nonverbal cue, such as guiding her hand or mouth north or south to another spot. Little by little she'll develop a working map of your erotic terrain.

The Inner Zones

As she gets closer to your genital area, try dissuading her—yes, you read that right—from going straight for the gold. There are many other surrounding areas where her touch can tease and entice you.

- **Your inner thighs.** These are almost invariably a good place for a turn-on. Thighs don't get touched much in the course of everyday events, and they're just asking for it. Have your partner pay them some attention by stroking them with her palms—or by grazing them teasingly with her fingernails, or by giving them a nibble or a lick.

- **Your perineum.** You read about this area with regard to stimulating your partner in Chapter 14. Your perineum, located between the scrotum and the anus, and loaded with nerve endings, is probably an under-explored area just as hers is. It's not generally an area where a man would stimulate himself during masturbation.

Have your woman try massaging the area, perhaps applying a bit of lubricant as she does so.

♦ **Your scrotum.** No one needs to tell you that this is a very sensitive and very fragile part of your body. In fact, you've probably spent a great deal of your life protecting it with athletic cups. But that doesn't mean your scrotum can't be a source of immense pleasure if gently caressed, licked, or sucked on by your woman. She might be afraid of causing you pain, so be sure to tell her you'll indicate if the pressure is too great (how could you not?) so she can make adjustments.

 Mood Makers

If your woman is game, have her hum while she holds your testicles in her mouth. It won't even matter if she can carry a tune.

The Back Way

Have you ever wondered whether there was the equivalent of a male G-spot? And if not, why did Mother Nature deprive you? Well, many people say there is such a thing: your prostate gland.

The prostate is a small gland, about the size and shape of a walnut. It is nestled in your pubic bone, where it is surrounded by pelvic muscles. It's said that the prostate gland can produce amazing orgasms when pressure is applied to it through the rectum.

Is it true? You'll never know unless you try. If you and your partner want to experiment with this kind of stimulation (consensus being absolutely necessary), it's advised that you start slowly. After a hot shower, so you'll feel clean, and some other kinds of foreplay, have your lover apply an anal lubricant, such as Anal-Eze. Then have your partner locate your prostate by inserting her index finger into your anus. If she inserts it as far as the second knuckle and presses forward in a "come hither" motion, she'll be able to feel the prostate through the front part of the rectal wall. If you enjoy the sensation you can have her press a bit more firmly and perhaps even remove and insert her finger in a thrusting motion.

Love Busters

If your woman would like to try stimulating you in this way but is squeamish about using her finger—or has long fingernails—try using a sex toy for penetration. Check out the some of the acrylic toys made specifically for anal play by browsing sex toy sights on the web (one such favorite is www.myplasure.com).

Anal play is not for everyone. Your response to prostate stimulation depends on your particular physiology. If you or your woman has a moral or aesthetic objection, there's no reason to pursue it. If you try it once and don't care for it, there's no need to do it again.

Fellatio: Giving Her the Lowdown

Finally we come to the topic I bet you've been waiting for: oral sex. Probably it will come as no surprise to you that most men are very enthusiastic about the idea of their woman performing oral sex on them. Why not? The act of fellatio offers direct, focused stimulation where you feel it most.

And it's incredibly sexy to watch a woman taking you in her mouth. Besides, you can just lie (or sit or stand) back and enjoy it.

Believe it or not, performing oral sex on a man actually has a lot of upsides for women.

- It can be a quick way of satisfying her man without mussing her hair or even taking off a stitch of clothing.

- Oral sex is a portable pleasure—perfect for experiencing intimate encounters in a variety of different locations.

- There's no birth control necessary.

- It's a way to gratify her man if she has her period and doesn't care to have intercourse at that time.

- It makes for great foreplay—because performing oral sex on a man without inducing orgasm can make him extremely hard.

- It can be very satisfying for a woman to see her man squirm and moan while under her control.

Last but certainly not least, if she performs oral sex on you, you might be inclined to reciprocate. Fair is fair, right?

But in spite of all this, some women are still reluctant to give oral sex a try. Sometimes even if a part of her really wants to do it, another part holds back—perhaps she has her reasons. But if you can talk about those reasons, calmly and non-judgmentally, you might find that your particular partner has a change of heart.

Understanding Her Inhibitions

One of the two most common objections to oral sex that women typically express is that they are afraid that they will gag. It's not an unreasonable anxiety. Mother Nature gave all of us a gag reflex in order to protect us from harming our throats with dangerous objects. A helpful tip you might give a woman who is fearful of gagging is that she can try breathing through her nose as she takes you in her mouth. Another thing she can do is to switch back and forth from oral to manual stimulation, giving herself regular breaks. In lieu of this, she can simply shift the angle of your penis periodically so that it rubs up against the inside of her cheek instead of the back of her throat.

The second of the top two objections that many women express is that they do not wish to swallow, usually because they think semen will taste bad and have an unappetizing texture. If this is the case, you can make it clear that whether or not she wants to swallow is her choice. (After all, it's not a deal breaker for you, is it? You can reach as intense a climax whether your partner swallows or not.) Sexual surveys show, in fact, that only 20 percent of women say they swallow at the culmination of oral sex.

There are a number of practical alternatives to swallowing semen. One is for the woman to let your semen dribble out of the side of her mouth. Another is to let you climax against her closed lips or against the smooth warmth of her cheek. Another is to switch from stimulating with her mouth to stimulating with her hand just before your orgasm. Then you can ejaculate into other sexy places, like her chest or her neck.

Mood Makers

Semen generally tastes a little salty. If you want your semen to taste sweet, eat a sweet dessert. It needn't be a whole Black Forest cake. Fruits such as honeydew, cantaloupe, kiwi, and strawberries will do very nicely. Sipping pineapple juice is another sweet solution.

Some women also feel squeamish about the smell of a man's genitals. But unless you've just come in from, say, a long day of bareback horse riding, you will just smell natural—a bit masculine and musky. Even so, offering to take a shower before oral sex will probably go a long way toward helping your partner overcome this inhibition. Hey, maybe she can even try performing oral sex *in* the shower.

Another common fear many women have is that they might hurt you during oral sex. (Some men fear this as well!) The trick to her not hurting you is simply for her not to use her teeth, but rather to pull her lips back over them. Once she masters this simple rule of thumb, she should be in no danger of doing harm or causing pain. Assure her, however, that if she were doing anything to cause you discomfort, you would tell her. (If there's a problem, just correct it and don't make a big deal out of it.)

And again, we get back to the problem of social conditioning. Some women think that fellatio is something that "nice girls" shouldn't do. But oral sex is more and more widely accepted in our culture as a natural, normal part of the sexual experience.

Many couples incorporate it into their lovemaking repertoire, either as foreplay or as an ultimate outcome. There's nothing "dirty" about a woman performing oral sex on her man. The taboo against it comes from outdated stereotypes and from not understanding what it's all about. Still, you mustn't be insensitive to this—or any other—objection. You won't please a woman by making her feel guilty or pressuring her into doing something that really doesn't fit in with her idea of a fulfilling sexual experience.

Raising the Subject

If you and your partner have never discussed fellatio, and if having your woman perform this act is an idea you're intrigued by, perhaps it's time to raise the subject. The trick is how, and when to do so. As with raising many delicate issues, timing can be nearly everything. Pick a time when your partner is relaxed and open, and when the two of you are feeling close.

- Don't introduce the subject when she's busy making dinner (whoops—you may find your supper splattered on the kitchen floor).

- Don't ask her when she's driving in heavy traffic (not if you want the car to stay on the road).

- Don't ask her via cell phone or e-mail—this definitely calls for the personal touch.

Be tactful. Don't just blurt out, "Honey, do you want to try going down on me later tonight?" If oral sex hasn't been part of your intimate repertoire, tell her you've been thinking about it, are curious, and that you're interested in her thoughts on the matter. Then give her some time to discuss it further and, if she would like, to think it over. Your sensitivity will be a turn-on in itself.

The Least You Need to Know

- Any man can help turn his woman into his dream lover by giving her tacit permission and overt encouragement to explore her wilder side.

- If you'd like your women to initiate sex more often, work with her on developing signals she can give you that indicate she's in the mood.

- Women might need help becoming familiar with your erogenous zones—and so might you—so have fun exploring them together.

- If you want your woman to give you oral sex, be sensitive to her inhibitions—never make her feel guilty.

Part 6

Lovers for Life

After sex comes … sleep? Well, yes, but this part of the book will offer tips for prolonging the mood a bit and ensuring a return engagement. It also includes a myriad advice for staying in the best possible shape so that you can keep on loving—in every way—for a long, long time. Finally, this concluding part takes a look at what keeps relationships solid in every sense. The ultimate goal is to please and be pleased for many years to come.

21

After the Loving

In This Chapter

- The body and mind after sex
- Keeping the physical love and mood going
- If you'd really rather sleep
- The pleasures of morning sex
- Intimacy between sexual encounters

When men are surveyed as to what activities they like to engage in immediately after lovemaking, taking a nap tops the list. Coming in second: having a snack. So the ultimate guy sex fantasy is having great sex, dozing off, and waking to find your smiling lover standing over you holding out a warm plate of nachos and a cold beer.

Good luck with that! This chapter is going to tell you what your woman would like to happen after lovemaking. It will also show you how, together, you can come up with some after-loving activities bound to make everybody happy.

Wow, That Was Something

It's a well-known fact that after a man ejaculates, he feels like sleeping. Why? No, it's not because you're insensitive or uncommunicative—no matter what anyone says. The answer is physiological.

Upon orgasm, humans release the hormone oxytocin, which normally makes us sleepy. In addition, we are recuperating from aerobic exertion. During sexual activity, heart rate and blood pressure become elevated. Now we want time to recover, and the body compensates by slowing down.

Mood Makers

To minimize sleepiness after sex, try consciously breathing through your orgasm by using the Tantric breathing methods described in Chapter 18. Typically, we tend to hold our breath during orgasm, and this is said to contribute to post-sex physical exhaustion.

But wait! If this is the case, why don't women just want to fall asleep after lovemaking? Well, some do—but most do not. In our case, I think it can be assumed that our drive to connect emotionally for the most part overrides our physical drive to snooze.

The post-lovemaking emotional element is also significant. After lovemaking both males and females probably feel more vulnerable with regard to their partners than at any other time. Men—who as a rule don't like feeling vulnerable—often deal with that feeling by gaining even more incentive to catch some z's. Women, on the other hand, want to process the feeling by solidifying their bond with their lover—usually by snuggling, or chatting, or both.

How to reconcile the difference in reactions? If you really want to please a woman with a chatty, cuddly post-sex penchant, you need to do *something*—even something small—to make her feel more emotionally secure.

One small gesture you can make is to be attentive to any immediate practical or aesthetic needs she might have. For example:

◆ If she is left lying on the "wet spot" on the bed, get up and bring her a towel or washcloth with which to cover and absorb it. (If you have thought to place one by the bedside beforehand, you're that much further ahead, aren't you?)

◆ If she needs to use the bathroom, offer her first dibs. (Yes, even if you need to use it also.)

◆ If she wants to use the shower, offer to let her go first—or offer to shower with her.

◆ If she's thirsty, offer her a glass of water or another beverage.

◆ If you've been wearing a condom, be sure to discard it in the trash (not by flushing, as it can clog a toilet). (Even in sexual matters neatness counts—and there are few things less "yucky" than a woman discovering a used condom between the sheets the morning after.)

◆ If she's been using a diaphragm, make sure she has the privacy she needs to remove it (she may be quite shy about doing this in your view).

These tiny displays of good manners require less than Herculean efforts, and pay a large dividend. It makes a woman feel cared for and protected when her partner puts her comfort before his own, and that's the sort of thing she really needs right now.

Afterplay

Another possible reason a woman may feel more wakeful than you after sex is if she has not yet achieved an orgasm. Or perhaps she has achieved one, but feels fully capable and desirous of experiencing another one.

In our culture, we tend to define sex as being "over" after the man comes. But a woman's orgasm is a more amorphous entity. Consider that even after you're thoroughly satiated, she may need or want an extra inning. Ask, "Is there anything else I can do for you?" If so, try a little afterplay.

Understandably, you may not be physically able to achieve another erection soon after you've had an orgasm, but that hardly means you're out of options. Your menu of choices includes:

◆ **Manual stimulation.** Surely you're not too tired to move one little finger. Move it slowly and teasingly back and forth along the length of your partner's labia. Then stroke her clitoris until she climaxes.

◆ **Watching.** If you're lover is so inclined, encourage her to masturbate while you observe. Now you don't even have to move that little finger!

◆ **Using sex toys.** If your partner still longs for penetration, it can be accomplished

 He Says/She Says

"For a long time, I resisted the idea of going down on my partner after we'd had intercourse, because I didn't like the idea of tasting my own semen. I started offering her a wet washcloth and then rubbing her with some strawberry-flavored lubricant. That did the trick. After these little amenities, I was happy to oblige."
—Gene, 41

without an erection. Afterplay is a great opportunity to experiment with sex toys such as vibrators and dildos.

♦ **Performing oral sex.** As you already know, most women just can't ever seem to have enough of this activity. If you still have strength enough to move your tongue, you can do it.

Never think of yourself as a "failure" if your woman still wants a little extra something once sexual intercourse has concluded. It only means she wants more of you. Besides, sex is not a race or a contest. It can go on for as long as both partners like. Pleasure, after all, is pleasure—regardless of how or when it occurs.

After-Talk

Knowing what you know about how much women enjoy talking to their partners, it won't come as any surprise to you that lots of women enjoy talking after making love. For you, it may well seem like there is nothing much to talk *about*. Men are action-oriented, by and large, and so you may feel like you've just, in effect, said it all. Why break the mood with actual words? Wouldn't that be sort of … redundant?

In a certain sense, you have a point. There are *some* things it probably is *not* a good idea to talk about after sex. Steer clear of topics that tend to cause stress in your relationship, such as finances or concerns about the kids. This is not a time to go over your tax return or to try to agree about where your kids should apply to college. Certainly you'll want to avoid any issues that generally lead to arguments. (Is your extended family coming for an extended visit. Now's not the time to break it to her.)

In general, this is not a good idea to analytically dissect the sexual experience you just had in minute detail. A discussion of technicalities ("I thought I found your G-spot, but it was two millimeters off from where I thought") won't serve to prolong romantic emotions and it's not exactly cuddly conversation.

Love Busters

Don't dilute your lovemaking experience by critiquing it afterward. Your woman wants to feel like she got an "A", not a C-plus."

In addition, this certainly is not a time to air any suggestions for improvement in your partner's lovemaking techniques. Precisely because a woman does feel vulnerable at this time, she may take even the gentlest suggestion as a sign of rejection—even if you truly didn't mean it that way.

Do, however, feel free to compliment your lover and to praise the lovemaking experience you both just shared.

Good Things to Say After Sex	Not-So-Good Things To Say
That was fantastic.	Better luck next time.
You were fantastic.	Are you coming down with something?
Remember our great first time?	We've come a long way since that first disaster, haven't we?
Wow, I felt really close to you.	You know, while we were making love I had this neat idea about installing a skylight over the bed.
You're the best I've ever had.	You know, you remind me a little of my first girlfriend—now she was *hot*.
When we do this, I feel young again.	Man, I'm pooped. Better get the old ticker checked out.
I wish we could stay here forever.	I need to check my phone messages.

Some couples find they tend to segue naturally after sex into a kind of easy, relaxed dialogue about plans for things they might do together the next day or down the road. Since you're both in a relaxed mood, the post-lovemaking period is a great time to daydream together about planning a special date, a weekend getaway, or a prolonged vacation. Try to imagine scenarios that would allow you to spend more intimate time together, so you'll get an opportunity to do this more often.

Even if those scenarios are not likely to occur right away, they are nice to think about—and they let your lady know how much you value your time alone with her. They also let her know that you're not going anywhere—that your thoughts of the future revolve around her.

More After Activities

Up for some other fun activities? There are a number of other things couples like to do to prolong a pleasant post-sex mood. Go ahead and try some of the following, or take the initiative and suggest some of your own.

- ◆ **Raid the refrigerator together.** If you're both feeling like a little nibble, give in to the urge. You can both head off to the kitchen. Or it might be especially pleasing to your partner if you were thoughtful enough to be the one to go foraging—bringing back a light, healthy snack (perhaps fruit, cheese and crackers) on a tray.

◆ **Snuggle up and watch T.V.** Although this is probably not the time to tune into the news (too serious, possibly even depressing) it's a great time for one of those romantic chick flicks. Rummage through your video or DVD library, or check out the American Movie Classics (AMC) channel if your local cable provider offers it—there you'll find some oldies but goodies featuring the likes of Bette Davis, Vivien Leigh, Doris Day, and Joan Crawford. It's also a good time to share a laugh, so you might want to check out a Jay Leno or David Letterman monologue, a *Saturday Night Live* rerun, or *The Daily Show* on Comedy Central.

Mood Makers

For some hot tips on how raiding the fridge together can prolong an erotic mood, rent the DVD of *9½ Weeks*. Mickey Rourke and Kim Bassinger provide some kinky ideas for furthering the food-love connection.

◆ **Listen to your favorite music.** Slip one of her favorite mellow CDs into a bed-side player. Cuddle and stoke her while you let the relaxing music flow through you.

◆ **Browse magazines or newspapers together.** Again, you might want to stay away from hard news. But this is a great time to peruse feature sections, human-interest stories, travel articles, and even recipes, sharing tidbits of information with each other and chatting as you read. For those with a literary bent, do the crossword puzzle together.

◆ **Give each other a massage.** Who wouldn't enjoy a gentle back rub and a bit of neck relaxation at a time like this? Massaging one another is a way to prolong your physical connection in a non-sexual way. But then again, who knows where it may lead? Perhaps without even realizing it, you and your partner will segue effortlessly into "round two."

◆ **Go out for a stroll together.** Weather permitting, throw on some casual clothes and take a walk through your neighborhood, or just go as far as the backyard. This may not feel like the right time for a full-fledged brisk power walk, but a breath of fresh air will re-invigorate you both. What the heck, you can even take the dog along if he's been feeling neglected.

◆ **Tell her an amusing anecdote or a good joke.** As discussed in Chapter 6, laughter fosters emotional bonding.

Feel free to float the possibility of any activity. The only criteria is that you think it might be pleasurable for both of you. If your mate is agreeable, that's all you need to know. And chances are she will be. But if she's reluctant, try another suggestion.

Really Sleeping Together

But if you really, really want to sleep, she may be a good sport and agree to your doing just that, even though she's more wide-awake. As long as she knows that your surrender to the sandman is nothing personal and she does not feel insulted, you've got nothing to worry about. Just try to mumble "I love you" or similar sentiments before heading off to the land of nod. Think of it as a kind of insurance policy for a happy re-awakening.

Of course there's always the possibility that *both* of you will be in agreement that right now is the perfect time to drift off to sleep together. If that's the case, you're all set. But do observe a few sleep-related niceties:

◆ Take a moment to straighten out and de-rumple the sheets.

◆ Make sure she has her share of the blanket or comforter.

◆ Make sure she has found her pillow—and fluff it for her if you really want to impress her.

◆ Blow out the candles you had burning to create a loving ambience.

◆ If you left some lights on while you made love, turn them off now.

◆ If you left any music playing, turn it off or set your system to automatically turn off later so that it doesn't replay all night long.

◆ Make sure the room is at a comfortable temperature; open or close windows or adjust the thermostat as necessary.

He Says/She Says _____

"I used to fall asleep on my husband's arm and he would invariably wake up in the middle of the night and say he couldn't feel it. Then he would wave the arm around a while, while it hung there like a wet noodle. So we devised a new sleeping position. He lies on his back and I lie on my side and slide my head into the crook of his underarm. I call it my "nook." I feel all safe and warm there, and he doesn't have the circulation in his arm cut off. This is a really great way to fall asleep."
—Regina, 38

Now assume a position—preferably one where your woman feels cradled in your arms. I know that sometimes this may not be the most comfortable sleeping arrangement for you—especially if she's putting too much of her weight on one part of your body. No one likes to wake up in the middle of the night feeling pins-and-needles in one of their extremities, or feeling as if there's a heavy weight in their chest, yet feeling unable to move for fear of disturbing their sleeping bedmate.

So you have two choices. One is to find a snuggle-worthy position that suits you both and allows you to remain cuddled in sleep—for example the spoons position, where you and lover lie nested, her back to your front, like spoons in a silverware drawer. The other is to let her cuddle contentedly any way she wishes to for a time, and then rearrange yourself when you feel you are soon about to drift off.

If the latter is your choice, that's fine—but, again, the key is to make sure your partner does not feel insulted or rejected. Give her a kiss, a hug, or a loving stroke—or all three—before you rearrange yourself in a more comfortable sleeping posture.

Morning Sex

So far, this chapter has been predicated on the notion that you and your woman are having sex at night, probably soon before bedtime. But have you and she ever tried sex in the morning? Many women—and men, too—actually say this is when they enjoy lovemaking the most.

From a physiological and biological point of view, morning sex makes sense for many reasons. Scientists say the body is most primed for sex—and females for fertilization—in the early morning on awakening. When we first wake up, levels of the hormones which stimulate the sex drive—progesterone and estrogen in women, and testosterone in both men and women—are up to five times higher than at any other time of the day.

In addition, many men awake with an erection in the morning. All men have erections while they dream, and the morning erection is the result of being wakened during, or just after a dream. It can be a very persistent erection indeed, and while in and of itself it is not a sign of arousal, its very presence and its attendant pleasurable sensation may result in arousal.

Finally, on a practical note, many people find that they are less likely to be interrupted during morning sex. The kids are still asleep, the cats and dogs are still snoozing, and the phone is unlikely to ring. No one has even started sending e-mails yet!

Morning sex may seem impractical if you're used to setting your alarm, jumping into a hot shower, dressing, and running off to work—or, on weekends, running off to sports activities, errands, or religious services. However, by setting that alarm a half hour or so earlier you can ease into the day with what many consider the most pleasant activity of all. Now you'll associate that heretofore annoying alarm beep or buzz with something wonderful instead of a series of onerous chores.

Concerned that you'll just get sleepy again if you have sex in the morning? Don't worry. Your *circadian rhythms* will counteract that tendency. Bright early morning sun-light has a powerful influence upon circadian rhythms, or biological clocks. Studies have shown that exposure to bright, early morning sunlight (between about 7:00 A.M. and 9:00 A.M.) for at least 15 minutes is perhaps the most powerful signal that sets our bodies on "go" for the day.

So, if you're both up for sex in the morning, enjoy yourselves, then open up your drapes or blinds and let the sun shine in. You'll be raring to go on and enjoy your day after a great start. But even so, don't forget to offer your woman some sweet words and a cuddle before you tran-sition to other important things.

Tongue Teasers

Circadian rhythms refer to natural patterns that repeat every 24 hours. The human body has more than 100 circadian rhythms. Each unique 24-hour cycle influences an aspect of the body's function, including body temperature, hormone levels, heart rate, blood pressure, and even one's pain threshold.

P.S. I Love You

Between sexual encounters—whenever you engage in them, and whatever the two of you like to do immediately following—it's a good idea to offer your partner little re-minders of how much you enjoy your lovemaking. In this way you'll be sure to secure a return engagement.

Some things you might do to have that return engagement occur sooner rather than later include:

♦ Leaving your partner a note by the bedside or on the pillow that alludes to how much fun you just had.

♦ Calling during the day to reiterate how great your encounter was.

♦ Sending a loving "thanks for the memories" e-mail.

♦ Sending flowers with a sly, charming note.

♦ Telling your partner how you thought about her and your lovemaking during your workday—during an important meeting, no less!

♦ Flirting with a wink, with "secret" smiles, and other kinds of body language.

♦ Planning a date so you know when your next special time together will be.

No woman wants to feel like sex is an isolated aspect of her life. She wants to know that it is an integrated part of her relationship with you. Anything you can do to let her know that the good memories linger will make her all the more enthusiastic for an encore performance—not to mention happier and more satisfied overall.

The Least You Need to Know

- After orgasm, both male and female bodies are exhausted—but the female remains emotionally revved up and wants to feel cared for.

- If a woman has not achieved orgasm before or during intercourse, try some afterplay—there are no "rules" about when sex ends.

- Many women like to talk after sex—even if you don't have the inclination to talk a lot, say something sweet and complimentary.

- There are many other things you can do to prolong a pleasant post-lovemaking mood, such as sharing a light snack, snuggling up with a video, or even going out for a stroll.

- If you're going to sleep and she's not, be sure to say something reassuring before you drift off; if you're both going to sleep observe bedtime niceties like straightening the sheets and offering a good cuddling position.

- One way to stay awake after sex is to have sex in the morning—scientists say it's the best time from a biological standpoint, and many couples enjoy this kind of a start to their day.

Chapter **22**

Staying Hot and Healthy

In This Chapter

◆ Men's top health risks

◆ Eating right and light

◆ Exercising for health

◆ Male supplements for an extra boost

◆ The importance of check-ups

Did you know that having a strong, satisfying relationship with your woman brings a health dividend as well? It's true. Men who are part of a couple tend to live longer and stay healthier than those who are alone. But as good as this news is, it's no reason to get complacent about your health. Your lady wants you in top shape for as long as you both shall live—and that can be a very long time if you take good care of yourself. This chapter is packed with information about enhancing your well-being and remaining her strong, virile honey for many years to come.

Knowledge Equals Health

When it comes to staying healthy, knowledge is power. Even if you are at the top of your game today, it's important to understand something about factors that can contribute to illness, as well as factors that can reduce your risks.

It's not always easy to ponder the thing that may take a toll on your health and longevity, but the rewards of doing so are immeasurable. Denial is a course of action that lots of men default to, but it's actually a self-defeating strategy—because most of the top health threats facing the American male are preventable.

The Heart Part

Heart disease is the number-one health threat to men in the Unites States today. Men have a greater risk of heart disease and have heart attacks much earlier in life than women do, says the American Heart Association. So all men—including you—need to take heart disease seriously. Genetics can play a role in heart conditions, but even if all your ancestors lived to be 100 years old, and spent their last days chopping wood and hauling water, don't imagine you're immune.

The good news is that fatal heart conditions can often be prevented. Healthy habits that reduce the risk of heart attack include weight control, exercise, eating a healthy diet, and reducing amounts of saturated fat and cholesterol.

Mood Makers

There are many good reasons to quit smoking, but if you won't do it for yourself, do it for her. If you both smoke, quit together for emotional support to reinforce your decision. In either case, your kisses will be sweeter.

If you smoke, stop. Please. Smoking kills more people through heart attacks and coronary artery disease than it does through cancer or emphysema. That's because smoking increases blood pressure and increases arterial plaque. It also increases the concentration of low-density lipoprotein (LDL) cholesterol (the harmful kind) in your blood while decreasing high-density lipoprotein (HDL) (the beneficial kind). By the way, those who smoke after a heart attack increase their risk of having another heart attack by 25 to 50 percent.

It's also a good idea to be aware of advance warnings of a possible heart attack. These include chest pain, shortness of breath, and fatigue. If you experience these symptoms, don't pretend that nothing's wrong. There's nothing manly about soldiering on in the face of such discomfort. Advance warning signs affect two thirds of all those who succumb to heart attacks, so don't brush them off.

Remember: Your physical heart belongs to you, but your emotional heart belongs to the woman you love and who loves you. If you've resolved to take better care of your heart and your overall health, let her know. She'll be only too happy to support you and help in way she can. Together you can become a team that addresses all the positive things you can do to keep your heart strong.

Other Parts

For men, cancer is the number-two ranked health risk. According to the American Cancer Society (ACS), the most common cause of cancer death for men is lung cancer. Prostate cancer is the second-leading cause of cancer death among males.

About one third of all cancer deaths are related to nutrition or other controllable lifestyle factors. You can reduce your risks by not smoking or chewing tobacco (never mind what any of your favorite baseball players do, or did), by exercising on a routine basis, and by eating a healthy diet. Cancer risk can also be minimized by limiting sun exposure and by limiting alcohol. In addition, regular preventive health screenings can catch many cancers in time to maximize the potential for cure.

The third ranked cause of death for men in the United States is stroke. Stroke is also one of the leading causes of disability among males. High blood pressure, smoking, lack of exercise, and a diet high in fat and LDL cholesterol contribute to the likelihood of having a stroke.

It might surprise you to know that the fourth-ranked cause of death for American men is accidents, especially motor vehicle crashes. So take care when you're behind that wheel—and try not to get too peeved if your wife or girlfriend reminds you to do so. Try not to drive when overly tired, and never mix drinking and driving. If you think you're a great driver and that anything that goes wrong is the other guy's fault, then watch out for the other guy.

The list of men's top ten health risks is completed by the following:

- ◆ Chronic lower respiratory disease (lung disease)
- ◆ Diabetes
- ◆ Influenza and pneumonia
- ◆ Suicide
- ◆ Kidney disease
- ◆ Liver disease (including cirrhosis)

Love Busters

It's not macho to neglect to buckle up. About twice as many men as women die in car accidents.

Notice how many of the conditions can be prevented or delayed by smart choices and a sensible, healthy lifestyle. Don't worry, no one wants to take all the fun out of your life. But a little indulgence is one thing, whereas over-indulgence can end your life prematurely.

Lighten Up

Everyone's heard the adage "the way to a man's heart is through his stomach." Ironically, we now know it's literally true. Eating well helps your heart. Eating a wide variety of wholesome, nutritious foods also can help you prevent cancer, diabetes, and other illnesses too numerous to tally. Moreover, a good diet can help keep your energy level and your libido high, while keeping your overall mood and self-image positive.

Mood Makers

An estimated 90 percent of American men do not eat a balanced diet. Be among the other 10 percent. Learn to shop for, order, and prepare satisfying, filling, and flavorful food—and still lower your intake of saturated fat, calories, and salt (excessive salt can contribute to high blood pressure).

But eating well can prove difficult for some men because of certain ingrained attitudes about food. Healthy food, unfortunately, has a bad reputation. To many of you guys, eating healthy still conjures up visions of facing a celery stalk garnished with a lettuce leaf. Understandably, you can get stomach pangs and tears in your eyes just thinking about it.

Real men want real food—and should have it. But healthy food can be appetizing, too. Don't make the mistake of opting for deep-fried corn dogs and heaps of hash browns because you can't see yourself eating "girlie food." Instead, learn the secrets of making wise ingredient choices.

Real Food, Smart Substitutes

Yes, you can still have the delicious, hearty fare you crave. But if you are doing some of the cooking at your house (see Chapter 13 for why this is a pleasing plan), use substitute ingredients that enhance a recipe's health quotient without diluting taste.

Lots of cookbooks feature healthy ingredient exchanges. It's a good idea to keep a few on the shelf for new ideas. Online recipe finders can also be a great help. Feel free to be creative, too. Think up your own healthy and creative substitutions. That's part of the fun of cooking real food the healthy way.

Some top substitution tips:

- Substitute condensed low-fat milk for whole milk.

- Use low-fat yogurt in place of heavy cream.

- Substitute flavorful spices like garlic, onion powder, oregano, basil, and sage—for salt.

- Sauté with olive or canola oil in lieu of butter.

- Use whole wheat instead of white grains.

- Use nonfat sour cream.

- Cook with egg whites in place of eggs.

Best of all, there's no need to relinquish those hearty Italian and Mexican dishes you love. Just rethink them a bit. If you're making lasagna, halve the cheese and add eggplant. For casseroles, halve the cheese and add vegetables like spinach, broccoli, and carrots.

> **He Says/She Says**
>
> "I couldn't believe it when my husband not only made me breakfast in bed but also explained to me that the omelet he'd whipped up was made from egg whites. He proudly told me he'd discovered that liquid egg whites are available in cartons, right next to the eggs at the supermarket—so he didn't have to waste time separating eggs. I practically swooned. After breakfast, we didn't get out of bed for a long time."
> —Allison, 36

Top Foods to Choose

Eating healthy is not only about knowing what to leave out, but also knowing what to put in. I'm not talking about esoteric health foods like seaweed and flax seed. It's amazing how many common foods promote good health. They are chock full of natural vitamins, minerals, and *phytochemicals*. Many of these substances are antioxidants that that can actually help your body defend itself against disease.

> **Tongue Teasers**
>
> **Phytochemicals** are chemicals produced by plants. They help to defend those plants against environmental dangers and also help protect us against harmful viruses and bacteria. They also prevent damage to DNA. Antioxidants protect cells against the harmful by-products of oxygen, called free radicals. They counteract these cellular by-products by binding with them before they can cause damage. Left un-checked, free radicals may cause heart damage, cancer, cataracts, and a weakened immune system.

A healthful diet should include as many of the following foods as possible. Every single one can be incorporated into flavorful dishes.

◆ **Tomatoes.** Studies show that cooked tomatoes found in ketchup, sauces, and soups contain the antioxidant lycopene, which can reduce the risk of prostrate cancer. So—hallelujah!—Ketchup, pasta sauces are all good for you. So is a nice bowl of tomato soup.

◆ **Garlic.** You learned in Chapter 13 that some say garlic has aphrodisiac-like properties. In addition, garlic's sulfur-based compounds, known as allyl sulfides, reduce cholesterol and protect the heart. Garlic has antibacterial and antifungal powers, too. To release its healthy potential you need to smash, mash, or mince it. Add it to those tomato sauces for a doubly nutritious whammy.

Love Busters

Although beans are good for you, you can easily avoid beans' side effects by using some Beano. Before consuming beans, or any other gas-inducing fare, place five drops on the bit you'll eat first.

◆ **Beans.** Like chili? Then beans are easy to include in your diet. They stabilize blood sugar and reduce your risk of high blood pressure, obesity, and cancer. Chickpeas count too, so dip some low-fat chips in a bowl of hummus for a hearty snack.

◆ **Nuts.** A handful of nuts makes a satisfying snack. It's true that nuts have fat, but it's the healthy kind of fat we all need: polyunsaturated and monosaturated. Don't limit yourself to peanuts. Instead, mix up your nuts. Pecans and walnuts contain ellagic acid, which appears to trigger a process that causes cancer cells to self-destruct.

◆ **Blueberries.** These pint-size goodies pack a punch. They contain more antioxidants than any other fruit or vegetable. They can help battle heart disease and cancer, and some studies show they may boost brainpower. Berries are not "girlie food." Hey, bears eat them. Toss them on cereals, bake them in a low-fat cobbler, or sprinkle them on a scoop of low-fat ice cream or frozen yogurt.

◆ **Spinach.** Popeye knew what he was doing. Spinach is loaded with iron and folate—an important B vitamin that lowers levels of a dangerous amino acid that irritates blood vessels. It also contains two phytochemicals—lutein and zeaxanthin—which seem to ward off the eye disease macular degeneration. If you don't want to eat it Popeye style, cook spinach in lasagna and stuffing.

◆ **Soy.** Soy helps prevent heart disease, cancer, and osteoporosis—the bone weakening condition that affects men, as well as women. Since soy is the chameleon of the food world, it comes in many forms and is easy to use in almost any dish. It can soak up all flavors and taste like just about anything. Look for soy burgers and soy chips for a start.

- ◆ **Oatmeal.** Oatmeal makes a wonderful breakfast because the protein in oats helps you feel full and can help prevent overeating later in the day. Oats contain a spongy, soluble fiber that sops up substances that produce cholesterol. They also contain hard-to-find vitamin E compounds.

- ◆ **Green and orange veggies.** Vegetables are great sources of all things healthful. Broccoli is a top green pick—one cup of broccoli contains more vitamin C than an orange. In the orange veggie category, a top choice is pumpkin. It lowers cancer risk and promotes healthy skin. So pumpkin pie is not just for Thanksgiving any more. By the way, sweet potatoes are another great orange food. Slice some up, French-fry-style, sprinkle with olive oil, and bake.

- ◆ **Salmon.** Wild salmon eat smaller fish, which in turn have eaten algae. The algae provide salmon with omega-3 fatty acids, which help the human heart by preventing plaque formation on arteries. Omega-3 fatty acids also reduce cholesterol, and may even protect against Alzheimer's. Other excellent fish and seafood choices include sardines, trout, sea bass, oysters, and clams. Try to eat fish three or four times a week.

What should you drink with all this healthful fare? Not sugar-laden soda. A glass of red wine per day may actually be good for you, because the grape skin it's made from counters hardening of the arteries. Green or black teas are also good, too. They're loaded with antioxidants. If you're not a hot tea fan, try it iced. You still get the benefits.

Does your lady say, "Too much beer, dear?" As an alternative to beer, try stout. It's not only flavorful but also loaded with healthful antioxidants. Its high concentration of B1 vitamins can lessen the risk of clogged arteries.

Mood Makers _____

Men need nine servings of fruits and veggies per day. On average, you guys eat only half that amount. The big key to eating them is having them around. Keep bowls of fruit and trays of veggies at eye level in the fridge. Many now come pre-cut at the supermarket. If they're prepared ahead of time, you'll start to instinctively grab for them. And don't forget to share some with your lady, because she needs them, too.

Shop So You Don't Drop

Even if you're unable to do a lot of home cooking, you can remain healthy by keeping an eye on what you buy. Reading labels on prepared foods is a great first step in elevating your food awareness. Food labels can provide useful information about the amounts per serving of fat, calories, dietary fiber, and several important nutrients, like vitamin A, vitamin C, calcium, and iron. They can also help you compare different brands of foods and their overall nutritional content.

Love Busters

Watch out for snack attacks! Trans fat, which can increase the risk of heart disease, is often found in snack foods like chips and crackers, as well as in vegetable shortenings, some margarines, and other foods made with or fried in partially hydrogenated oils.

Food labels also contain information on what kinds of fat are in the food. Polyunsaturated and monounsaturated fats are required to maintain robust health, but saturated fat should be avoided.

A recent addition to food labels is information on trans fat. The Food and Drug Administration (FDA) has ordered manufacturers to list trans fatty acids, or trans fat, on the nutrition facts panel of foods and some dietary supplements. Basically, trans fat is made when manufacturers add hydrogen to vegetable oil—a process called hydrogenation—to increase shelf life and flavor stability. The FDA has confirmed that trans fat, like saturated fat, increases the risk of coronary heart disease.

Supplements for Men

Even a really healthy diet can leave a few gaps, so it's a good idea to take a few dietary supplements, like a good multi-vitamin. Make sure it includes the antioxidants E, C, and beta-carotene, as well as vitamin B6 and the mineral zinc—both of which are beneficial for prostate health. Don't forget a supplemental dose of calcium, too.

If you want an additional boost, consider some herbs that are believed to contribute to male well-being. Some are meant to treat specific men's problems; others are generally useful for men who are beset by stress and often on the run. Some herbs frequently recommended for men include:

- **Red Clover.** Red Clover, a member of the pea family, contains powerful antioxidants that fight off cancerous growths. Red Clover inhibits enlargement of the prostate gland and the symptoms that accompany it.

- **Saw Palmetto.** This herb is from a small palm tree native to the Atlantic seaboard. It is the most popular and most researched prostate herb. Studies show that saw palmetto shrinks enlarged prostates and relieves urinary problems.

- **Ginkgo Biloba.** This herb, used for centuries in Chinese medicine, comes from a tall, hardy, deciduous tree. It stimulates the mind, helps concentration, and acts to alleviate the symptoms of depression. Gingko also reputedly increases circulation to the penis.

- **Tongkat Ali** (Eurycoma longifolia). Its name means "walking stick" in reference to its impact on male sexuality. Research has shown that this substance contains plant chemicals that support healthy testosterone levels. It also supports a high energy level and mental alertness.

- **Muira Puama.** Muira Puama has been shown to increase both male and female sex drive, as well as help men maintain erections. Muira Puama may also help balance sexual hormone levels.

Herbs are natural substances and have been used medicinally by countless societies for thousands of years. Do be aware, though, that herbs are unregulated substances. It's wise to do your own research, to use extreme caution with regard to dosage amounts, and to obtain all herbs from a reputable source.

Sexercise

Feeling better, looking better, and even loving better are not only about what you put into your body, but also about what you do with your body. Unless you've been living in a sealed-off biosphere devoid of news from the outside world, you already know that exercise is a good thing—in theory. But are you putting that theory into practice, and are you exercising as much and as often as you should?

It's been noted that if you could put the benefits of exercise into a pill, it would be the most powerful healing medicine on Earth. Ah, but you can't. You have to get up and do it. (Nope, lifting a bowl of pretzels and a T.V. Guide doesn't count.) Should a man consult his doctor before starting an exercise program? Yes. But it's a shame no one ever consults a doctor before becoming glued to their sofa and the widescreen T.V.

More often than not, the hardest part of exercising is deciding to start. After you begin, though, exercise is self-reinforcing. The more you do it, the more of it you want to do. That's because you get a cornucopia of benefits, including:

- **A much healthier heart.** Exercise strengthens your heart so it can pump blood more efficiently and bring much-needed oxygen and nutrients to the rest of your body. This is one of the main reasons why you generally feel refreshed and energetic after exercising. Exercise also prevents the onset of high blood pressure and lowers blood pressure that's already high. Exercise also increases the concentration of HDL (good) cholesterol and decreases the concentration of LDL (harmful) cholesterol in the blood.

Love Busters

When a man gains weight, he tends to accumulate fat around his waist in the abdominal area. Having a waist size greater than 40 inches can increase your risk of high blood pressure, diabetes, heart disease, and stroke. Plus, it's harder for us ladies to get our arms around you.

◆ **Better breathing.** The respiratory system benefits from exercise, which promotes deep, rhythmic breathing. An active person's lungs actually develop greater capacity, so you're better able to take in oxygen to nourish your cells.

◆ **Weight control.** As you exercise, your body works harder and requires more fuel (calories). Even after you stop exercising, the body continues to burn calories at a somewhat increased rate for hours.

◆ **Lower blood sugar levels.** As muscles contract during exercise, they use sugar for energy. To meet this energy need, sugar is removed from the blood during and after exercise, which lowers your blood sugar level. Exercise also reduces blood sugar by allowing the body to use available insulin more efficiently. Lower blood sugar levels can help prevent or control adult-onset diabetes, also known as type II diabetes.

◆ **Strong bones and muscles.** Bones respond to the force of muscles at work. Strength-training and weight-bearing exercises help preserve bone mass and may even increase bone density.

◆ **Better balance and coordination.** By strengthening your muscles and bones, you can also improve your balance and coordination, reducing your risk of falls.

◆ **Uplifted mood.** Exercise stimulates the production of endorphins—brain chemicals that produces feelings of well-being. It also activates the neurotransmitters serotonin and norepinephrine. The levels and balance of those neurotransmitters play a role in how people respond to daily events. When you are depressed, the level of serotonin, norepinephrine, or both may be out of sync. Exercise can help synchronize those brain chemicals.

◆ **A higher sex drive and more sexual stamina.** The cardio endurance, muscular endurance, and flexibility that result from exercise come in handy in the bedroom. Studies have found a direct correlation between physical inactivity and a lack of potency. Exercise can increase your potency, and it can also make your sex life more pleasurable.

Thirty minutes or more of physical activity on most days is the minimum needed to improve fitness and enjoy all the benefits of regular exercise. The investment of your time will pay off in spades. Exercise will help you live longer and live better. Your overall quality of life will improve. The stamina and strength gained with regular exercise will make daily tasks—from going up and down stairs to mowing the lawn— much easier on your body. You'll feel more relaxed, and sleep better at night. You'll also feel proud of yourself—as you should.

Finally, exercise can offer you and your partner more years together. In a study of Harvard graduates, men who burned 2,000 or more calories a week by walking, jogging, climbing stairs or playing sports lived an average of one to two years longer than those who burned fewer than 500 calories a week by exercising.

Mood Makers

Don't forget that sex burns calories! A 180-pound man can burn about 10 calories per 5 minutes of vigorous sex. And the more vigorous it is, the more calories burned. Keep it up for an hour and a half and you're down nearly 200 calories.

Doctor, Doctor

Even those with the healthiest diets and exercise regimes may have times when they're under the weather. When you're feeling sick, your wife or girlfriend may encourage you to visit the doctor. But will you? Quite possibly not. In fact, you might also be reluctant to get regular medical check-ups. Study after study has shown that women are far more vigilant about check-ups than men. Every year, women make 150 million more trips to doctors than men do.

Key Medical Screenings

I know, I know. If it ain't broke don't fix it, right? No. The price of delay and denial is high. For example, one in nine men will be diagnosed with prostate cancer, yet few will have the easy and painless digital rectal exam and prostate specific antigen blood test to detect it.

Top health experts from the U.S. Preventive Services Task Force have made the following recommendations, based on scientific evidence, about which screening tests you should have:

- **Cholesterol checks.** Have your cholesterol checked at least every five years, starting at age 35. If you smoke, have diabetes, or if heart disease runs in your family, start having your cholesterol checked at age 20.

- **Blood pressure.** Have your blood pressure checked at least every two years.

- **Colorectal cancer tests.** Begin regular screening for colorectal cancer starting at age 50. Your doctor can help you decide which test is right for you. How often you need to be tested will depend on which test you have.

- **Diabetes tests.** Have a test to screen for diabetes if you have high blood pressure or high cholesterol.

- **Depression.** If you've felt "down," sad, or hopeless, and have felt little interest or pleasure in doing things for two weeks straight, talk to your doctor about whether he or she can screen you for depression.

- **Sexually transmitted diseases.** Talk to your doctor to see whether you should be screened for sexually transmitted diseases, such as HIV.

- **Prostate cancer screening.** Talk to your doctor about the possible benefits of either a prostate-specific antigen (PSA) test or digital rectal examination (DRE).

Some men need certain screening tests earlier, or more often, than others. Talk to your doctor about which of the tests listed above are right for you, when you should have them, and how often. Each screening also gives you an opportunity to talk with your doctor about your health-related behaviors, and to establish a working relationship with a physician in the event a condition is discovered.

No Excuse for Excuses

I bet you have plenty of excuses for not checking out your health. Most men do. One third of American men have not had a checkup in the past year. Nine million men haven't seen a doctor in five years.

Take a look: (Do any of these seem like your particular excuses?)

- "I'm too busy with work to go to the doctor."

- "I don't want to hear a lecture about being out of shape."

- "Exams are embarrassing—I hate being poked and prodded."

- "Even if I am feeling less than great, I don't want to seem like a complainer."

- "I'm afraid I might find out something I don't want to hear."

Sure, you can rationalize any one of these. And your resistance is perfectly under-standable. Since boyhood you have probably gotten the message that "real men" are self-sufficient and that if they have a problem they ought to suck it up and shake it off. But it's time to overcome that conditioning. Let your logic prevail. Prevention and early detection are critical aspects of maintaining your good health.

Love Busters

If your partner is nag-ging you to get a checkup, don't get defensive and don't just "yes dear" her. remember that's her way of saying, "I love you and want to keep you around."

When in doubt, remember the words of Mickey Mantle: "If I'd known I was going to live this long, I would have taken better care of myself."

The Least You Need to Know

- ◆ Most of the major health threats facing men today can be prevented or mini-mized by sensible lifestyle choices.

- ◆ Real men can still have real food—just make wise ingredient substitutions, read the labels, and include choices known to boost energy and immunity.

- ◆ Exercise is an excellent way to prevent illness, trim down, and boost energy and libido—once you start, it is self-reinforcing.

- ◆ No matter how balanced your diet, a few good supplements can help fill in any gaps.

- ◆ Many men resist regular medical check-ups and screenings, but the price of avoidance can be much too high.

Chapter 23

Remaining Forever Hers

In This Chapter

- The chemistry of falling, and remaining, in love
- The three aspects of long-term love
- The perils of lop-sided love
- Gauging your levels of passion, intimacy, and commitment
- Creating a legacy of love

When you fell in love with your woman, everything seemed exciting and new. You felt so alive, so lucky, so overwhelmed by this unexpected experience. But here is love's great paradox: the better the relationship goes, the more the initial burning excitement cools. Now what?

Fortunately, intimacy and commitment grow even as initial passion takes on a more mellow nature. And, with the right attitude, passion itself can be periodically rekindled. The nature of long-term love is the topic of this final chapter.

After Love's Lightening Bolt

For every man and his woman, falling in love is a unique experience. But the emotional and biological path that love takes is remarkably consistent in every case.

What prompts a male to hunt for a mate? Initially, lust. What prompts a woman to do the same? Primarily, the longing to bond with an attractive, reliable mate and begin making familial attachments. But each gender, underneath their primary urges, also wants what the other wants.

When lust and longing for attachment converge, individuals can find they've gotten more than they bargained for. They're each infused with the heady sensation that accompanies the merging of physical and romantic love—and the process of merging with one another. They both narrow their focus and decide to stick with one exceptional partner—one they feel can absolutely fulfill all their dreams.

At each of these stages, brain chemicals shape our behaviors and our reactions to our beloved. First, as the French say, we are hit with the "lightening bolt" of love. We may describe the feeling as *ooh-la-la*, but what's actually happening is that our levels of dopamine and norepinephrine are soaring. The flipping of these chemical switches causes us to experience exhilaration. We are so elated by and preoccupied with our lover that even our basic needs for food and sleep are diminished.

Although we sometimes refer to this stage of a relationship as "lovesickness," we are actually the opposite of sick when in the initial, breathless stage of love. Bernie Seigel, M.D., a physician, author, and researcher noted for his work in the field of mind-body connections and healing, contends that people who are falling in love have a physiological response to their emotions that makes them stronger and more physically resilient in certain ways. Lowered lactic acid levels in their bloodstreams make them less tired, and increased endorphin levels render them less sensitive to pain.

Tongue Teasers

Researchers say that **cuddle chemicals**—the hormones vasopressin and oxytocin—facilitate the drive for long-term, familial attachments.

But the surge of elation-inducing brain chemicals is, by nature, impermanent. This kind of intensity occurs only when we have an experience that is new and previously *unknown*. Once we get to know the object of our affections better, the chemical rush subsides. A preponderance of dopamine and norepinephrine is then replaced with hormones that some researchers call *cuddle chemicals* that stimulate bonding.

Cuddle chemicals give us a delightful warm, fuzzy feeling. They're deeply satisfying. But, hey, what happened to that lightening bolt charge? To find it again in its purest form we'd have to go out and hunt for someone new. But if you really value the relationship you're in, and the woman you're in it with—that's not such an appealing prospect anymore.

All long-term lovers find themselves in such a situation. Their choice is either to stay and nurture the bond they have forged or go off and cavort with a new love object. If the latter were your choice you wouldn't have read this book, now would you? Clearly you're the kind of guy who sticks. But every now and again you wish you could recapture the lightening bolt that started your relationships off with a jolt. What's to be done? To find the solution, let's look at an enlightening theory about the elements of long-term love.

The True Love Triangle

Throughout the ages, love has always been easier to write ethereal sonnets about than to quantify in concrete terms. However, Dr. Robert Sternberg, a Yale University psychology and education professor, has done an exceptional job of defining lasting love in practical terms. He does this in what he calls his triangular theory of love.

Lasting love, Sternberg says, consists of three elements. The first is passion; the second, intimacy; and the third, commitment. Each component is invaluable and indispensable if a relationship is to endure.

Side One: Passion

Passion, of course, is indispensable because it ignites love's initial fire. Trying to forge a long-term relationship without a burst of passion is like trying to cook a roast without lighting the oven.

Ah, but what happens when the roast is done and the oven cools? As the noted psychologist Theodore Reik wrote, "Love can outlast passion .... It can survive, but only if it changes its character, or rather, if it gains real character." Love's "character" comes from the other two sides of Sternberg's triangle: intimacy and commitment.

Side Two: Intimacy

The word intimacy comes from a Latin root meaning "innermost." That seems logical, because intimacy is love's deep emotional component. Intimacy involves having warm, friendly feelings for another. It involves divulging our own feelings, listening to our partner's, and believing that it is safe to do both.

Intimacy involves the ability to be empathic, and to see the world from our partner's point of view. Somewhat paradoxically, it also involves the ability to give another person enough space to be him- or herself and to grow as a separate individual.

There is another curious, somewhat paradoxical element to intimacy as well. Over the years, a couple's intimacy may seem to be fading, even as it grows stronger and stronger. Sometimes, you need to consider a relationship quite carefully before you can determine which way the trend is going. For example, after many years together the actual number of hours a couple spends conversing in words might lessen, but they may have developed many other ways of communicating with one another that transcends words. Their emotional and spiritual bond might allow them to deeply touch one another in ways that are not obvious to outsiders. Sometimes what a long-married couple communicates with a smile is more than what newlyweds say over the course of a long verbal discussion.

Mood Makers

Research shows that although men talk more about valuing autonomy, they also value intimacy. Though men might not have been as well trained to seek and sustain intimacy, the capacity for intimacy is not really a gender-related trait.

Whereas passion draws people in toward love, intimacy can initially put them off. It is spooky, in a way, to have someone in your life who knows you as well as, or maybe better than, you know yourself. As attracted as we might be to another, there can be a part of us that wants to throw up a barrier. Even in long-term relationships, there can be times when we resist complete openness, because we don't want to feel so exposed. But until one is ready to accept that a certain amount of transparency and vulnerability go with the territory of true love, such a love will fail to thrive.

Side Three: Commitment

Commitment, the final element of the long-term love troika, is love's glue. It keeps us around even on those days when we might not feel like being around. On those days it may feel that our glue is "Crazy Glue," but it still serves it purpose.

Commitment represents not only the wish but also the determination to make a relationship last. Commitment is a decision made and honored. That decision says you will stay by someone's side even when immediate gratification might be gotten elsewhere. Yes, even if it means being less than ecstatically happy for a while.

We stay in a committed relationship because we have made a promise, but we also stay because we have faith. We believe, deep in our heart, that the eventual substantial rewards of staying outweigh those of making a change.

> **Love Busters** _____
>
> Don't bolt—even when passion is on the back burner and you think it would be easier to have an intimate conversation with a Martian than with your woman, commitment is what sees you through. Remember your promise.

Lop-Sided Love

There are many times during any long-term relationship when one element of the love triangle or another takes the lead position. There are times when the level of intimacy might be high, with passion simmering almost imperceptibly in the background. There are instances when there is more distance between two partners than one or both would like, yet commitment remains stalwart. These shifts are normal and natural. Love always works so long as three pillars support it.

Relationships that lack a crucial element, however, do not add up to long-term satisfaction. The equations work out quite differently, in fact.

- Intimacy and passion together produce romantic love, but without commitment that love will be transient—perhaps a tenderly remembered affair.

- Intimacy and commitment without passion produce a genial, companionable love—like the love of best friends.

- Passion and commitment together produce a shallow love—the stuff of whirlwind romance that, in retrospect, seems poorly thought through.

You wouldn't want sizzle without steak. But you wouldn't want steak without sizzle either. It's only when all three aspects underpin a relationship that it will be mature and complete.

A Review for You

Throughout this book, you've been given lots of ideas for concrete actions you can take to keep your partner and yourself happy, and your relationship solid. Do you know which of these contribute to love's three elements? I'll bet you can make some pretty good educated guesses, but—as you remember from your school days—it's always a good idea to review.

Keeping It Fresh

Passion thrives on novelty. Adding new things to a familiar relationship drives up levels of happy-making brain chemicals all over again.

Several studies show that couples that make it a point to step outside their routines, shake things up, and embrace new adventures report a higher level of satisfaction with their partners and their relationship.

Among the things you can do to enhance your relationship with new experiences are:

- Trying new pastimes together

- Visiting new destinations, near or far

- Learning new skills together (like signing up for those dance lessons)

- Surprising your woman with a special night out—or in

- Getting her a gift for "no reason"

- Flirting and teasing in unexpected ways

- Dressing up super-sharp and looking your very best for her

- Complimenting her on some change she's made to her physical appearance

- Trying new lovemaking techniques or toys—or both

He Says/She Says

"I think the most dangerous thing any two people can do to their relationship is to get stuck in a rut. Whenever my wife and I feel that happening, when we are getting too complacent, one of us takes the lead in shaking things up. Our rule is 'change something—anything.' It seems to work, because we have been going strong for thirty years."
—Tim, 54

You might think that in mentioning sex at the end of this list, I deliberately saved the best for last. But the truth is that passion consists of much more than sex. Besides, doing all the other things on this list will only make sex that much more intense.

Keeping It Real

Intimacy may seem like a somewhat amorphous term, but there are many concrete ways of cultivating it. Anything that contributes to feelings of emotional warmth constitutes an intimate gesture. Likewise, so do things that contribute to each partner's sense that they are understood and valued for who they are.

Some things you can do to keep your intimate connection strong:

- Making spontaneous thoughtful gestures to show you care
- Being sure to spend time alone together, despite busy schedules
- Doing your fair share of household and parenting chores
- Helping her learn to relax and take a break
- Conversing more—not only about your relationship, but about things in general
- Listening well and responding thoughtfully
- Laughing together
- Being gracious and polite to her
- Showing respect for her friends and family
- Devoting more time to sensual experiences and to foreplay outside of the bedroom
- Prolonging your loving mood after lovemaking itself
- Accepting your partner's flaws
- Handling even your disagreements with fairness and sensitivity
- Making up after quarrels

Notice that an intimate relationship is not one that is free of conflict. In fact, just the opposite is true. Intimacy should be steady and strong enough to accommodate conflict, which is a natural part of the interaction between two individuals.

Mood Makers

Seinfeld fans may recall a very funny episode about "make-up sex" being especially exciting. It's true. Coming together, literally and figuratively, after a quarrel adds a certain pizzazz, in part because the two of you have felt separate for too long, and in part because it is a great means of blowing off any residual steam. Just be sure you and your partner are both ready to forgive and forget in this powerful way.

Keep On Keeping On

Commitment is something that is often expressed symbolically, such as in the presentation of an engagement or wedding ring, or the public exchanging of vows. Such symbols are important, but they lack meaning unless they are backed up with an attitude that says "I'm in it for the long run." Commitment is both a promise *and* a process.

Things you can do to live your commitment every day include:

◆ Valuing fidelity and remaining physically faithful to your woman

◆ Persevering in the relationship even when things are not going smoothly

◆ Actively rekindling affections after difficult times or periods of estrangement

◆ Supporting your woman as she faces life's challenges

◆ Using your relationship as an anchor as you face life's setbacks and disappointments

◆ Celebrating the way you and your partner both change and evolve throughout your years together

◆ Staying healthy and fit so that you can both have as many active, enjoyable years together as possible

He Says/She Says

"You know my philosophy of commitment? When the going gets tough, the tough don't get going."
—Phil, 50

◆ Accepting that while you will both grow older, things can continue to get even better

It's always good to remember how committed you are. But what's the best time to do so? Not when you are in the throes of a passionate interlude or a stretch of comfortably warm and fuzzy intimacy. Stay committed when the chips are down.

Checking Your Balance

How is your relationship doing with regard to passion, intimacy, and commitment? Keep track for a week and see. At the end of each day, give yourself a checkmark when you've done something to please your woman that falls into more than one of these categories. If you think there's some overlap—for example, you did something that you consider intimate *and* passionate—go ahead and give yourself a check in both. (You've gotten this far, and I think you deserve some extra credit!)

	Mon	Tues	Wed	Thurs	Fri	Sat	Sun
Passion	___	___	___	___	___	___	___
	___	___	___	___	___	___	___
	___	___	___	___	___	___	___
Intimacy	___	___	___	___	___	___	___
	___	___	___	___	___	___	___
	___	___	___	___	___	___	___
Commitment	___	___	___	___	___	___	___
	___	___	___	___	___	___	___
	___	___	___	___	___	___	___

It's important to have your relationship supported by all three pillars. Nevertheless, you should be aware that any given week represents only a slice of a relationship's totality. If your tally is heavy on one or two elements, but lacking elsewhere, it is probably just the particular phase that you and your partner are in. Don't do anything drastic! Just see if you can make a little extra effort here and there and then take a new week's tally in 30 days.

Love's Legacy

Apart from keeping tabs on your relationship in the present, being hers forever entails thinking about what is yet to be. What are your goals for the future? Do they match up with hers? And how well do they need to?

Antoine de Saint-Exupery, the author best known for his philosophical fable, *The Little Prince*, said, "Love does not consist in gazing at each other, but in looking together in the same direction." This is a profound, and very accurate, sentiment. If your vision of the future is that the two of you will remain exactly as you are right now and that your relationship will stay the same, it's time to reconsider.

As time goes by, you and your woman will have many mountains to scale, both as a couple and as unique individuals. For every triumph, a new test will await. You will each have to modify certain dreams you held dear, and generate new aspirations as you move on. You will have to be prepared for setbacks, but also for surprise and serendipity. You will make many new discoveries—some of them via careful planning, some via happy accident.

There are parts of life's journey you each will have to make alone, but the support of your woman for you and yours for her will serve as an ever-present source of strength. After the solitary struggles, you can fall once again into each other's welcoming embrace, delighted to see how each other has grown.

As long-term partners, you will want to periodically re-evaluate your goals and your overall mission as a couple. In the early years, your joint mission may include making a home together and starting a family. Later, it may include participating to a greater and greater degree in the life of your community. Later still, it might be to support one another as children leave the nest, and as you grow older.

Mood Makers

How do we know when our love is going as it should? As Italian sociologist Francesco Alberoni put it, "Because we repeatedly fall in love with the same person."

Ultimately, part of your shared mission with your woman will be to leave a legacy. Maybe you want to leave the world the legacy of well-adjusted offspring, and a home that's been welcoming and well cared for. Maybe you want to leave spiritual or social traditions that will be honored and embellished by your descendants. Maybe you just want to be remembered as really cool role models—tolerant parents, good neighbors, and loyal, fun-loving friends.

In any case, discussing and creating your legacy, and updating your mission, is something you and your woman can enjoy doing at regular intervals—to be sure that your general goals for the long-term future coincide. Having shared goals is of immense value, even though each of you will contribute to them in your own individual way, as well as together.

That said, of course, the future is about tomorrow. Don't let it eclipse today. Whatever your dreams and goals, remember each day to appreciate your woman and let her appreciate you. Every now and again, do something a little wild and crazy. Throw out the rulebook, and have a blast.

Remember, nothing is outside the realm of possibility when you love your woman for who she is and when you love yourself for who you are, too. Never stop being grateful for all the wonderful things your lady brings to your life and never stop bringing wonderful things into hers.

May the two of you never stop pleasing one another.

The Least You Need to Know

- ◆ Powerful brain chemicals make us feel elated when we fall in love—and can be rekindled periodically—but there's more to any love that supersedes transience.

- ◆ Long-term love consists of intimacy, commitment (these two make up the "steak"), and passion (the "sizzle"); all three are important for long-term satisfaction.

- ◆ Happy and mature relationships transition through phases when one or two of love's aspects are most in evidence, but a relationship that lacks any single aspect is in danger of extinction.

- ◆ A couple should have evolving goals and missions, and should agree on the legacy they will leave—although none of this should take precedence over simply enjoying one another.

Appendix **A**

Pleasing Gift Resources

For any occasion, or none at all, here's a list of gift ideas to delight her and suit her every whim.

Jewelry & Watches

EVP Design
www.finejewelryart.com
831-336-8835
Fine assortment of unique jewelry designs. Handcrafted and designed rings, bracelets, necklaces, and earrings.

Tiffany's
www.tiffany.com
1-800-843-3269
Classic, beautiful jewelry. Famous for style and tradition.

Fortunoff
www.fortunoff.com
1-800-Fortunoff
Diverse collection of fine jewelry (including engagement rings) and excellent prices.

Kay Jewelers
www.kay.com
1-800-877-8169
Specializes in gold and diamonds, wonderful fine jewelry. The website has a diamond buying guide to learn about color, size, shape, and weight of diamonds before you purchase one.

Macy's
www.macy's.com
Check local telephone listings.
Great quality precious and semiprecious jewelry, including broaches, watches, rings, bracelets, and earrings. Site has a great gemstone buying guide. This is helpful if you're not sure which stone to choose.

Bloomingdales
www.bloomingdales.com
Check local telephone listings.
Great selection of brand name jewelry from Kate Spade to Burburry.

Overstock.com
www.overstock.com
1-800-The-Big-O
Great selection of well-priced precious and semiprecious jewelry. Special section of website devoted to designing your own jewelry.

Target
www.Target.com
Check local telephone listings.
For the tasteful, hip man on a budget. Great selection of semiprecious and costume jewelry.

Carroll's Fine Jewelry
www.carrollsfinejewelry.com
carrolls1895@earthlink.net
206-622-9191
Seattle's oldest family owned jewelry store. Want a more personalized touch to your gift? Try this site for fine jewelry, wedding jewelry, and watches.

ebay
www.ebay.com
E-mail through site.
Huge selection of jewelry. Constantly stocking new jewelry. Great prices and unique selections.

Fossil
www.fossil.com
1-800-449-3056
A classic blend of American style and craftsmanship. Fossil watches are gorgeous and she will definitely appreciate one.

Princeton Watches
www.princetonwatches.com
1-800-572-8263
Princeton Watches offers a fine collection of watches. Many designer names represented.

Swatch
www.swatch.com
Regional phone numbers listed on site.
Swatch takes the prize for fun and funky. Always trendy and in style, Swatch is a great place to find her a gift.

Omega
www.omega.ch
1-877-839-5224
Hailed as one of the most beautiful and elegant watch companies in the world, Omega offers various pieces of timeless beauty.

Chocolate and Gourmet Goodies

Godiva
www.godiva.com
1-800-9-Godiva
Among the best chocolate in the world. Try the truffles and biscuits. Site features a buying guide so you can choose a box with her favorites.

Lindt Chocolates
www.lindt.com
Check local telephone listings.
An alternative to Godiva, fine selection of very rich chocolates and coffee flavored chocolates. Creamy and delicious.

Gabriel Teas
www.gabrielteas.com
304-598-8903
Assortment of gourmet goodies, teas, cookies, chocolates, and coffee.

L.A. Burdick Chocolate
www.burdickchocolate.com
1-800-229-2419
The handmade chocolate is delicious and crafted into most eye-pleasing, whimsical shapes. The tiny chocolate mice are a favorite.

Gevalia
www.gevalia.com
1-900-Gevalia
Whether it's flavored coffee, gourmet goodies, or coffee accessories, Gevalia is an excellent retailer of fine pampering products.

Harry & David
www.harryanddavid.com
1-877-322-1200
From gift baskets to chocolate to baked goodies, Harry and David offers the best selection of healthy and indulgent treats for her. Bonus: this store has a last minute gift section and quick shipping options.

Cherry Moon Farms
www.proflowers.com/cherrymoonfarms
1-888-378-2758
Gift baskets, gift towers, monthly fruit clubs, gourmet desserts, and wine.

Lake Champlain Chocolates
www.lakechamplainchocolates.com
1-800-465-5909
Beautiful hand-crafted chocolates and gift baskets. Site features a wedding chocolates guide and ideas about when to give chocolate as a gift.

Gertrude Hawk Chocolates
www.gertrudehawkchocolates.com
1-800-822-2032
Fine chocolates, including a special sugar free and low-carb chocolate section.

Flowers

1-800-Flowers
www.1800flowers.com
1-800-Flowers
Flowers are perfect for the girl who has everything. 1-800-Flowers offers a wide variety of floral arrangements that can be sent just about anywhere in the world.

Proflowers.com
www.proflowers.com
1-800-776-3569
Proflowers offers a nice selection of arrangements and gift baskets. Proflowers promises to ship "fresh from the field."

Books

Amazon.com
www.amazon.com
One of the biggest bookstores on the planet, Amazon offers huge savings and a marketplace where you can locate out of print, collectable or rare books. If she's a book nut, Amazon is the place to shop for her.

Barnes and Noble
www.barnesandnoble.com
1-800-THE-BOOK
Barnes and Noble is also an excellent bookstore and features a wide variety of books, DVDs, CDs, and journals.

Borders
www.borders.com
Check local telephone listings.
Borders is one of the best bookstores with an extensive music section, as well as an excellent stock of books.

Music

Ez-tracks.com
www.ez-tracks.com
E-mail through site.
Ez-tracks makes buying her electronic music easy. Offers a wide variety of songs to choose from at great prices.

Coconuts
www.coconuts.com
Check local telephone listings.
Offers a wide variety of DVDs, CDs, and electronic accessories.

Walmart
www.walmart.com
1-800-966-6546
Great prices, great music. Walmart has a good selection of popular music.

Apple-iTunes
www.apple.com/itunes
1-800-275-2273
iTunes is one of the best places to download songs. Hundreds of hits for her iPod or MP3 player.

Best Buy
www.bestbuy.com
1-800-888-BEST-BUY
Best Buy has excellent prices on a wide variety of electronics including CD players, iPods, MP3 players, and portable handheld devices. Best Buy also carries an extensive selection of CDs, cassettes, and DVDs.

Target
www.target.com
Check local telephone listings.
Great prices on electronics including CD players and stereos, and a large selection of CDs for her.

Gardening

Smith & Hawken
www.smithandhawken.com
1-800-940-1170
Upscale items not just for the well-appointed garden but also for the well-dressed, well-prepared gardener.

Gardener's Eden
www.gardenerseden.com
1-866-430-3336
An excellent resource for the woman interested in outdoor entertaining, plant artistry, and garden hideaways.

Home Depot
www.homedepot.com
1-800-349-4358
Home Depot is one of the best resources for gardening equipment, as well as plants, seeds, and lawncare items.

Sears
www.sears.com
1-800-349-4358
Sears always offers reasonable prices on lawncare and gardening tools. Wide selection of items.

Lowes
www.lowes.com
1-800-890-5932
Lowes also offers a large selection of gardening equipment, home care items, plants and seeds.

Elegant Housewares

Williams-Sonoma
www.williams-sonoma.com
877-812-6235
Williams-Sonoma is the store for cooking enthusiasts and carries an extensive line of high quality kitchen accessories and appliances.

Crate and Barrel
www.crateandbarrel.com
1-800-967-6696
Stylish and chic housewares at affordable prices.

Pier 1
www.pier1.com
1-800-245-4595
Pier 1 offers candles, furniture, and housewares from all around the world. Treat the exotic woman in your life to something unique.

Yankee Candle
www.yankeecandle.com
1800-243-1776
Women love candles and Yankee Candle has the best candles on the market. There are tons of scents to choose from or buy her a gift card.

Pottery Barn
www.potterybarn.com
1-888-779-9156
Pottery barn offers a huge selection of housewares, deck furniture, and accessories. Hint: this store also creates monogrammed towels and linens for that personalized touch.

West Elm
www.westelm.com
1-866-West-Elm
West Elm features a huge variety of upscale furnishings, linens, candles, wall décor, and lighting, as well as home accessories.

Clothing

Macy's
www.macys.com
Check local telephone listings.
The name Macy's is synonymous with style and quality. With several departments to choose from, a gift certificate from Macy's would be her dream come true.

Nordstrom
www.nordstrom.com
1-888-282-6060
Nordstrom is the place for name brand and designer women's clothing. Over 400 brands are displayed on the website.

Express
www.expressfashion.com
Check local telephone listings.
Trendy and stylish clothing for her. Treat the model in her to a runway look.

Ann Taylor
www.AnnTaylor.com
1-800-DIAL-ANN
Classy, elegant, and high quality clothing that she will love. Has a good petite section.

Banana Republic
www.bananarepublic.com
1-888-BR-STYLE
High quality, high fashion. Lots of cute classic looks, including suits, accessories, and casual wear.

Gap
www.gap.com
1-800-GAP-STYLE
Classy and stylish clothing. A woman's favorite.

Bloomingdales
www.bloomingdales.com
Check local telephone listings.
Bloomingdales is famous for brand name style and high fashion.

Eddie Bauer
www.eddiebauer.com
1-800-625-7935
Is she into casual comfort? Eddie Bauer offers a fine line of causal clothing with a touch of preppie.

Talbots
www1.talbots.com
1-800-TALBOTS
Beautiful, high fashion clothing for all age ranges. Includes a special petite, misses, and larger size section.

Old Navy
www.oldnavy.com
1-800-OLD-NAVY
Trendy fashion for her at excellent prices.

Lane Bryant
www.lanebryant.com
1-800-228-3120
Beautiful, chic clothes for sizes 14 and up.

Lingerie

Love Fifi
www.lovefifi.com
1-866-LUV-FIFI
Huge assortment of gorgeous lingerie, bras, hosiery, panties, corsets, and sexy shoes.

Victoria's Secret
www.victoriassecret.com
1-800-411-5116
Classic and trendy lingerie, bras, and panties. She'll always love something from Victoria's.

Fredrick's of Hollywood
www.fredericks.com
Check local telephone listings.
Sensual and delicate lingerie, corsets, hosiery, shoes, and accessories in regular, petite, and plus sizes.

My Diva's Closet
www.store.yahoo.com/mydivascloset
714-523-3320
Is she a party animal? Get this party started at My Diva's Closet. They offer a great collection of lingerie, wigs, sexy costumes, club wear.

Big Gals Lingerie.Com
www.biggalslingerie.com
1-866-501-6355
Is your lady big and beautiful? Big Gals Lingerie offers a selection of plus size lingerie for the most voluptuous woman.

Biggerbras
www.biggerbras.com
1-877-475-8110
More plus size bras and lingerie for the full-figured woman.

Lingerie of Hollywood
www.lingerie-of-hollywood.com
1-877-473-3070
Help her feel like the star that she is. Lingerie of Hollywood offers various styles and shapes of lingerie, including custom designed corsets for the Renaissance Woman.

1 Lingerie Store
www.1lingeriestore.com
1-800-206-7230
1 Lingerie Store offers a wide assortment of baby-dolls, and exotic lingerie.

ThePlayboyStore.com
www.store.playboy.com
1-800-993-6339
Lots of fun outfits for her. Has she ever wanted to dress like a playmate? Here's your chance to make her one.

Pajama World
www.pajamaworld.com
603-520-0136
Offers a wide assortment of casual lingerie, silk and flannel pajamas.

Pajama Gram
www.pajamagram.com
1-800-GIVE-PJS
This store offers a beautiful selection of pajamas that are delivered right to your lady's door in a beautiful organza hatbox. This is one of the cutest gifts she will ever receive. Pajama counselors are standing by to assist you.

Jeannie Nitro Bone Church Gothic Clothing
www.jeannienitro.com
602-279-0497
Help her look and feel like a princess or goth queen with clothing and lingerie at Jeannie Niro. This store features a wide variety of elegant goth, fetish and fantasy wear.

Female First
www.femalefirst.co.uk/lingerie
01942 720 377 (British)
This site offers many articles on lingerie, in addition carries a great variety of movie inspired lingerie for your favorite diva.

Stationary and Related Items

American Stationery Company, Ltd.
www.americanstationery.com
1-800-822-2577
American Stationery Company offers a wide variety of fine personalized stationery and accessories. In addition, they offer personalization and low, factory-direct pricing.

Paperchicks
www.paperchicks.com
1-866-663-4659
Huge chick-approved supply of stationery with great prices and personalization.

Iprint.com
www101.iprint.com
650-474-3939
A variety of personalized letterhead and other printing supplies. Hint: go romantic and get her a mug with a picture of you two or a favorite inscription.

The Jungle Store
www.thejunglestore.com
1-888-621-2249
Does your lady favor a particular animal? Whether it's an anteater, bear, tiger, or a cow, the jungle store has a variety of adorable stationery products.

Chelsea Paper
www.chelseapaper.com
888-407-CPCO(2726) x115
Chelsea Paper features elegant note cards, gifts, and wedding supplies. This store will also monogram stationary.

Fine Stationery.com
www.finestationery.com
1-888-808-FINE
Fine Stationary.com offers a really cute selection of note cards, personalized and non-personalized stationery. Great prices.

Horchow.com
www.horchow.com
1-877-944-9888
Horchow has a great selection of novelty note cards, stationery, labels, and embossers.

Luscious Paper
www.64.182.1.116/lp/index.php
201-656-5874
Luscious paper is the perfect store for the lady scribe. Beautiful hand-bound journals, quill pens, and inks adorn the shelves, as well as gorgeous paper from around the world.

Walter Drake
www.wdrake.com
1-800-858-4979
Walter Drake carries and extensive line of note cards, labels, memo pads, and stationery items. This store is happy to personalize her gift. Excellent prices.

Leather Goods

Coach
www.coach.com
1-800-222-6224
The Coach store sets the mark for quality designer handbags and accessories.

R.D. Gomez
www.rdgomez.com
1-800-440-0699
R.D. Gomez Leather Goods come from a long tradition, passed down among generations since the first Iberian goat hides were fashioned into pouches and wallets. Today, R.D. Gomez represents one of Spain's finest leather houses.

LeatherTree.com
www.leathertree.com
1-800-792-7002
Huge assortment of leather goods. Excellent prices on satchels, purses, backpacks, wallets, jewelry, duffels, tote bags, and desk sets.

LeatherUP.com
www.leatherup.com
1-888-467-0222
Biker chic, bad ass, or stylin' woman. This site has what she needs. Lots of variety- leather skirts, jackets, boots, blazers, and accessories.

Natural Reflections
www.naturalreflections.com
585-374-2520
Natural Reflections has a great assortment of leather accessories and specializes in belts, handbags, buckles, and wallets.

Darnier
www.danier.com
1-877-9-Danier
Darnier carries fine quality leather products.

Rawlings Sports Accessories.com
www.sportsaccessories.com
1-866-587-7678
Specializing in messenger bags and backpacks, Rawlings offers superior craftsmanship with leather goods.

Classic Country Comforts
www.classiccountrycomforts.com
1-888-228-9970
CCC carries the finest quality imported Australian made products including Outback, Duster Style Coats by the original Driza-Bone Company which are made from oil- skins. These coats are waterproof, windproof, and warm. Today, an authentic Driza- Bone coat is an Australian icon renowned for its quality and durability.

Seductive Lingerie Shop.Com
www.seductive-lingerie-shop.com
734-673-1250
Lots of great leather lingerie for her at fabulous prices.

Day Spa Treatments

Georgette Klinger
www.georgetteskinger.com
1-800-Klinger
Fantastic day spa with a variety of different services and locations. Get her a facial, massage, or body wrap and pamper that princess.

Spawish.com
www.spawish.com/vip/ak
856-273-8877
This awesome site allows you to purchase spa gift certificates redeemable all over the country. Treat your lady to a manicure, water therapy, or shiatsu massage that she will never forget.

Electronics

The Sharper Image
www.sharperimage.com
1-800-344-4444
All the latest and greatest electronic toys including personal massagers and portable hand-held devices.

Brookstone
www.brookstone.com
1-800-846-3000
An alternative to The Sharper Image, Brookstone also carries a variety of electronic goodies.

Circuit City
www.circuitcity.com
1-800-843-2489
From iPods to DVD players, if she's into technology, Circuit City has everything she could want. Excellent prices.

Perfume

Sephora
www.sephora.com
1-877-737-4672
From perfume to makeup, Sephora has an amazing selection of beauty products for your lady. This store caters to all price ranges from designer brands to their own label.

FragranceNet.com
www.fragrancenet.com
1-800-727-3867
Offers a nice selection of fragrances for her and specializes in perfume.

Perfumes Boutique
www.perfumesboutique.com
516-292-4757
Also specializes in perfume and body fragrances.

The Kama Sutra Company
www.kamasutra.com
1-800-216-3620
Huge assortment of massage oils, fragrances, gels, body paint.

The Body Shop
www.thebodyshop.com
1-800-263-9746
Fragrances, hair care, foot care, skin care, makeup, and aromatherapy items, The Body Shop has what she wants.

Victoria's Secret
www.victoriassecret.com
1-800-411-5116
V.S. has a beautiful collection of fragrances and makeup. Try "Love Spell" body spray to make her go wild.

Sports and Outdoor Equipment

The Sports Authority
www.thesportsauthority.com
1-888-801-9164
The Sports Authority has *everything* to make your athletic girl smile. From tennis to yoga to running to camping, Sports Authority has your gift covered.

Eastern Mountain Sports
www.ems.com
1-800-463-6367
For the nature enthusiast, EMS carries an extensive line of quality outdoors wear, camping supplies, kayak equipment, and biking gear.

Dick's Sporting Goods
www.dickssportinggoods.com
1-877-846-9997
Dick's also has a wide variety of sporting equipment and supplies at great prices.

Modells
www.modells.com
1-866-835-9129
Modells carries a tremendous selection of sporting equipment, as well as athletic clothing.

ParagonSports
www.paragonsports.com
1-800-961-3030
Also carries a wide array of sports equipment and supplies.

Tickets

Ticketmaster
www.ticketmaster.com
Phone numbers listed by state on site.
Musical theatre, classical theatre, opera, ballet, sports, music and all other events can be found at Ticketmaster. It'll make all the difference to get her great seats at her favorite events. Who knows? You might even find something you would both enjoy.

Selectaticket.com
www.selectaticket.com
201-909-9700
Though not as well known as Ticketmaster, Selectaticket also offers great prices on sports events and other related happenings.

Ticketweb.com
www.ticketweb.com
E-mail through site.
Another great site to purchase tickets to her favorite events. Excellent for concerts.

Tickets Now.com
www.ticketsnow.com
1-800-927-2770
This site has a healthy variety of various ticket opportunities. Especially good with sports and music events.

Appendix B

Sexy Destinations

A change of scenery is a surefire pleaser. Here's a list of suggested getaways that can turn just about any of her travel fantasies into a wonderful reality.

Bed and Breakfast

Bed and Breakfast Online
www.bbonline.com
615-868-1946
It's easy to locate a convenient close getaway, or to find a more distant bed and breakfast inn anywhere in the country with this online search site. Choose from over 5,000 B&B's. The site features over 20,000 photos and offers over 4,000 special packages.

Bed and Breakfast.com
www.bedandbreakfast.com
E-mail through site.
BedandBreakfast.com is a comprehensive worldwide listing of bed and breakfasts, country inns, urban bed and breakfasts, guesthouses, lodges, cabins, historic hotels, small resorts, guest ranches, and even charming farmhouse accommodations. Surprise her with a print-it-yourself bed and breakfast gift certificate.

Cruises

Celebrity Cruises
www.celebrity.com
1-800-647-2251
Celebrity cruises offer first class ambience at affordable rates. In addition to fine dining, entertainment, and casino gambling, they offer an unusually wide range of adult activities including acupuncture and spa services. You can bring the kids along without lamenting your own lack of alone time. Celebrity's Youth Program offers a full compliment of age-specific activities and entertainment around the clock.

Royal Caribbean Cruises
www.royalcarribeancruise.com
1-866-562-7625
Royal Caribbean cruises are a tad more casual than Celebrity, though owned by the same parent company. Adults are assured more activities than they can possibly get to in a typical 7-day run, so consider 10 days. Kids are also well taken care of, and even enjoy the onboard rock-climbing walls on some of the ships. Check out their website for virtual tours of their cruise ship fleet and experience your vacation vicariously before you go.

Princess Cruises
www.princess.com
1-800-PRINCESS
Princess cruises offers a wide variety of destinations, including Bermuda, the Mediterranean, and Alaska—where you can cuddle with your sweetie and sip hot chocolate as you take in the Hubbard Glacier and some amazing wildlife. Their website offers a cruise dictionary for newbie's.

Carnival Cruises
www.carnival.com
1-888-CARNIVAL
Carnival cruises, the "fun ships," feature voyages to Bermuda, the Panama Canal, Europe, Hawaii, Mexico, and the Caribbean. Carnival offers activities for every cruiser and age group. The crowds tend to be on the more boisterous side, but if you and your woman are in a mellow frame of mind, you can enjoy a relaxing massage.

Holland America Cruises
www.hollandamerica.com
1-888-Sail-HAL
Between fine cuisine, intriguing ports of call, and spacious accommodations, Holland America offers a unique, high-end cruise experience.

Disney Cruises

www.disney.com

1-800-951-8332

Enjoy a cruise in spectacular Disney style. Disney cruise ships are state-of-the-art, and their programs are well suited to the entire family. The cuisine is delicious and the restaurants varied and inventive. The kids? You'll never see them!

Windstar Cruises

www.windstarcruises.com

1-877-STAR-SAIL

Windstar truly is 180 degrees off the typical cruise experience. The Windstar passenger sees the world from a romantic sailing ship with luxurious accommodations, a casual yet elegant atmosphere, and exquisite service and cuisine. The ships are small, with far fewer passengers than large ocean liners. This means less crowding and access to exotic ports that are off the beaten path.

Windjammer Cruises

www.windjammer.com

1-800-327-2601

Indulge in the fun of a barefoot adventure with your lover. If you've never felt weathered teakwood beneath your soles, now's your chance. Windjammer's spacious decks are a focal point of activity. Atmosphere onboard is relaxed and comfortable—so you both can let your hair down.

Hiking, Biking, and Adventure

Country Walkers

www.countrywalkers.com

1-800-464-9255

Want to walk across Montana, Wyoming, Utah, or Maine? How about Chile, Bhutan, New Zealand, or Crete? The destination site of this organization reads like a comprehensive world atlas. For over a quarter of a century they've enabled travelers to experience the most breathtaking sites in the world, on foot. Trips include accommodations three meals a day, and between-hike transport by bus, boat, train, plane, gondola, or funicular. Visit the website for a vivid description of a typical day.

Scott Walking Adventures

www.scottwalking.com

1-800-262-8644

Change your mind-set entirely as you immerse yourself in the world's most beautiful venues with like-minded inquisitive and environmentally aware travelers. You can choose from trips that are easy, moderate, or challenging. You can choose something as tame as fall foliage hiking or something as exotic as a trek across Iceland. In winter, you can even snowshoe across Canada. Check out the website photo albums.

The Wayfarers
www.thewayfarers.com
1-800-249-4620
Inspiring coastlines, world-class wine country walks, and lovely mountain vistas are all on the menu. Your woman might especially enjoy this organizations culture walks, which combine walking with other interests such as gardening and cooking.

VBT Deluxe Bicycle Vacations
www.vbt.com
1-800-245-3868
VBT led the way in designing bicycle tours that both invigorate and pamper. They still offer the incredible bike tours of Vermont, which helped build this organizations' fine reputation. But you also try everything from Hawaii to the California wine country to European destinations. For a doubly amazing journey, combine a bicycle and barge tour of Alsace-Lorraine, and explore the medieval towns near the France/Germany border.

Carolina Tailwinds
www.carolinatailwinds.com
1-888-251-3206
Bike America the beautiful, including the Shenandoah Valley, the Outer Banks, and—for real enthusiasts—the Blue Ridge Mountains. This organization knows how to balance exercise with relaxation. Trips feature exquisite cuisine and comfortable, charming inns.

Links 2 Love
www.links2love.com/ski_vacation.htm
E-mail through site.
White snow, warm cabin fires, and the need to cuddle for warmth makes ski vacations great romantic getaways. This site will help you find the perfect one for you and your snow bunny, in places like Colorado, Utah, and California. There's more to it than hitting the slopes: hot tubs, hot cocoa, warm fireplaces.

Just For Fun
www.jus4funusa.com/ballooning.html
E-mail through site.
This company provides romantic hot air balloon rides for two (or more can be accommodated if you insist). Vistas include Northern California wine country, Palm Springs, and San Diego.

Specialty Travel

www.spectrav.com

1-888-624-4030

For those of you into walking on the wild side, this portal offers a variety of different options to connect you with vacation sites that will get your blood pumping. Are you two history buffs? Try an archeological excursion. Perhaps you have been dying to go on safari together. Whatever the adventure, this site can match you up with a great vacation match.

Spas and Retreats

Spa Finder

www.spafinder.com

212-924-6800

Browse this worldwide online directory to find the perfect spa vacation. Check out their "romantic" and "adults only" categories for spas that feature such sensual amenities as couples massage and candlelight dinners. Gift certificates are available.

Rancho la Puerta

www.rancholapuerta.com

1-800-443-7565

A truly unique spa resort, Rancho la Puerta, just south of the Mexican border about an hour from San Diego, Rancho la Puerta qualifies as one of the world's first true eco-resorts. It provides a variety of different activities for you and your partner including artistic workshops, nature walks, meditation, and an astounding variety of fitness workouts. The beauty and sage-infused fragrance of the surrounding land will transport you and your spouse to a realm outside the ordinary. Special couples weeks are available in fall and spring.

Canyon Ranch

www.canyonranch.com

1-800-742-9000

Since 1979, Canyon Ranch has set the standard for health spas all over the world. Every Canyon Ranch experience is an opportunity to explore your potential for the highest possible quality of life with the one you love. Canyon Ranch has resorts in the Berkshires and in Arizona.

Amansala

www.amansala.com

info@amansala.com

Located on the remote beach of Tulum, Mexico, the chic eco-resort, Amansala, is best known for its six-night Bikini Boot Camp program, which is limited to 25 men and women. In between beach power walks, Pilates, yoga, and meditation, swim or snorkel in nearby freshwater swimming holes and visit mysterious Mayan ruins.

Cal-A-Vie
www.cal-a-vie.com
1-866-259-1647
Cal-A-Vie is nestled on 200 acres in a secluded valley 40 miles north of San Diego. The spa accommodates only 24 guests each week, and they are housed in private Mediterranean-style villas. Many consider one of the week's highlights to be the Friday night cooking class, given by a renowned chef.

Mirabel
www.Mirabel.com
1-866-MIRABEL
This Scottsdale, Arizona, spa has been featured on *Oprah* for its weekend couples workshops. Even if you eschew the workshop, Mirabel is well worth a visit for it's gorgeous setting and comprehensive fitness and tennis programs.

Retreat Finder
www.retreatfinder.com
1-800-889-6906
Whether you are on a quest for inner peace, or simply a good yoga workout, this site helps seekers find what they're after. Search here for yoga resorts, meditation retreats, and panoply of inner-peace related sojourns. But do steer clear of the monasteries if a second honeymoon is what you had in mind.

The Chopra Center
www.chopra.com
1-866-260-2236
Located at California's La Costa Resort and Spa, The Chopra Center is a health and wellness retreat that integrates the mind-body techniques and Ayurvedic (Indian healing) principles set forth by internationally acclaimed author and philosopher Dr. Deepak Chopra.

Omega Institute
www.eomega.org
1-800-944-1001
This peaceful, Eden-like oasis in Rhinebeck, New York, offers a plethora of retreats and workshops to expand mind, body, and soul. They sometimes offer workshops in Tantric sexuality.

Island Oases

Club Med
www.clubmed.com
1-800-248-5463
Club Med is a feast for all the senses. Its secluded villages—in sensuous beach locales such as the Bahamas, Cancun, and Bora Bora—feature all-inclusive dining and a potpourri of beachy activities, such as snorkeling and windsurfing. Choose romantic retreats or family friendly clubs. If you choose the latter, your kids will be royally entertained—and kept out of your hair.

Sandals
www.Sandals.com
1-888-SANDALS
Sandals is a collection of 12 of the most romantic reports on the Caribbean's best beaches, created exclusively for couples in love in Jamaica, St. Lucia, Antigua, and the Bahamas. Enjoy an astounding array of land and water sports, including unlimited golf and scuba diving.

The Grand Lido
www.supeclubs.com
(877) 467-8737
With two Jamaican locations, this resort and spa offers all-inclusive high-end pampering and oodles of island charm.

Grand Pineapple Beach
www.allegroantigua.com
1-800-858-4618
Love is always in bloom at this Antiguan resort, with its 4-mile white-sand beach. Walk hand-in-hand through 25 acres of lush gardens and experience romantic seclusion. Getaway here are all-inclusive, featuring sumptuous cuisine, themed buffets, unlimited refreshments, entertainment, dancing, and exciting activities for day and night pursuits.

Palm Island
www.grenadines.net/palm/palmhomepage.htm
1-800-858-4618
Craving extreme privacy? Situated in the island chain of St. Vincent and The Grenadines, Palm Island is located on its own private 135-acre island hideaway at the end of the Windward Island group of the Eastern Caribbean. It has 37 intimate guest rooms and features island motifs, custom rattan furnishings, and luxurious amenities. The vantage point from your private balcony or patio provides a sweeping panoramic view at every turn as far as the eye can see.

Jakes, Jamaica

www.all-jamaica.com/hotels/jake_descr.html

E-mail through site.

This laid back boutique resort is set by the fishing village Treasure Beach and features 15 pastel cottages nestled into the landscape, some with decks just above the lapping sea. Two restaurants serve fresh seafood and spicy, authentic Jamaican cuisine. A music business entrepreneur partially founded the resort, resulting in a comprehensive library of world music for you to dance to—or just relax to.

Atlantis Resort

www.atlantis.com

1-888-528-7155

Whether your fondest vacation fantasy revolves around a fishing boat, a casino, a snorkeling reef, or a spa, you can fulfill it at the Atlantis mega-resort, nestled within the beauty of the Bahamas. There are lots of diversionary kids' activities, but there are also lots of couples that eschew bringing the tykes along.

Beaches

www.beaches.com

1-888-BEACHES

Beaches all-inclusive resorts include all the fun, adventure, and luxury that families want most, elevating the family vacation to world-class standards on the Caribbean's best beaches. Because all the other families will have kids in tow, your offspring will have lots of company aside from you.

European Tours

Gate 1 Travel

www.gate1travel.com

1-800-682-8333

This site features vacations filled in romance and splendor. Specializing in Italian getaways, Gate 1 will transport you and your partner to the Italian countryside, or the bustling streets of Rome.

Alitalia

www.alitalia.com

1-800-223-5730

If Italy is your destination, few do it better than Alitalia. From beautiful Florence to Venice to Naples, this will be one vacation experience that neither you, nor your partner will forget.

Europe Tours

www.europtours.com

1-800-882-3983

With a European tour, you and your spouse will journey back to explore history. This company provides full-service tours to Greece, Italy, Turkey, Great Britain, Spain, and France. They have been in the travel business for over 25 years and enjoy a good reputation.

Tour Vacations to Go

www.tourvacationstogo.com

1-800-680-2858

Vacation options include single country tours of Spain, Greece, Germany, Austria, Portugal, Switzerland, Holland, Norway, Russia, Poland, Turkey, and Iceland. Take your beloved to a fairy tale castle in Germany, the imperial cities of Eastern Europe, or the pristine alpine vistas of Switzerland.

Contiki Tours

www.contikitours.com

1-866-CONTIKI

Experience culture, food, and people of Europe in a fun-filled fast-paced European tour. From Greek Island hopping in spring to watching a midnight sunset in Scandinavia's summertime or strolling through piazzas anytime, Contiki offers the perfect vacation package for you and your partner. Contiki Tours are specifically geared toward younger couples.

America's Sexy City Hotels

The Bishop's Lodge (Santa Fe)

www.bishopslodge.com

505-983-6377

Surrounded by acres of steep hills, red earth, and piñon trees, The Bishop's Lodge is located in its own private valley only a few minutes from intriguing, historical downtown Santa Fe. The scenic, spacious SháNah Spa and Wellness Center at the Lodge offers esthetic services and treatments inspired by the healing traditions of the Pueblo tribes that once lived in this part of New Mexico.

Hotel del Coronado (San Diego)

www.hoteldel.com

1-800-HOTELDEL

The Hotel del Coronado in San Diego, California, is situated along 31 oceanfront acres on Coronado Island. A National Historic Landmark, The Del is considered one of America's most beautiful resorts. Since its opening in 1888, The Del has attracted filmmakers, presidents, and royalty. Today, the legend continues to unfold with the recent unveiling of the dramatic enhancements of a $55 million restoration, featuring an oceanfront lawn, new seaside restaurants, bar, re-designed Victorian rooms, and the Cottages at North Beach, offering exclusive beachfront accommodations.

The Ballastone Inn (Savannah)

www.ballastone.com

E-mail through site.

Entering this painstakingly restored 1838 mansion is like being sent back in a time machine to an era of true grace and sincere hospitality. The romantic hotel is furnished with antiques and authentic reproductions; each room is decorated with designer fabrics. To compliment the original architectural motifs of the Inn, Salamander wall coverings and historic Savannah colors were tailored by renowned Savannah artist. Don't miss afternoon tea in the lush garden.

The Pierre Hotel (New York City)

www.fourseasons.com/pierre

212-940-8109

Just across Fifth Avenue from Central Park, a stroll from the most fabled attractions of New York, The Pierre offers top drawer service—with the charm and comfort of a European residence, accented by original 1930s detailing and the art of *trompe l'oeil*. A New York landmark hotel, The Pierre is a testament to understated elegance.

Miss Celie's Old Victorian Inn & Spa (New Orleans)

www.oldvictorianinn.com

1-800-725-2446

This unique bed and breakfast first opened in the 1880s to pamper socialites. Guests are greeted with hot tea or chilled lemonade, which only hints at the pampering to come. Though the French Quarter lies immediately out the front door, this is another world entirely. Note: this venue is not designed for overly macho sensibilities. The four guest rooms are decorated with ruffles, lace, teddy bears, and period furnishings. But the morning's aromas of fresh-baked breads, biscuits, coffee cakes, eggs, bacon, and home fries are enough for most guys to compensate.

Bellagio (Las Vegas)

www.bellagio.com

1-888-987-6667

This opulent contemporary European-styled enclave is complemented by ornate fountains with a choreographed water ballet, botanical gardens, a fine arts gallery, and an attentive staff. Throughout the resort, guests will enjoy sweeping vistas of the magnificent lake and elegant pool area. Bellagio's 36-story tower features 3,000 luxurious guest rooms, including 270 suites. Sumptuous fabrics, traditionally styled furnishings, and European artwork and antiquities will give each room a lavish yet comfortable and residential feel. The resorts design was inspired by the idyllic village of Bellagio, which overlooks Italy's magnificent Lake Como.

Clinton South Beach (Miami)

www.Clintonsouthbeach.com

305-938-4040

This ultra chic and sexy resort features cool cutting edge design that blends art deco with a unique contemporary spin. Guests should ask about perks like boat rides and free entry to local clubs. For the young and the young at heart.

The Majestic (San Francisco)

www.thehotelmajestic.com

415-441-1100

Constructed in 1902 as a private residence, San Francisco's Hotel Majestic offers romantic refuge from the city's bustle in the charming Victorian neighborhood of Pacific Heights. With its distinctive bay windows, Edwardian styling, and ideal location near the cable cars and high rises of downtown, the hotel ushers guests into another era enhanced with vintage architectural details and adorned with French and English antiques. Here you'll be treated to the gracious traditions of yesteryear—but with all the essentials of today.

Outrageous Second (or First) Honeymoons

Caesars Pocono Resorts

www.caesarspoconoresorts.com

1-877-822-3333

Want to swish down the slopes hand in hand with your snow angel and then cuddle up afterward in front of a warm fire? Here's the perfect place. Caesars Pocono resorts feature a wide variety of couples activities and yes, for those of you into it, they even feature champagne glass hot tubs.

Taveuni Island Resort (Fiji)

www.taveuniislandresort.com

1-866-828-3864

A young New Zealand couple that found this remote island whilst on honeymoon in Fiji, 28 years ago—and decided it would be the perfect place to build a romantic resort. Second honeymooners get special packages and special care in this verdant paradise, complete with cascading waterfalls, rare birds, and hidden lakes.

The Lodge at Koele (Hawaii)
www.laniahotels.com
1-866-656-7125
This Hawaiian honeymoon getaway is situated in the big island's dramatic uplands, where guests will discover sublime extravagance and serenity. You can renew your vows—or take your first set—sheltered among towering Cook pines and Banyan trees. The breathtaking 102-room Lodge has enchanting rustic Hawaiian ambiance and engaging collection of rare artwork. The atmosphere is both refined and thoroughly relaxing. Activities include hiking, horseback riding, tennis, golf, mountain biking, and archery.

Amangani (Jackson Hole, Wyoming)
www.tablethotels.com
E-mail through site.
Amangani (which means "peaceful home") lies across the valley from the Teton Pass. The 40-suite, three-story resort is set on the cliff-edge of a butte. Its roof, crafted of cedar shakes, flows like a natural outcropping. Amangani's rough rock exterior blends so well with the awesome landscape that at night the lights from its windows appear to glow from within the mountain. You can go for broke and rent the 600+ square feet Grand Teton Suite with its breathtaking views of the Grand Teton, king-size bed, and sunken tub.

Ventana Inn and Spa (Big Sur, California)
www.ventanainn.com
1-800-628-6500
Tucked into a hillside overlooking Big Sur's dramatic Pacific coastline, this is a secluded honeymoon for the discriminating. The Inn has 12 unique buildings, housing 60 enchanting, romantic rooms and suites, most with fireplaces and many with private hot tubs. All-inclusive honeymoon packages are available.

Ashford Castle, Ireland
www.celticcastles.com/castles/ashford
44-870-050-3232
Seven hundred year-old castle sits amidst some of the world's most spectacular scenery in the countryside outside of Galway City—commanding the water's edge and with 350 acres of private woodland. In this romantic honeymoon backdrop, you can fish, golf, play tennis, trail walk, ride horses, and even try your hand at falconry. It goes without saying that you'll be treated like royalty.

Cayo Espanto, Belize

www.aprivateisland.com

Located off the coast of Belize, Cayo Espanto is a spectacular and exceptionally private retreat. With only four villas and a staff-to-guest ratio of one-to-one, you will always feel you have the island to yourself—in fact, you *can* rent the whole island for a wedding or vow renewal ceremony! There's a private, sea front freshwater pool in every villa, romantic dining on a personal veranda, and alfresco showers, too. Days begin with breakfast brought to you in bed. Afterward, enjoy world-class snorkeling, scuba diving, fly-fishing—or just stay in bed for lunch and dinner.

Honeymoons By Sunset

www.honeymoons-by-sunset.com/RenewalOfVows.html

1-800-308-2518

This site offers expert assistance and ideas from second honeymoon consultants who specialize in helping you find the perfect destination at which to renew your wedding vows. It's also great for first-time honeymooners.

Love Tripper

www.lovetripper.com

E-mail through site.

Trip planning ideas for first and second honeymoons and other getaways. The couple that founded this site travels the globe in search of its most romantic places. The site features an e-newsletter as well.

Romantic-Escape.com

www.romantic-escape.com

E-mail through site.

Another site with many links to and idea about couples who love and who love to travel.

Glossary

Achilles' heel   A vulnerable spot that can cause extreme hurt. The term comes from the ancient story of Achilles, which tells of a great warrior immune to all moral wounds except in the heel area that was untouched by the magic waters that protected the rest of him.

affiliative behavior   Behavior that indicates friendly intent, such as smiling, laughing, and engaging in pleasant shared pastimes. With regard to parenting, it is sometimes used in contrast to attachment behaviors, which foster a complex, more emotionally charged bond.

androgenetic alopecia   The technical term for male pattern hair loss (MPHL). "Andro" refers to the androgens (testosterone and dihydro-testosterone) necessary to produce the condition, which usually begins with hair recession in the temporal areas.

antioxidants   Substances that protect cells against the harmful by-products of oxygen, called free radicals. Antioxidants counteract these cellular by-products by binding with them before they can cause damage. Left unchecked, free radicals may cause heart damage, cancer, cataracts, and a weakened immune system.

arm candy   Gossip and society columnists popularized the phrase, which initially referred to an attractive woman who was escorted by a gentleman so that others could eye her appreciatively. The term was first used to describe Marilyn Monroe in a walk-on role she played in a party scene in the 1950 film, *All About Eve*. Today, in the name of gender equality, good-looking men are sometimes referred to as arm candy, too.

attachment behaviors   Behaviors that foster a lasting emotional bond, such as communicating in ways that foster abiding trust.

Brazilian wax   A grooming technique that removes all female pubic hair except for a vertical strip in front.

buffer zone   In military terms, this is a neutral area that lies between hostile forces and reduces the risk of conflict between them. More colloquially, the term refers to any means designed to form a barrier that prevents potential conflict or harmful contact.

chi   A name for the lifeforce, the vital energy that runs throughout the human body along paths known as meridians. Those who believe in the concept of chi say that an imbalance in this energy can lead to fatigue, listlessness, and even disease.

cunnilingus   The act of performing oral sex on a woman. The word is derived from the Latin *cunnus* meaning "vulva," and *lingere*, "to lick."

dry orgasms   Male orgasms in which semen is not ejaculated. Orgasm and ejaculation are functions that are activated by separate parts of the nervous system. Although they often do occur simultaneously, each of these functions can be experienced independent of one another.

eating unit   The term nutritional sociologists use to define couples who regularly share food and dine together. The food choices and eating and exercise habits of each member of the eating unit affect those of the other.

facial symmetry   A term used to indicate that the left and right sides of the face match up, appearing perfectly balanced.

Hollywood wax   A grooming technique that removes all female pubic hair from the genital area.

lubrication   Commonly known as "getting wet," this term refers to a process that occurs within 10 to 30 seconds of a woman becoming sexually aroused. The vascular engorgement of the tissues that lie beneath the vaginal wall begin the process.

metrosexual   An urban, heterosexual male who is fashion-conscious, has a strong aesthetic sense, and spends significant time and money on his appearance and lifestyle. He is the target audience of men's magazines.

missionary position   A commonly practiced man-on-top sexual position. It got its name from Christian missionaries in the South Pacific and Africa. The missionaries maintained that based on their interpretation of the Book of Genesis, in which man is said to be the superior gender, this was the heavenly ordained way to make love.

paraphrasing   A way of letting a speaker know they're being heard by restating their message, as well as the emotion behind their words, and then reflecting it back to them.

pheromones   Natural scents that, although undetectable to the conscious mind, serve as powerful forces of sexual attraction. Pheromones are produced by glands nears a person's armpits, nipples, and groin. Although research is inconclusive, they're probably detected by something called the VNO (vomeronasal organ), a small cavity in the nose.

phytochemicals   Chemicals produced by plants. They help to defend those plants against environmental dangers and also help protect humans against harmful viruses and bacteria. They also prevent damage to DNA.

placebo   A placebo can be any treatment or substance believed by its administrator to be without effect. Yet those who receive the substance may experience intense effects, which they attribute to it. In controlled scientific experiments, placebos are often sugar pills or starch pills. The word is from the Latin, "I shall please."

political correctness (PC)   Speaking and behaving in a way that gives no offense to any segment of the population. Being "PC" means showing that one is without prejudice or preconceived notions.

Tantra   Sacred practices which can be traced back at least to the Indus Valley civilization that was contemporary with the Sumerian and the beginnings of the Egyptian Old Kingdom. The term is derived from a Sanskrit word meaning "woven together."

unconditional love   Love without conditions or judgment. It isn't predicated on the fact that the object of one's love always be or act or look a certain way. It only requires that they exist.

vanity sizing   The practice of resizing clothing so that customers feel like they are thinner than they used to be—without shedding a pound. This practice is becoming more and more popular as the general population ages.

yin and yang   These words from the Chinese Taoist tradition represent the blending of male and female energies. Yang, which represents the male aspect of universe, is necessary to balance and complete yin, which represents the female aspect of creation.

Index